HELP! I Married ~~An~~ ~~Alien~~ A Comedian

A memoir of life in the circus lane of marriage to a stand-up comedian

Carolyn V. Hamilton

SWIFT HOUSE PRESS
Las Vegas, Nevada

SWIFT HOUSE PRESS
7380 S. Eastern Avenue, Suite 124-216
Las Vegas, Nevada

ISBN 978-1-7337209-2-2 Trade Paper Edition

www.carolynvhamilton.com

Photo credits in this book:

Brian Janus, Ed Foster and Carolyn V. Hamilton

Editor, Kathryn M. McCullough

Foreword

John L. Smith

My career as a standup comic was mercifully brief. It consisted of participating in a celebrity roast in 2012 at the South Point Hotel and Casino showroom of legendary Las Vegas comedian Cork Proctor on the occasion of his 80th birthday and the publication of his hilarious memoir, *My Mind is an Open Mouth.*

That's right. I actually opened for Cork Proctor, the man affectionately dubbed "The Oral Assassin" for his occasionally bruising improvisation. The guy makes Don Rickles sound like Barney the Dinosaur. Of Proctor's style, a beard-stroking Las Vegas entertainment columnist once warned, "If he keeps it up with this filthy sludge, it will be a wonder that he fails to get socked either physically or by a lawsuit. He causes walkouts with his remarks."

Walkouts … and lots of laughs.

Those who knew Cork offstage realized he had another side. He was warm-hearted and charitable. In fact, that aforementioned comedy roast raised thousands of dollars for Opportunity Village, the Las Vegas nonprofit that for decades has helped adults with intellectual challenges. Turns out Mr. Acid Tongue was a softie.

You didn't have to know Cork well to discover his secret to a happy life. Her name is Carolyn V. Hamilton. At various times over the decades Carolyn has been his friend, girlfriend, lover, wife, ex-wife, nurse, and navigator on an amazing adventure she captures in the pages that follow.

A talented writer and artist, Carolyn gives readers a backstage pass to the downright insane world of a working comic from the showrooms and lounges of Las Vegas to cruise ships in distant ports of call. Suffice to say it's not all grins and giggles working amid jangling slots and at times belligerent tourists. That insight alone is worth the price of admission.

But don't be misled. *Help! I Married a Comedian* is a love story. Well, at moments it's a love-hate story, but then all real love stories are that way. It's a story of real people, both funny as hell, learning to adjust and roll with life's punches while embracing the adventure of it all.

Carolyn learned early in their relationship in the parking lot of the Gold Coast Hotel Casino that their personal life wasn't off limits when Cork took the stage. In fact, on many nights it was the material. Cork told Carolyn about advice he'd received years earlier from Shecky Greene: "Whatever happens in your life, take it right out on stage and make it funny."

Take what happens in your life and make it funny. That sage advice from a comedy hall-of-famer actually applies to real life, too. It's something Carolyn and Cork have known for many, many years. The hard times are always better with laughter, and a good margarita.

Carolyn takes you through the packed houses and the Strip variety shows that are a hit on Tuesday and closed by the end of the week. Cork was nothing if not indefatigable, and Carolyn was in his corner for every round.

With a refreshing candor and clipped language that's earthy and honest, she guides us quite literally on a trip around the world to many places I can't even pronounce. We're talking Ankara to Paramaribo, people, and places where they serve monkey stew. Hey, I received 10,000 frequent flyer miles just reading the manuscript.

Their relationship really took off, so to speak, after Cork left show business in 1999 and they joined the U.S. Peace Corps, serving in Suriname. It's in South America. You can look it up.

"What are you thinking?" comedian Sandy Hackett asks them when he learns of their Peace Corps plan. But everyone in their large circle of friends knew that it sounded like something they would do.

Today they live in the Andean town of Cuenca, Ecuador, where presumably Cork keeps busy making the locals laugh and Carolyn works fulltime explaining his behavior to strangers.

If you can't fly south for the winter and see the "Cork and Carolyn Show" in person, reading this book is the next best thing.

* * *

John L. Smith is an award-winning Las Vegas journalist and the author of more than a dozen books. He was inducted into the Nevada Press Association Hall of Fame in 2016. His most recent book is *The Westside Slugger: Joe Neal's Lifelong Fight for Social Justice.*

HELP! I Married ~~an Alien~~ A Comedian

TABLE OF CONTENTS

PART THREE - The Peace Corps

One Room Marriage, Continued
The Money Argument
Hello Outside World
Rainy Season
The Urine Cure
The Secret is Out
New Country Director
Vacation to French Guiana
Cork's Solution

PART FOUR - And Then...

Back in the US of A
Puck's Fate
Christmas With Trombones
Special Collections
The Saga of the Cell Phones
Craig
The Fifteen-Year Tune-up
Auctioneering School
Never Drink and Dress
Middle of the Night
The Art Studio
Las Vegas First Topless Wedding
The Garden Nazi
No More Landlording
Edith the Housesitter
Puppies
From Paris to Amsterdam
The PT Cruiser
The Turkey in the Driveway
The Atrial Fibrillation
The Bionic Book
A Wedding & a Tsunami in Thailand
The Sally Rand Model
Naming My Novel
The Citizen's Police Academy
Why Not Move to Thailand?
Sedonas on the Boulevard
Lunch in Barstow

HELP! I Married ~~an Alien~~ A Comedian

"Men are stupid and women are crazy. And the reason women are crazy is because men are stupid."
-     **George Carlin**

INTRODUCTION

The anatomy of a marriage – or any loving adult relationship, for that matter – can be both wonderful and weird.

That certainly goes for marriage to a professional comedian, during which I have seen more comedy than one woman should ever be subjected to in her life.

After his performances, women would approach me and often say, "I'll bet he's fun to live with" or ask, "Is he like this at home?"

I developed a stock answer, delivered with a laugh: "Only on Tuesdays."

How can I introduce to you the ADHD/obsessive compulsive personality that is Cork Proctor? A comparison to an alien from outer space seems logical.

Once Cork starts to obsess on a subject, he talks it and talks it and talks it. He won't let it go – he's like a bulldog with a dictionary in his mouth. He's the only man I've ever met who can talk and give head at the same time. He can change subjects mid-sentence. On occasion he has made me think of a talking ferret.

He's also witty, curious about everything, exceptionally well-read, a brilliant story-brainstorming partner, and a ready-at-any-given-moment travel companion. He's honest and sensitive and he can still make me laugh.

It took Cork Proctor almost ten years to ask me for a date. On the rebound from a four-year relationship with a woman twenty-five years his junior, I crafted a greeting card for him that read, "What do older women have that younger women don't?" and inside, "— a mysterious past."

Cork doesn't remember everything exactly the way I do. In every marriage there's a his and her version of events, so here's my official disclaimer: this is *my* story. This is *my* version of my life with and marriage to the alien-comic-from-outer-space, Cork Proctor.

PART ONE - Prenuptial Bliss

The Oral Assassin

On a hot August evening in 1980 Rich, my partner in Newman & Hamilton Advertising, and I had been invited to attend a roast at the Las Vegas Press Club, a dark, smoky bar on Charleston Boulevard in the old Fox Plaza Mall. The roastee was Darrell Dryer, State Assemblyman and News Director at KNUU News Radio, and the roaster was Las Vegas' resident actor and comedian, Cork Proctor.

Las Vegas had less than half a million residents and two major communities governed the town: the business community and the casino industry. With the willingness of both to support non-profit endeavors, a cross-over network of friendships thrived. Indeed, the entire state of Nevada seemed small. As a public relations friend said, "Where else can you trick-or-treat at the Governor's mansion?"

Cork Proctor's style of comedy was off the top of his head. He likes to say he "has no act." He opens his mouth and witty and brilliant and funny stuff comes out. The media called him, "The poor man's Don Rickles" and "The Oral Assassin." He worked fast and sharp, with a "take-no-prisoners" persona.

In the audience, Cork singled out my former boss, KNUU general manager Joe McMurray and said, "You know what's good about you, Joe?" Pause. "You'll never need Preparation H because you're a perfect asshole."

Laughter exploded in the room. Darrel laughed, Joe laughed, Rich laughed, I laughed, and I thought, *Jeez, who is this guy? Who can get away with saying stuff like that?*

I didn't know much about Cork Proctor. I'd seen his name on a few hotel/casino marquees, but my day job in advertising kept me sensibly away from the famous Las Vegas Strip and late-night shows, so I had never seen him perform.

High from laughter, I was intrigued by this tall, slim, good-looking comedian who exuded a playful, magnetic charm. Besides, I've always been a sucker for a great story-teller. When he invited me to come see his show the next night at the Royal Inn, I tried to be "cool." I said, "I might do that."

Monday night, dressed to the Vegas nines, I drove to the Royal Inn, eager for an evening of more laughs. I walked into the lounge to see stage curtains closed. On an easel rested a hand-painted placard (before computers, there was sign-painting). "SHOW DARK MONDAY NIGHTS."

My disappointed lasted maybe five minutes. I thought, *He's cute, he's funny, and he's probably one of those egotistic guys who likes to see how many girls he can get waiting for him all over town.* I already had two boyfriends, so I dismissed the comedian possibility and drove home to read a good book.

Calling All Carolyn Hamiltons

Fast forward to 1987. My partnership with Rich Newman had ended, and I had returned to my first career love, graphic design. I had created a print design company, Graphic Communications.

One afternoon after a client presentation I returned to my home office and checked my answering machine for messages. To my surprise I heard a sexy male voice.

"Hi. This is Cork Proctor, and I'm looking for the Carolyn Hamilton who owns the ad agency. I want you to know you've been my fantasy for ten years. If you are she, please call me back at 361-5454."

If you are she? Who speaks like that—with such perfect grammar—these days?

I remembered our meeting seven years earlier at the Press Club. I remembered seeing him on the disastrous press night for an ill-fated show at the Silver Slipper called *Bullshot*, and seeing him emcee the 1981 Las Vegas Addy Awards at the Desert Inn. It seemed like years, though, since I'd seen his name on a Strip marquee.

Curiosity aroused, I called him back. He invited me to breakfast at the Showboat Golf & Country Club.

A date? I thought he was calling to look for advertising work in commercials.

The day of our breakfast date I wore flat shoes with my dress. Later he told me he thought I wore flat shoes because I didn't know how tall he was. Interesting how a man can make the shoes you wear all about him!

During our breakfast he talked and I listened. He told me how he had called every Carolyn Hamilton, Carol Hamilton and C. Hamilton in the phone book to find me. One of the women had called him back and asked, "Even though I'm not the Carolyn Hamilton you're looking for, can we meet?"

He informed me upfront that years before he had had a vasectomy. "Done in Florida by a Cuban gardener with a weed-wacker."

His conversation often trailed like this: "I'm left-handed, dyslexic, and I have a redundant prepuce. You don't smoke, do you?"

I found him witty, charming, and compellingly attractive.

After we both declared we had never smoked cigarettes, he said, "If you'll go out with me, I promise you you'll never be bored."

Years later I would remember these words and remark, "On more than one occasion I wanted to *kill* him, but I have never been bored."

* * *

On our second date he took me to lunch at the Thai Room, where we sat next to each other in a booth. We ordered beers. Before the food came, I noticed he'd slouched in the booth, the lower half of his body under the table so that now I was looking down at him. I had a vision of him sliding the rest of the way, disappearing under the table. Was he uncomfortable to be with me? Perhaps positioning himself for a quick exit under the table? Or was he just incredibly relaxed? This was the beginning of many unexplained mysteries that came with Cork Proctor.

Because he was on the rebound from a four-year relationship with a woman twenty-five years his junior, I crafted a greeting card for him lettered, "What do older women have that younger women don't?" and inside, "— a mysterious past."

Dinner on Firethorn

Cork owned a three-bedroom house in Wishing Well Estates, a horse-friendly planned community. When he invited me for dinner at his home, I had reservations. It was *dark* way out there on Eastern Avenue, way out past Warm Springs, south of town, with no street lights. Not a lot of housing developments or businesses there in the eighties. I would be alone with a man I didn't know well in a strange house. Still, I was attracted and *no* seemed not in my vocabulary.

The plan was to have dinner and then watch the 10 p.m. airing of an episode of the TV show, "Crime Story," in which he had a speaking role.

In the low living room lighting I didn't immediately notice the clutter. In the brightly-lit kitchen, however, I couldn't help wondering where we would eat. Books and mail and pens and stamps and magazines and newspapers covered the oak dining table. The kitchen smelled of heavenly roast chicken, and Cork had prepared enough salad for a large family, into which he'd thrown every possible vegetable.

He removed the chicken from the oven, plates and silverware from cupboards and drawers. In one sweeping movement he cleared enough space on the table for us to eat. We enjoyed a fine meal and retired to the living room to watch the TV show.

This will be romantic, I thought. *He will sit next to me and put his arm around me. He might kiss me. Whoo-ha!* With that in mind I positioned myself on one end of his cozy couch. He turned on the TV and seated himself in a rocking chair on the other side of the room.

Hmmm... maybe not.

We watched the show, I thanked him for a nice evening, he made no move to kiss me, and I drove home wondering what had just *not* happened.

* * *

16

Cork drove a big, beige, 1986 Ford F250 extended Supercab pickup. His personalized license plate read, QUE HUEVOS. Literal Spanish for, *what eggs*. In the Mexican street slang he'd picked up as a child in East Los Angeles it meant, *what balls*.

The state of Nevada has rules about what you cannot say on a license plate. No profanity or blatant sex terms. If they didn't understand your plate request, you had to explain it on a form. Cork had written, "*Que huevos* is Spanish for *what eggs*, and I raise Cornish game hens."

Here's your license plate, Mr. Proctor.

Guys Ask the Darndest Things

Cork had given up running for walking and invited me to accompany him on several walks. We covered his neighborhood, my neighborhood, and some nice residential areas. Often, we walked in the early morning, before the notorious high desert heat took over the day.

During these walks I listened to him talk about his past. Stories about growing up in Orange, California, living with his Wisconsin grandparents, serving in the Navy, becoming a drummer, and later a comedian. He described a lot of odd gigs—"gigs" is musician-speak—he had taken in his early career. He had even appeared in costume as Ronald McDonald for a McDonald's in Reno.

I learned he had been married before to a nice Lutheran girl from Washington State (like me!), Louise, and had two daughters in their early twenties, Kathy and Luann. He told me about the divorce in the seventies, and how he had moved from Reno to Las Vegas to work as a comic. He said he had slept for a while in his car, but he had never missed a child support payment.

A man who never smoked and never missed a child support payment? I was soooooo impressed.

We talked about mutual media friends in radio, television, and advertising. He asked me if I knew Loretta St. John, Kenny Laursen, Diane Ellis, Ronnie Fabre, Freddie Bell and the Bellboys—all prominent lounge entertainers. When I said I did not, he said, "You gotta get out more."

"Hey, I have a day job that starts early. I don't hang out all night on the strip."

My initial concern that at the fifty-four he might be a little too old for me—I had just turned forty-three—had disappeared. But there was something else.

Cork confided his dream was to get a trailer and go on the road "to see America." He had already purchased a used Nomad trailer that rested in his driveway. It sounded like he planned to give up his house for this trip and would be gone indefinitely.

He had introduced me to his friend and travel agent, Ann Geno, whose husband was a guitar player. One day I said to Ann, "I'm not sure I want to get into a relationship with someone who's going to leave town."

Ann laughed. "Oh, don't worry. He's been talking about going to see America for ten years. He's not going anywhere."

* * *

In the course of my dating life, men have asked me to do some odd things. Cork asked me to go see his psychiatrist. "So you will know exactly what you're getting into." He would pay. Good sport that I am, I agreed.

Tad Corbett was a big, energetic, outspoken Texan with a strong drawl. He and his wife Priss rented a condo on the Las Vegas Country Club, and that is where I went to meet him.

"Waaaaaell, we cain't talk about Cork," Tad said. "Thay-et's confidential information. But we cain talk about *yeeew*, and why yew're attracted to Cork."

He gave me a personality test called the Minnesota Multiphasic Personality Inventory (MMPI), a psychological test used by licensed psychiatrists to assess personality structure and traits.

Afterwards he held the long sheet of results in front of me and showed me a line meandering from top to bottom down the center of the page. Half way down the page the line veered off dramatically to the right, then returned pretty much to the center.

"See-ya thet line that goes waaaay off to the side?" he asked. He pointed a big finger to where it veered off to the right. "Thet's the part of yew that's attracted to Cork."

In the course of our conversation Tad asked me, "Have you seen Cork's back bedroom?" I had, and had been amazed by the collection of boxes and stuff that filled it. The door to the room opened just far enough to be able to pass into the room, and a little pathway went to the center of the stacks. "Thet room represents hees *mind*," Tad explained.

The Courtship and the Consummation

After several months of long walks and romantic dinners and late evenings in lounges without so much as a kiss, my girlfriends began to question if I thought Cork was gay.

"I don't think so." I named two women I knew through the marketing and public speaking communities that he had dated. "I think if he was gay, someone would have told me by now."

From the stage Cork joked about his redundant prepuce and his vasectomy—"a bilateral misterectomy done in Florida by a Cuban gardener with a weed whacker." Now every time I heard a hardware commercial on KNUU for weed whackers, I thought of Cork.

In mid-November, in an attempt to encourage more intimate relations, I made him a custom greeting card with some black lace inside cut in the shape of a teddy. Inside I wrote, "This is just a note to let you know I liked what I saw when you took your shirt off. One of these days when you least expect it, you and I will merge fantasies."

In the afternoon of December 1st, I was visiting the house when Cork invited me to take a nap with him. *Hey,* I thought, *this is IT!*

In his bedroom he drew the shades, we both took off our jeans and wearing only our underwear climbed into his big bed.

Then, *nothing.* Not a move. *Ridiculous,* I thought. *I'm ready and this is going to happen.* It didn't take too many moves on my part to get the idea into both his big head and his little head.

I laughed to myself. How many women can say they slept with Ronald McDonald?

Later, Tad would tell me, "Cork's shy. He never seduced anybody. They all seduced him."

* * *

Now that we had officially consummated our relationship, we couldn't keep our hands—and other parts—off each other.

I had told him honestly up front I had reservations about entering into a relationship with a man who would be gone all the time. He had replied, "I promise you I'll never be gone more than five months that you won't be able to come visit me during the time." In this instance, he kept his word.

Now he had a multiple-week cruise gig again with RCCL. He called suddenly to tell me he was flying home from Florida, and fly home he did—for eleven hours. We had lunch, took a "nap," had dinner, and eleven hours later he flew back to Florida.

Afterward I sent him a card in which I wrote, "Hello, welcome home, goodbye, have a nice trip. Life is timing, logistics and coordination. But hey, I'm not bored."

***

At some point I also remember telling him, "No matter how much I might fall in love with you there are two things I will never do for you. I will never help you rob a bank and I will never take it in the ass."

The Missing Passport

Katherine Engle, a tall ex-showgirl and one of Cork's ex-girlfriends, was between jobs and needed a place to live with her horse. Cork rented her the middle bedroom and she parked her horse in a corral in the large stone-walled backyard.

I liked Katherine, and when Cork left town for jobs, she and I and Ann Geno often went out together in the evening to lounges and shows. She even referred me for a huge graphic design job with a local builder.

One night, Cork and Katherine and I had just had a nice dinner. Cork was scheduled to leave at 1:10 a.m. on a red-eye to Miami for another cruise gig. And he couldn't find his passport.

"Some professional traveler you are," Katherine joked. But it wasn't a joke. He could fly to Miami on his drivers' license, but he couldn't board the cruise ship without a passport.

Good sports that we were, Katherine and I helped him search the house. We went through the pile of magazines and papers and mail and phone notes on the kitchen table. We looked through drawers in the kitchen, drawers by the bed, drawers in the bathroom. In the freezer, I found an exploded beer bottle and the missing lid to his blender.

The clock ticked so loudly it could have been laughing at us.

"Did you look in your truck?" Kathy asked.

"Yes, I looked all through the truck. It's not there."

We asked the usual questions, where did you have it last? Where do you normally keep it? Where did you see it? He answered that he kept it in his safety deposit box, but he brought it home for this trip.

Another half hour of searching proved futile. Kathy reasoned out loud. "If you brought it home, that means at some point it was in your truck," she said. "Are you *sure* it's not there?"

Cork was adamant and annoyed with the repeat question. "I'm telling you, dammit, it's not there."

We continued to search. At 11:30 p.m. Katherine announced, "I'm going outside and look in the truck."

Five minutes later she returned, passport in hand. I could feel the air in the room relax. Cork's expression had been determined, but never worried, and now he displayed an innocent grin.

"Where'd you find it?"

"In the door on the driver's side."

First Class Male

I swear Cork single-handedly supported the entire US postal system. With greeting cards and thank you cards and letters. He had a collection of mismatched motel and hotel stationery and pens and stamps. He also had a collection of rubber stamps he liked to stamp on the outer envelopes. One was a cartoon character and the word, *YOW-ZA!*

From a stationary store I ordered a personalized rubber stamp for him that read, FIRST CLASS MALE. It was the kind that was self-inking—all you had to do was stamp it on the paper. He loved it.

After I gave it to him, I left the room for a few minutes. When I returned, he stamped and stamped and said, "Look. It doesn't work."

Now that I knew him better, I became immediately suspicious.

"What did you do to it while I was in the bathroom?"

He grinned with boyish innocence. "Well… I had to take it apart to see how it worked."

"Show me what you did."

He took it apart again and I could see that when he had reassembled it he had put the little ink pad plate back in upside down. Putting it back in the correct position fixed the issue.

Swiss Kriss

Drugs were never Cork's thing. But being a bit of a hypochondriac—"Oh my God I have a hang-nail. Do you think it might be *cancer*?"—and sometime health nut, I believe he was addicted to the herbal laxative Swiss Kriss. Got a hangover? Take Swiss Kriss. Got an upset tummy? Take Swiss Kriss. Got a headache? Take Swiss Kriss. Got turned down for a gig? Take Swiss Kriss.

One afternoon without thinking I mentioned some physical complaint and Cork said, "Take some Swiss Kriss." In the bathroom I found the bottle of tablets in the medicine cabinet. What is it about human nature that we never read the *instructions*? From the bathroom I called to Cork in the kitchen, "How many of these should I take?"

He called back, "Oh…about a dozen."

Being the gullible Lutheran girl from Seattle, I counted out twelve tablets and with a big glass of water swallowed them.

About two hours later, the cramps hit. For the next few hours I would stop what I was doing and double over with waves of abdominal pain. When nature finally took its course, I sat on the toilet while it seemed like everything I had ever eaten came out. An exhausting experience.

I came out of the bathroom mumbling, "Swiss Kriss…never again…"

"Jesus," Cork said, "How many of those did you *take*?"

"Twelve."

"You're only supposed to take one or two."

"I *asked* you, and you said, *oh about a dozen*."

Again, that innocent look. "It was a joke."

Now I turned angry. "How would I know that? You have to be careful what you tell me because I'll believe everything you say. I'm a simple Lutheran girl from Seattle. We don't grow up with jokes."

Kiss and Tell

It was in the parking lot of the Gold Coast Hotel Casino where I first learned never to tell a comedian anything you don't want to hear again thrown back at you as a joke, either privately or onstage.

Cork told me Shecky Green's early career advice to him had been, "Whatever happens in your life, take it right out on stage and make it funny." I had already seen evidence of that with his onstage remarks about the Very Young Girl Friend: "She's making an updated version of that old Marlo Thomas TV series, 'That Girl.' They're going to call it 'That Cunt.'"

So we could spend a long, cozy, romantic night together without him being nervous with Katherine in the house, Cork got us a room at the Gold Coast.

The following morning, gentleman that he is, he walked me to my car in the parking lot. There he took me in his arms and kissed me. Then he whispered, "I can't believe I'm kissing the lips that kissed the dick of Neil Glover."

During our walks and dinners, we had each happened to mention the names of previous lovers. The whole state of Nevada being a small community, it wasn't unusual for us to know a lot of the same people.

As it happened, long before I met Cork I had "affairs" with two prominent Nevada businessmen whose names I decided right there in the Gold Coast parking lot he would never know. I could imagine the potential jokes!

So, I guess this isn't a "tell-all" memoir after all . . .

Wonder Lungs and the Washer and Dryer

Cork began to refer to my boobs as, "Wonder Lungs." He had noticed that in my house on Boca Chica I lacked a washer and dryer, so for Christmas he gifted me with both. I had already realized that on Cork time, things didn't often happen exactly when one would think they would. The washer and dryer did not arrive *before* Christmas.

On New Year's Eve, he picked them up and loaded them into the bed of *Que Huevos*. On one side of each large cardboard box he wrote in heavy felt pen, "Merry Christmas, W.L." He was cutting behind a corner 7-Eleven when he got stopped by one of Metro's finest and given a ticket for something like cutting through a parking lot to another street.

"I thought they had gas," he explained to the officer.

Smarter than the average bear, the cop said, "No, you didn't."

My observant friend, Joe Bauer, later said to me, "That Cork's a pretty smart guy, to give you a washer and dryer."

"How so?" I asked.

"If you get mad at him and have a fight, you can't throw a washer and dryer at him like you could, say, a diamond choker."

Doing It in the Parking Garage

What is it with men that they are fascinated by the idea of sex in unusual places?

One afternoon I accompanied Cork to the McCarran Airport to see him off on a flight to San Juan, Puerto Rico to board another cruise ship. On the way in his truck, he voiced the idea that it would be fun to screw on the top level of the parking garage. Was it the fact that I wore a skirt that day—easy access—that gave him the idea?

Good sport that I am, when he explained how he would bend me over the railing, overlooking the main airport driveway access, I said, "Why not?"

Because most people like to park in parking garages as close to the ground floor as possible, we were the only people on the top level, so I was only mildly nervous about being "caught." I figured all those people I saw down there on the main level, busy with getting wherever they were going, would never be looking *up*.

During the deed, I said, "I don't think I can cum."

"That's okay," he replied. "I can cum enough for both of us."

His next idea was to do it among the bushes in front of the Post Office on Warm Springs. The reality was that the bushes were spaced too far apart to hide anything, so scratch that idea.

Cork had brought adventure into my life. After the airport parking garage scenario, I sent another hand-made card, thanking him for a recent gift of *je reviens* perfume, a fish tee-shirt, and "the new way of looking at the McCarran parking garage."

In teensy print at the bottom I wrote, *Made in the USA and willing to be made in other exotic locales.*

Friends

It says something about a man who doesn't have any long-time, close friends, and something about a man who does. Cork did not lack in the friends department. He introduced me to friends he had bonded with over old cars in high school forty years earlier.

Jim Reber, a great self-taught artist, had married his high school sweetheart, Delores Lewis, and remained in Las Vegas. For several years he illustrated billboards for Donrey Outdoor Advertising, had the vision to purchase a lot of property on the cheap, and had become a millionaire.

Cork described Jim and Dee as "the finest Mormon couple I ever met, who never once asked me to join the church."

Robert Mackenzie, a retired supermarket manager, lived in a condominium in San Diego. His father and Cork's father had worked as accountants together at a company called War Assets, a federal agency that liquidated millions of dollars worth of planes. After three years in the marine corps, "Mack", who as a kid had worked in local markets, went into the supermarket business.

Mack had an older brother, Roy, who had been in the marines and then became a Las Vegas policeman. "He happened to be the cop who arrested me," Cork says, "when I was sixteen and stole that car."

In 1949—their senior year at Las Vegas High School— Cork, Reber and Mack had all quit school. When they walked out of class together, the teacher asked, "Where are you going?"

Cork quipped, "To LA to get our shoes built up."

When Mack came to Vegas to visit us, the house became like a living zoo. He had a wicked sense of humor, and when he was with Cork, I dubbed them, "The Circus Twins."

Cork also introduced me to his close showbiz friends. Carme Pitrello, a talented Italian singer/comedian had been a friend since the early sixties and had appeared with Cork in the seventies in a show at the Union Plaza, *Natalie Needs a Nightie*. Carme lived in an old house in the desert on Haven Street even further south than Cork's house in Wishing Well Estates.

Carme always called Cork either "Alfie" (for his real first name, Alfred) or "Cock."

I met comedy magician Jac Hayden, who lived in a trailer behind Carme's house, and had a flare for party decoration. Carme threw a lot of parties at his house, and Jac would create

26

novel and clever decorations. It was there I would meet so many entertainers who had performed in burlesque, casino lounges and popular afternoon shows.

Cork's friend comedian Bernie Allen had previously been half of the comedy team Allen and Rossi, had appeared in the movie, *Raging Bull* plus several television series in the sixties and seventies. In France in World War II he'd been wounded in the legs by shrapnel, and had a wonderful ability to live life in the moment, to the fullest. Bernie helped the homeless and, like Cork and all his comic friends, was always ready to appear for free for any fund-raising benefit in town.

Bernie's motto was, "God loves everybody."

One afternoon Cork and I and Bernie were driving somewhere in QUE HUEVOS and Bernie was on a rant about President George Bush (Sr).

I couldn't help myself. I guess I inherited this trait from my dad, who could say the most nonsensical things with a deadpan face.

"But Bernie," I said, "Doesn't God love everybody?"

"Of course, He does."

"So, doesn't it follow that if God loves everybody, He loves George Bush, so we should love George Bush, too?"

Cork jabbed me with his elbow but it was too late. I had already fed more fuel to Bernie's fire.

The things all of Cork's friends had in common was their positive outlooks and love of laughter and a good joke. I loved their company.

Half a Cruise

In February 1988 Cork invited me to fly to Miami and go with him on RCCL's *Song of America*. As an entertainment employee with a private cabin, he could bring a guest for free as long as they shared the same cabin.

My first cruise, ever!

As soon as I finalized my flight, I wrote him a short letter:

I arrive in Miami 2/27 8:35 a.m. Eastern Airlines. If I don't hear from you before then, I'll call the office or cable the ship or send a carrier pigeon to be sure you remember I'm coming. (I'm the tall brunette with the big tits and growing interest in sex in unusual places.)

The cruise was all I had ever imagined. Gourmet food in the dining room. Stunning sunsets. A Las-Vegas style stage show—I marveled at how those dancers could do their steps with the occasional and without-warning ship heave to the right or left.

I learned the typical cruise joke: "What time is the midnight buffet?"

Cork performed in the Sky Lounge. He began his shoot-from-the-hip act with *where-you-from?* with an older couple in the audience. Each question he asked of the husband was answered immediately by the wife.

The husband had had open heart surgery, and Cork could see the "zipper, a livid red scar."

Cork spoke to the husband, "Well, apparently you've had open heart surgery."

The wife hacked, "Yeah and he's doin' great."

"Well, look at you, you've got a medic alert bracelet." The husband let Cork pull his arm up for a closer look. "And how unique to have a medic alert bracelet that says, (big pause for effect…) Give me head until I'm dead."

* * *

When I met the captain of the *Song of America*, I asked, "Is it true the captain of the ship can marry people?"

"No," he replied. "I can't."

"So, what's the craziest, oddest experience you've ever had as a cruise ship captain?" I asked.

This is the story he told:

> "On one cruise one of the passengers, an older gentleman, died. Now you have to understand we are at sea and we have to keep the body cold until we get to Port. So we cleared out the beer locker and put his body in there. I asked his wife if there were any special arrangements he had made in advance for his passing. 'Oh', she said, 'he always wanted to be buried at sea.'

I said, 'We can do that.' So, we arranged for a special memorial ceremony with the ships pastor and we buried him at sea.

Now when we arrived at Port there was a woman on the dock waiting for him who said *she* was his wife. I realized he had been on the cruise with his girlfriend. And I had to explain to his wife that not only had her husband died, but there was no body because we had buried him at sea."

* * *

My first-ever cruise only lasted four days. The company had scheduled Cork to disembark in Puerto Rico and fly back to Miami.

Cork had a theory about cruise ships—they could well be a laundry for the mob. Some Italian singer had told him it would be a perfect place to launder money, with no American constraints, no IRS connection, no American ports of call, ships based in Panama or another foreign port, lots of cash flowing through the ship casinos.

Later when Cork ran the Gold Coast Comedy Lounge, one night he saw in the audience an RCCL executive he knew, watching his show in the company of a known mob boss.

Early on I decided Cork has some sort of sixth sense. Many times I've seen him say to someone in the audience, "You look like you're in law enforcement" and the guy would turn out to be a prison guard, or "You look like a nurse" and the woman would be a nursing trainer. He told me about earlier experiences where he'd joked about a restaurant being in foreclosure, or a store owner being gay, only to discover later these things were true.

So, I could well believe the possibility of a cruise ship-mob connection.

* * *

Before we flew back to Vegas, we visited Vizcaya, an early 1900s American villa in the Grove area of Miami that had been built for a winter home by bachelor and retired millionaire

James Deering, who lived in Illinois and ran the Deering Harvester Company.

On the shore of Biscayne Bay, Deering indulged his interest in landscaping and plant conservation. He styled Vizcaya after eighteenth-century Italian villas, with elaborate European-styled gardens of hedges, mazes and fountains. Romance and enchantment oozed from every architectural detail.

In the 80's, Vizcaya's Café and shop were in rooms that had once been Deering's smoking room, billiard room and changing rooms for guests. We enjoyed lunch in the cafés buffet-style restaurant. As we passed with our trays by the food selections, Cork asked the pretty young Latin server behind the counter, "Are you open every day?"

She gave us an exquisite smile. "*Si*. Monday through Friday."

"So how do we get from here to the zoo?" he asked.

She thought he was asking about the soup.

"*Mee-na-stro-nee*."

Talk about looking for coffee in the supermarket pantyhose section.

Rubber Sheets

On this post-cruise road trip through southern Florida, we established a pattern where each evening we would pass a strip of motels, I would see one I liked and say, "Pull in here." Cork would park, I would get out of the car, go into the office, look at the room, and make a deal.

On the fifth day I grew tired of this routine. I suggested to Cork that this evening he would be the one to find a motel, look at the room, and make the deal.

At six o'clock we were driving on the freeway and we saw a major offramp with lots of motels. Cork pulled off and drove into the first motel closest to the freeway offramp. I waited in the car while he went in to look at the room. A few minutes later he returned and announced this is where we would spend the night.

To say the room was drab would be kind. Faded blue grey walls, dark carpeting of an undeterminable color, and twin beds. I noticed the television was bolted to the wall.

I sat down on one of the twin beds. A strange crunchy sound I'd never heard in a bed before. I pulled back the thin coverlet and felt a strange material under the sheets. A pull back from the corner of the sheets revealed a fitted rubber pad. No mattress pad, only the mattress topped by the rubber pad topped by the thin sheet.

"I have a surprise for you," I said. Cork gave me a quizzical look. "Look! Rubber sheets! You sure can pick 'em."

I had never before slept on rubber sheets and it became an experience I never want to repeat.

No hot romance that night.

The Milford Track

On one of our walks, Cork had asked me if I would like to go with him to walk the Milford Track in southern New Zealand. He had airline miles with Continental. He raved about how beautiful New Zealand was, how amazing the track was, how wonderful the people are, what a great adventure it would be. Had he been there before? No, but he'd read all about it in *National Geographic*.

I was discovering that Cork had a tendency to see television documentaries or read about a place and decide he had to visit.

Having never heard of the Milford Track, I went to the library to do research.

The Milford Track, in Fiordland National Park in New Zealand's South Island, began in a town called Te Anau. From there we would hike three thousand feet up over McKinnon Pass to Milford Sound. We would see glacier-carved fiords, beech forests, lakes and powerful waterfalls.

I discovered there were two ways to walk the track. One was with a small group and two guides. The other was "free-walking", less expensive because you carried in all your own supplies—food, tent, sleeping bag, etc. Naturally Cork wanted to "free-walk" it, but I insisted on the guided tour.

31

"If I see an interesting flower or a strange bird, I want to be able to turn to someone knowledgeable to tell me what it is." Besides, I hadn't been camping since I was in the Girl Scouts, and the idea of carrying in tents and sleeping bags and food and cooking gear overwhelmed me. Cork finally agreed to the guided tour.

At the library I also read in a *National Geographic* magazine that in 1974 a hut blew off the mountain and four people were killed.

You want me to go *where* and do *what*?

* * *

We flew from Las Vegas to Los Angeles to Auckland, New Zealand. From there we flew to Christchurch in the South Island.

In the Auckland airport Cork lifted my suitcase and exclaimed, "Jesus, what do you have in here? An entire library?"

That was the moment we reached our most important travel agreement. I said, "You will be responsible for lifting and keeping track of your own bags, and I will be responsible for lifting and keeping track of mine. We will each carry our own passports and tickets. I don't ever want to hear, 'where are the tickets? I thought you had them...' "

March was the end of the season for the Milford Track when it would close for New Zealand's southern hemisphere winter. Because of rainy, inclement weather at the top of McKinnon Pass, one of the items issued to walkers was a big yellow slicker.

As a joke I said, "I'm really not going to need this because I'm not going to have rain at the top of the pass."

And I didn't—the weather at the top of the pass was cool and clear and afforded the most majestic views I had ever seen.

"I can't believe this," the guide remarked. "I've never seen such good weather this late in the season!"

* * *

After we walked the Milford Track there was the opportunity to take a scenic flight in a seven-passenger, single-engine plane over the top of Sutherland Falls, a famous waterfall southwest of Milford Sound.

With water falling nearly two thousand feet, Sutherland Falls is the second largest waterfall in New Zealand. In 1880 a Scottish settler, Donald Sutherland, discovered the falls and proudly proclaimed them the tallest waterfall in the world.

Cork, not a fan of small planes, opted to stay on the ground, but I was eager for this adventure. Spectacular views of fjords, forests and snow-topped mountains were my privileged reward.

The source of Sutherland Falls is Lake Quill, at the top of an old volcano, named after the first explorer to climb up the cliff face and find it in 1890. The pilot told the story of the first pilot to land on Lake Quill in a small pontoon plane. "He was so excited by the experience, he invited his best friend to go up with him. The second time he landed on the lake he couldn't get out because he didn't factor in the weight of the second man in the small plane. This time there wasn't enough room from one wall of the lake to the other for him to take off successfully."

"What happened?" I asked.

"He circled the lake a couple of times to gain speed and flew out over the top of the falls where there was a break in the volcano walls."

Bermuda on the *Nordic Prince*

The following spring Cork invited me to Bermuda during one of his runs for RCCL on the *Nordic Prince*. I would fly to New York, where we would meet and together board the ship. This would be my first week-long cruise. To Bermuda!

Like many north Americans confused by geography, I had thought the island of Bermuda, a British territory, was in the Caribbean. No, that's the *Bahamas*. Bermuda is off the Eastern coast in the North Atlantic.

The *Nordic Prince* docked on Front Street, with its high-end shops, in the capitol of Hamilton. I loved the architecture of pastel-colored colonial buildings and houses with eye-blinding white roofs, all constructed from stone. And businessmen wore suit jackets, white shirts and ties, and Bermuda shorts with socks up over their calves.

This will be soooo romantic, I had thought. As it happened, on the *Nordic Prince* that week was the annual *Romantic Times* Book Lovers Convention for romance writers. Everywhere on the ship wandered ladies in flowing dresses and floppy sun hats. I met the magazine's founder, Kathryn Falk, and she gifted me with an autographed paperback of her book, *How to Write a Romance and Get It Published*.

As part of her convention, Kathryn had arranged a day tour to 300-year-old Verdmont Historic House and Garden in Smith's Parish and invited Cork and I along as her guests.

White mullioned windows framed in black punctuated the salmon color of this mansion full of pristinely preserved furniture and artifacts, with gardens of herbs, fruit trees, ancient rose bushes, and an expansive view of South Shore.

"Wow. Look at all those palm trees," Cork said. "If you have to be a slave, this would be a great place."

From Verdmont, on a road overlooking the sea, we visited a roadside shrine. A tiny one-room building, we were able to go inside, but only five people at a time. The doorway was small, the head jamb low. Inside, Cork made comic observations.

On the way out, he banged his head hard on the head jamb.

"Oh my God," I exclaimed. "Are you all right?"

He rubbed his head. "That's what I get," he whispered, "for doing *shtick* in a holy place."

* * *

"Let's walk to the beach," Cork said one morning.

Immediately suspicious, I asked, "How far is it?"

"Not far."

"How far?"

"Not that far. What's the matter with you? I thought you liked to walk. C'mon. It'll be fun. We'll see a lot of cool stuff along the way."

I was reluctant to commit to a walk of indeterminant length in hot, tropical sun, but in the end I acquiesced. We donned swimsuits and coverups, packed a book to read for each of us, towels, and other beach paraphernalia, and began our walk to the beach.

In the hot, tropical sun.

The first few blocks were interesting. We passed hand-hewn stone walls, profuse little purple Bermudianas (the national flower of Bermuda), little shops, historic plaques, and limestone cottages.

But even with a hat and sunglasses, I soon became fatigued. I wanted to be lying on a towel in Bermuda's pink sand, not hiking in Bermuda's heat.

"How much farther?" I asked Cork.

"Five minutes."

Okay, I can do that.

Fifteen minutes later I said, "That's enough. I'm getting a taxi."

My pronouncement annoyed the master walker. "What? It's not that far! You can walk."

"You're missing the point. I don't *want* to walk. I want to *be* at the beach."

Miffed, he said, "Fine. Get your taxi. I'll see you there."

Minutes later I sat in a comfortable, air-conditioned cab headed toward Bermuda's famous pink sand.

At the beach, I spread my towel, slathered on tan cream, and opened my book.

Forty minutes later, a shadow over my book pages announced Cork's arrival. I thought he looked flushed, but he said he had enjoyed the walk.

We spent the rest of the morning relaxing in the pink sand.

* * *

We visited the largest wildlife sanctuary in Bermuda, Spittal Pond Nature Reserve in Smith's Parish. This previously-privately-owned area stretching along the south coast originally had proved unsuitable for development due to large parts being salt marshes.

A winding trail climbs to horizon-wide views over the south shore. Strong winds buffeted the cliff where we stood to view the ocean. It proved difficult to take any photos because I had to hold my straw hat on my head with both hands.

Helpful Cork said, "Here, let me hold that for you."

It seemed like only seconds later I looked down to see my favorite straw hat bobbing atop the crests of waves crashing against the rocks below. My *favorite* straw hat…

"Sorry," he said. "I'll buy you a new one."

Cork Does His Taxes

Harboring bad fantasies of the very-young-girlfriend in his bed with someone else while he was on the road, Cork sold his Wishing Well tract home and moved into a duplex on the south side of the airport. The owner of the property, retired sea captain and widower John Meyer, had acquired two duplex structures from the owners of the old El Rancho Vegas, when that vintage strip hotel casino had been demolished.

April 15 approached and Cork busied himself after the move, assembling all of his receipts to take to his long-time tax accountant, Sue Lambros. "She's kept me out of jail for years," he said. This tax organization consisted of spreading out little pieces of paper all over the living room carpet.

In the middle of this process he had to leave town for another job. He would be gone two weeks. One day after he left, I received a call from John Meyer. "You'd better come right over. There's been a flood. Cork's apartment is flooded and I think there are some papers you'll want to recover."

When I opened the front door, I saw a soaked carpet, a gazillion little pieces of paper beginning to float. John gave me a plastic sack, and with squishy steps I moved about the living room, picked each piece of paper with care, dried it as best I could, and placed it in the bag.

Cork was due home in two days and there was no way John would have the exploded water heater fixed and the carpet dry enough for Cork to stay there. So, for the first week he would be home I rented a weekly apartment for him.

The night he came home I picked him up at the airport and announced, "You're not going home."

"Where am I going?"

"To the Budget Suites on Paradise Road." In the room at the apartment complex, I presented him with his bag of tax receipts.

The next day, so he could finish the paperwork for his tax filing, he spread them all over that carpet.

Warehousewarming

I'd been operating Graphic Communications out of a bedroom in my house on Boca Chica, and felt like I wasn't really in business since I didn't have a "real" office. I thought it was time to get serious. Plus, the house overhead was more than I was now able to handle, and I needed to make a serious financial decision. In September I rented a warehouse in the newly-constructed McKellar Business Park on Eastern Avenue.

I'd always fantasized about living in an office space. I sold my house and exchanged the swimming pool and spa for a car phone and other exotic business toys.

Although it was illegal in Clark County to live in a business space, one of my typesetting sources told me, "It's no big deal. I know a dozen other artists doing the same thing."

Because the commercial building was new, I had the option to design the architecture of my space. I had the McKellar guys build a formal office space in the front, with a load-bearing ceiling, and leave the space above it open to the rest of the warehouse. That way I could get a ladder and put a mattress up there that wouldn't be seen. I also told them "Part of what I do in my business is photograph models, so I need a shower in the bathroom and a hook-up for a washer and dryer in the warehouse so I can wash photography backdrops." The builders, construction guys who had no idea what I was talking about, agreed to everything.

The space looked good, filled with the furniture from my house. My dining table was now my desk. On September 30, 1988 I hosted an afternoon "Open Warehouse Party", provided wine and fat markers, and everyone signed one huge warehouse wall.

While I saw my warehouse space as an artistic, bohemian environment for a creative person who made a living as a graphic designer, Cork saw it as a big garage. And what goes in a big garage? A car. Could he park one of his cars in the rear space by the big roll-up doors? He would pay me a small storage fee.

No.

Fire Inspection

Because the McKellar warehouse was new construction, the building had to be inspected and signed off by the fire department. The property manager told me the day and time the fire department representative would come to inspect the interior of my office.

Alarmed, I called our fire captain friend, Tony, to come by the warehouse for coffee and alert me to any possible violations I could fix before the inspector arrived. Tony didn't see any problems.

As an artist, I've always loved craft fairs. Inspired by an artist I'd met at a Steve Powers fair at Cashman Center, I had begun to decorate hats and make earrings. In a few days I was scheduled to leave for a crafts fair in San Diego. The day of the fire inspection, hats decorated in rhinestones, leather, feathers and lace covered the tops of all my work tables.

Imagine my surprise to welcome the fire department inspector, a uniformed woman. She asked me more questions about my hats and earrings and the craft fair than about how I had my warehouse—secret home—space arranged. She never questioned my plug-in appliances: coffee maker, toaster, hot plate, oven, or microwave. She never saw my ladder or mattress in the open top level of the office space. It didn't look like there was anything up there but open space.

I gave a sigh of relief when everything passed the fire department inspection.

* * *

The following month temperatures dropped. Las Vegas has a short fall. Oven-hot till mid-October, two weeks of fall, and by November first the desert is into winter.

In my lease, which I had signed with a woman representing McKellar Development, I had asked for a swamp cooler for summers and a heat pump for winters. Now I had no idea where the heat pump was or how to turn it on. When I asked, she had no idea, either. Together we discovered that the power company had said a heat pump would not work with a swamp cooler, and they had never installed it.

What would I do for heat? Cork suggested Home Depot's finest—a $300 portable fireplace made of wrought iron with a brick interior and glass heat-proof door, all designed with safety in mind for mobile homes. I loved the idea, the leasing agent had no objection, and Cork and I went shopping for a cord of firewood.

Comedy Under the Balls

The Gold Coast Hotel Casino west expansion opened in February, 1989. Owner Michael Gaughan offered Cork the new West Lounge (it had no creative name) to host a comedy club.

The expansion also included a bowling alley upstairs, and often in the lounge you could hear the balls hitting the pins. Because it was an open lounge with no cover charge, it attracted quite a mixed crowd. A bar in the center had seats with video poker games, guaranteeing part of the crowd would be sitting with their backs to you.

Cork would ask people to turn around, saying, "I can't get laughs out of your ass," but often they wouldn't pay attention. It turned out to be a tough comedy venue. "They don't pay, they don't care," he said.

One day I asked, "So how did it go last night?"

"Good. Nobody threw anything."

Still, we had a lot of fun in that lounge. He was able to hire whoever he wanted to appear with him. Naturally he first hired his friends, then only comics who were recommended by comedian friends he trusted.

Between the tough room and the bowling alley upstairs, he began to refer to the lounge as, "Comedy Under the Balls."

In his Gold Coast endeavor, Michael Gaughan had fifty-two partners. In the lounge Cork joked, "Imagine! Fifty-two partners! I don't know whose ass to kiss."

Bermuda Revisited

When RCCL offered Cork four weeks of straight work on the *Nordic Prince* from New York to Bermuda, he said, "How would you like to go with me back to Bermuda for a week?"

I couldn't say "yes" fast enough.

I knew he'd offer a week to each daughter. That left one week to invite someone else. Cork liked to host friends to accompany him on his cruise gigs. So, I wasn't surprised when I heard him on the phone inviting a friend to go with him for a week to Bermuda, who was thrilled to accept. I was surprised when I heard him on the phone inviting a second friend, also thrilled to accept.

"Wait a minute," I said. "You've invited four other people and you've only got four weeks. What about my week?"

"Oh, you don't care," he said. "Besides, you've already been to Bermuda." His nonchalance stunned me. He headed for the bathroom and I followed.

"But you *invited* me. I said, *yes*. How can you go back on your word?"

"I'm not going back on my word."

In front of the bathroom door I stood my ground. "Well, I'm *going*. You call someone else back and retract your invitation."

I don't remember how he handled it and who of his invitees didn't go, but I will never forget how he vented his anger at me with snotty remarks and a cold shoulder. The more he vented, the more determined I became.

"Look," I told him. "You don't have to spend any time with me. The cabin has twin beds. You don't even have to sleep with me, but I'm going, because *you promised*."

Cork has always prided himself on keeping his word, so I imagine that's why he didn't tell me outright I couldn't go. I had called him on "keeping his word." But he made it clear he didn't have to like it.

That week in Bermuda turned out to be the most miserable vacation in my life. The snotty remarks and cold shoulder continued and, avoiding him as much as possible, I did have some pleasant time by myself. I befriended another girl, who had just discovered her cruise employee boyfriend was sleeping with one of the other waiters. We commiserated, but had some laughs as well.

When Cork and I returned to Las Vegas, he returned to his previous boy-charm, amusing self. For him, it was as if nothing unpleasant had ever happened.

Bourbon Street Showdown

Bourbon Street, a small hotel casino on Flamingo Road across from the MGM, had an intimate lounge on one side of the casino that regularly featured singers and bands.

Cork summed up the manager this way: "You know he is really lucky—normally they would have killed him for stealing, but somehow he managed to tap dance his way out of it."

The week Bobby Morris' Dixieland Band appeared there, Cork was invited to come by one evening and sit in on the drums. The evening was scheduled with several of Cork's musician and comedy friends, and Ann Geno, to gather for a fun evening of music and laughs.

Would I like to go? Absolutely!

"I'll pick you up at four o'clock tomorrow afternoon," Cork said.

I so looked forward to this. Never a dull beat when this group got together. I'd had a busy week and was ready for fun.

4:15. No sign of Cork. *Musicians and comics can be a little off-schedule personally,* I told myself.

4:30. Still no sight of Cork. No phone call. Mild annoyance began to set it.

4:45. I begin to worry. *Has he been in an accident? Is he laid up in a hospital somewhere, unconscious? Are doctors fighting to save his life?*

5:00. I have passed worry to the full state of pissed off. Is it possible—just possible—he *forgot*? Forgot he said he'd pick me up to take me to Bourbon Street?

Nah, couldn't be…yes, it could be.

5:15. Time to act. I couldn't call all the hospitals, but I could call Bourbon Street and see if he was there. I asked the hotel switchboard to page "Cork Proctor."

Minutes passed while I forced myself into a pseudo cool state.

"Hi, it's Cork." I knew that confident voice.

"Did you forget to pick me up?" I asked.

"What? I can hardly hear you. It's noisy here."

He was right about that. Casinos by nature generate high-energy noise.

"DID YOU FORGET TO PICK ME UP?" I screamed.

"We're all here in the lounge," he said. "Come on down and join us!"

"I'll be right there." He probably didn't hear my words because of the background noise and the fact that while I was saying it, I hung up.

During my twenty-minute drive to Bourbon Street my anger grew. No way was I going to put up with being treated like this. No way was any man going to treat me with such indifference, no matter how cute or funny he was. This was it. It was over. So I told myself.

In the lounge I walked up to the first row where Cork and Ann Geno and several friends sat. I stood in front of him and screamed, "You forgot to pick me up! No man is ever going to treat me that way! We're through." I held out my hand, palm up. "Give me back my door key!"

Cork looked startled. The others looked fascinated. He pulled the key I had given him from his pocket and placed it in my hand. I turned and stalked out.

The thing was that Bobby Morris' Dixieland Band was so loud no one could hear my words. Cork had probably read my lips. I'm sure I had looked like a big, angry, flapping bat.

* * *

The following week we had a dive trip to Cabo planned. I didn't call Cork, and he didn't call me. I hated to miss that trip, but I was still so angry and confused by the erratic way he treated me, I refused to do anything I felt would be a compromise. But I missed him terribly. My world seemed so dull without him.

Our breakup lasted three weeks until he called "to see if (I) was okay." I invited him over for dinner, and we easily fell back into our previous relationship.

He told me he had taken another woman on the Cabo trip, and it had been a disaster. She had become angry when he wouldn't sleep with her.

He never apologized for forgetting to pick me up to go to Bourbon Street, and we never discussed my public bat display.

Danger and Comedy

In late spring of 1989, we took a road trip in *Que Huevos* to California's Napa Valley.

Years before I had been to the wine country in Sonomo, and I always say, "If you can't afford a European vacation, go to California's wine country."

In front of us, driving through that pastoral scenery, was a truck with a winery logo. In the flatbed laid a massive drive shaft disconnected from a big diesel caterpillar tractor, roughly six feet long, six inches in diameter and looking like it could weigh two or three hundred pounds.

The thing hadn't been tied down well, and when we all rounded a corner, it slid off, hit the ground, and even though Cork had already slowed down, we ran over it.

"He was goin' too fast," Cork stated.

We all stopped and got out of our respective trucks. Cork was so angry he said later he "wanted to punch him out" but the winery driver was just a kid who didn't have a clue what he was doing. Frightened, he couldn't have been more apologetic. There was no damage to *Que Huevos*, and a few minutes later we were back on the road.

The flat bed of the winery truck was the same height from the ground as the dash of Cork's truck. "Two hundred feet closer," Cork said, "and that drive shaft could have gone right through the windshield and killed us both." Cork's driving skills probably saved our lives.

"Same shit, gettin' in a hurry," Cork repeated all the way to the restaurant we'd picked for dinner.

* * *

That evening we stopped at a charming French restaurant in the wine country. By now I had discovered that in restaurants it often happened that Cork would do *shtick* with the waitress, the waitress would erupt in giggles and laughs, and then screw up the food order.

In this restaurant, the owner herself waited on us. Perhaps because the French see humor differently, she never smiled at any of Cork's quips. I could feel his frustration at not being able to get a laugh out of her. After a few exchanges like this she said, "You should not try to do comedy."

Indignant, Cork rose from the table, left the restaurant, and brought back from his truck his comedy brochure with its glowing testimonials from people like Shecky Greene and Dick Clark and Phyllis Diller. He would prove to the French woman that he actually *worked* as a comedian and other people actually thought he was funny.

Thanksgiving in Valley Forge

Eventually Cork got bored and gave up his gig managing the Gold Coast Comedy Lounge for a contract to appear in *Caribbean Carnival* in the Lily Langtree Theater at the Sheraton Valley Forge.

I discovered the show producer, Greg Thompson, lived and had his offices in Seattle. In fact, he had gone to Roosevelt High School the same years I had. He had been a year behind me. I grabbed my 1959 Roosevelt High School yearbook and discovered the picture of Greg. A fresh-faced freshman with neat dark hair, white shirt, white sport jacket and black bow tie. I took the yearbook to Kinko's and had them blow up and print the tiny photo on letter-size paper. I mailed it to Cork at the Sheraton Valley Forge.

He told me he showed it to the cast, who loved seeing this different image of their boss. They only knew him in his present long-haired, leather-jacketed, high-heeled boots, eighties rock-star persona. They borrowed the picture from Cork, made copies, and sent them to their friends who were appearing in Greg's other shows in Bermuda, Japan, Reno and Las Vegas. For about six months, everywhere Greg went, he saw his high school photo plastered all over the backstages of his shows.

When I flew to Valley Forge to spend Thanksgiving with Cork, I met Greg for the first time. I had been afraid he'd be mad at me for the publication of his high-school-yearbook photo, and was relieved that he took it in good humor.

* * *

As soon as I knew I was going to Valley Forge for Thanksgiving I told all my friends I couldn't wait to see the snow where George Washington, during the American Revolution, had spent his famous winter.

They assured me there would not be snow in Pennsylvania that early in the winter, but I was determined to have the complete experience!

Mid-afternoon on Thanksgiving Day it began to snow. Before dinner we visited the Valley Forge National Historic

45

Park, little cabins hand-built by Washington's troops in different styles according to what part of Appalachia—or wherever in the south—they had come from. Smaller than the average American single-car garage, each cabin contained a small fireplace and small bunkbeds for up to six men. That day the park rangers shivered in their revolutionary costumes.

Later the TV newscasters reported this was the first time it had snowed in Valley Forge on Thanksgiving Day in fifty years! *Another Carolyn-the-weather-goddess phenomenon*, I thought.

Between shows we indulged our travel curiosity, visiting the Philadelphia Museum of Art for an exhibit of Robert Mapplethorpe's controversial black and white photography, and dining at the Italian-villa-style Kennedy-Supplee Mansion, now a gourmet restaurant.

One week on the show's dark days we went to overnight in the 1870 bed & breakfast, the Wedgewood Inn, in New Hope, that year's Bed & Breakfast of the Year. We enjoyed quite a romantic evening there.

We visited Doylestown's Mercer Museum, and saw their new, exciting acquisition: a nineteenth-century Vampire killing kit. This small wooden box lined with green felt contained a pistol, a box of "flowers of garlic" powder, a crucifix-shaped wooden stake, and a mold for making the traditional silver bullets.

"How much do you think an insurance company would charge today," Cork mused, "to insure you against vampires?"

In New Hope we dined at Chez Odette. While I looked forward to a savory French meal, Cork was excited to see "the place where Jessica Savage ate it in a 1982 Oldsmobile station wagon."

Jessica Savage, a prominent NBC reporter and award-winning news journalist, had dined there that foggy October night in 1983 with Martin Fischbein, vice-president of the *New York Post*. There had been heavy rain, and Fischbein drove out the wrong exit from the restaurant parking area, up the towpath of the old Pennsylvania Canal, and went off the edge fifteen feet to land upside down in shallow water and deep mud, which sealed the doors. They both drowned.

Cork remembers, "It was just me and you and the waitress, so Odette's must have been a laundry for the mob."

Carter Power Sports Party

Friends Charli and Dave had purchased a property on East Tropicana Avenue and build a large sports vehicle dealership. In June 1986 they threw an opening party, inviting advertising contemporaries and news media and friends, on a Friday night at 6 pm.

"What time would you like to leave?" I asked Cork.

"I don't want to be the first one there," he said.

"Okay, so what time would you like to leave?"

"What difference does it make, what time we get there?"

"It seems like a simple question," I snapped.

"We'll get there when we get there."

Exasperated at being unable to get a straight answer or have a sensible discussion, I said, "Let me rephrase that. It's Friday night and there will be a lot of traffic on Tropicana, so I plan to leave at 5:45 p.m. Perhaps you'll join me."

"I'll think about it," he said.

At 5:45 I announced, "I'm ready to leave now. Are you coming with me?"

"No, I'll be along later."

Of course, when I arrived at the party, where we knew nearly everyone there, the first question I was asked was, "Where's Cork?"

"He's coming later."

I had just made my way to the bar and ordered a glass of wine when I turned and saw Cork come through the entrance. I waved and he joined me at the bar, and we spent the rest of the evening together chatting and gossiping with media friends and stuffing ourselves with hors d'oeuvres.

A little after 8 o'clock I said to Cork, "I think I'm ready to leave now."

"Yeah, me too," he said.

We left and drove home at the same time, each in our separate cars.

The Graduation Dinner

Cork's oldest daughter Kathy graduated in June 1989 from San Diego State University with a Masters degree in Public Health, Public Health Education and Promotion. Former US Surgeon General C. Everett Koop was the commencement speaker. I was most impressed by this man who at seventy-six talked about being in his fifth career.

After the graduation ceremony the woman of the day, her sister Luann, their mother Louise, her paramour, Henry, Cork and I went for a celebratory dinner at an upscale seafood in Seaport Village. The seafood was succulent, and champagne was the drink of the day.

When the (large) check arrived, Henry reached for it. Cork reached as well and said, "I'll get that."

"No," Henry said, "I insist."

"It's my daughter's day and I'd like to pay."

"Really. It would be my pleasure."

Luann leaned into me and whispered, "This is when I like being a girl. We don't have to get involved in this."

High Voltage

In August of 1990, Cork joined another Greg Thompson production, this one at Las Vegas' Dunes Hotel Casino. In *High Voltage*, a sexy stage show based on a radio theme, Cork's comedy was presented in front of a world map, seated at desk with a Styrofoam coffee cup, as "newscaster."

Cork closed his twelve minutes with a bit he wrote: a rundown of "The Top Ten Shows on the Strip." He followed each show name announcement with a one-line description.

The number one show on the Strip that year was "Siegfried & Roy at the Mirage Resort and Casino," featuring the German-born duo of magician entertainers, a bevy of showgirls and white lions and tigers. Cork ended "The Top

Ten Shows on the Strip" with this line: "And the *number one show* on the strip – voted the most-visited show in Las Vegas – *Siegfried & Roy at the Mirage Resort and Casino!* ... Two ex-cruise ship waiters who make giant white pussies come and go."

* * *

Whenever we went to see other main room shows, maître d's who recognized Cork would always want to show us to seats in a front row. But Cork preferred to sit in the last two or three rows because he liked to be able to see the entire room. "This way, I can get a handle on the audience as well as the show. I can get a good barometer on what's working in the show and what isn't from how the audience is reacting." I could see his viewpoint.

The Dunes showroom was configured to include a balcony. So, when we went to see Mitzi Shore's late night *Comedy Store* there, being in the back row meant we were under the balcony, in the darkest part of the showroom.

From the stage, because of the way it's lit all lights focus on the show, and no one onstage can see the audience. Maybe a few people in the first row, but the rest of the audience is experienced as just applause in darkness.

It was customary that when a celebrity was "in the house" —meaning he was in the audience—the entertainer would interrupt his show at some point to introduce said celebrity and elicit a round of applause from the audience.

Someone had hipped the comedy show emcee, Argus Hamilton, to the fact that Cork was in the house.

"Las Vegas comedian *Cork Proctor!*"

The house lights came up and just as Cork began to rise from his seat, a guy in the third row stood, waved his arms, turned and bowed to the audience, which dutifully applauded. Because of the balcony, the house lights didn't illuminate the back rows, and Cork couldn't be seen. Argus Hamilton, blinded by the stage lighting, couldn't identify the audience even with the house lights up. He assumed the guy in the third row was Cork. He thanked him, the lights went down, and the show went on.

On the Road With Crafts

Hats and earrings sat on every surface in the warehouse, waiting to be packed for yet another week-end craft festival. The morning we were scheduled to leave to drive to Tucson, I rose early to pack, stoked some logs in my snappy Home Depot wood stove and put on the coffee.

At 8:30 a.m. Cork called. His voice sounded urgent. "Get dressed quick! The fire department is on its way!" He told me he had just pulled up in front of my door.

I threw on some sweats, opened the front door and let him in. Several neighbors in the business complex stood on the grass in front of my office, watching in alarm the black plume of smoke rising from the roof. I'm sure they were hoping their businesses were adequately insured against fire damage.

Moments later a big fire truck arrived behind the building. I rolled up the back door to let them in. Three firemen in full gear, looking like unrecognizable astronauts, rushed in dragging a fire hose as thick as my leg. They shoved it inside the tiny door of the portable fireplace and turned it on full force. Water and ash flowed onto the floor. Specks of ash exploded into the air and settled all over my hats and earrings.

My phone rang. "Hi, it's Tony." Tony's fire station was the closest one to the warehouse. "I'm sure you're wondering why I'm not there with my men. You see, today a guy called in sick…and I don't have a full complement to answer calls…so the guys who are at your place are from another station…because I couldn't send my guys…"

"Tony, I'm a little busy here right now," I said, exasperated. "Call you back." I hung up.

The firemen left, the neighbors dispersed, we cleaned up the mess as best we could—clean-up is apparently not on the list of fire department duties—drank our coffee, dusted off the hats and earrings, and left in Cork's latest vehicle, a 1986 yellow El Camino, for Tucson, only a half hour later than we'd planned.

* * *

On the Arizona side of Hoover Dam we had an amazing surprise. Luckily there was not much traffic because we saw the body of a man spread-eagled in the middle of our lane.

Cork pulled to the side of the road and got out to see if he was dead.

He nudged him in the leg. "Hey man, are you okay? You might want to get out of the traffic."

The man twitched and moaned something I couldn't hear. He sat up, and Cork helped him to his feet. Together they stumbled to the side of the road. He assured Cork he was okay and he had "just been walking."

The man had no suitcase, and Cork figured he was drunk and had passed out crossing the highway.

Garza Blanca

In the first year of our relationship I had taken Cork on a vacation to a timeshare I owned in Puerto Vallarta. Vallarta Torre sat on the beach north of a row of fancy beach hotel resorts.

The first afternoon we had moseyed down the beach, stopping at each beach-front hotel to sample their two-for-one margaritas. We had enjoyed the wide-open veranda restaurants and lounges, various musical entertainments and a spectacular sunset ribboned in red and purple and accompanied by the rhythmic roar of the waves.

In the darkness, we decided to cut through the last hotel to the main road and walk that way back to Vallarta Torre, assuming it would be well-lit. What we didn't realize was that further north the road split before Vallarta Torre, and we got lost. No road signs. Fewer street lights. In the darkness Cork announced he had to pee. Not a hotel in sight.

On a small bridge over a stream of muck that ran into the ocean, he unzipped and let go. Even with no one in sight, I felt nervous, imagining us being arrested and detained in a Mexican prison. Who knows how much we would have to bribe to get out?

During our margarita-filled happy hours, we must have been handed the sales flyer for the "FREE BUFFET BREAKFAST." Held in one of the exotically-decorated upscale hotels, its "price" – nothing is ever really *free* – was that first we would have to listen to a sales pitch for a vacation timeshare, Garza Blanca.

Listen to an hour sales pitch for two free buffets? No big deal. We can do that, we agreed.

Garza Blanca was a gorgeous ocean-front resort south of Puerto Vallarta's Old Town. The unit we liked was a brick casita with its own private swimming pool and view of the ocean. I envisioned romantic, moonlit, nude swims in the pool. Cork envisioned inviting his daughters for a week's vacation.

With mixed feelings I watched him slowly succumb. Our relationship was new, and I figured it wasn't my place to advise Cork on how *not* to spend his money. I told myself it was none of my business how he wanted to spend it.

By the time we got to the "free" buffet, he had committed $9,000 to buy the Garza Blanca timeshare. We were told it was the same unit owned by Gladys Knight for a different week. Great sales pitch.

* * *

In December we flew to Puerto Vallarta to spend a week in Cork's new timeshare. Our stone villa had a slanted high ceiling of natural *vigos* and *latigas*, and we loved the private swimming pool. We enjoyed fresh seafood dinners and strolled the Malecon at sunset and downed copious margaritas.

We signed up for a diving trip that took us to Las Animas, a private beach at the southern end of Banderas Bay where film director John Huston had a house with a wide front veranda. The 1964 film "Night of the Iguana" had been made there.

Surrounded by mountains of jungle, Las Animas is only accessible by boat. The dive company provided a sumptuous buffet lunch on the beach.

At the end of the day the boat ride back to the dive shop in the north part of town took an hour. From there we would take a taxi back to Garza Blanca. On the top deck, I spread out my towel, opened my paperback novel and prepared for a nice, relaxed trip. I did not know Cork had chatted up the boat captain, and found out the boat would pass the private Garza Blanca beach.

So why couldn't we just grab our dive gear and jump off there and swim in? The dive captain told Cork that would be no problem, he could stop the boat while we dived off.

The warm sun and gentle purr of the engine lulled me into complete relaxation. Then, "Hey, grab your stuff. We're getting off! Here's your B.C. and fins. Put all that" – he indicates my towel and book – "in this plastic bag!"

"What? What are we doing?" I fell straight into confusion.

"We're getting *off*. We'll swim in," Cork said. "We don't need to go all the way back to the dive shop. *Hurry up.*"

The boat was already slowing to a stop. The captain waited for us to get our stuff together while the other divers watched with interest. Everything we had for diving—except my novel—wouldn't suffer from getting wet, so this turned out to be an easy adventure.

Over the side we went and paddled towards the Garza Blanca beach. When we emerged from the water, we startled everyone on the beach. Fifteen minutes later we were in our room, showering and washing salt water from our bathing suits and dive gear and planning which restaurant we would visit for margaritas.

Cork Moves In

Eventually we agreed it seemed practical—and fun—for Cork to give up his little duplex bungalow at John Meyer's and move into the warehouse with me.

My only caveat was no *furniture* on the upper space over the offices, to which he agreed. I wasn't too confident about that ceiling construction, even though I'd asked the builder to make it "load-bearing."

Cork got some friends to help him move in one day while I was out tending to my clients. When I returned, there in the upper space, among the boxes, they had placed his heavy wooden coffee table and a bedside table.

I wondered, *What part of 'no furniture' did he not understand?*

Now I had a choice: make a big deal out of it to prove a point, or say nothing and let it go. I decided I didn't want to create a fight over something as silly as furniture. I told myself, *Ninety percent of what we worry about never happens, and the ceiling is probably not going to fall in from the weight.*

That is how I rationalized the fact that he had paid no attention to my request.

Thanksgiving in the Warehouse

For Thanksgiving, we planned to cook dinner in the warehouse for Tad and Priss, my girlfriend Cam, Cork's young comedian friend Kelly McDonald, John Meyer and Mack who was visiting from San Diego.

Because I had no stove or oven, I had purchased an electric roaster from a woman who had bought a camper and was selling everything to go on the road to see America. I had misjudged its size and now discovered the turkey I'd purchased was too big for it. The lid wouldn't close.

Cork, a guy with strong MacGyver genes, took two logs from the woodpile and two cans of cranberry sauce to weight the lid, and with a bungee cord he secured it to the roaster.

The warehouse was toasty warm from the woodstove—now that I'd learned the hard way how many logs to put in at one time—and the turkey came out great.

Cork said, "In all my life I've never had to strap a woman down, but now I can say I've strapped a turkey down."

"Who's that in the window?"

Another live show producer for whom Cork worked was Dick Francisco. Like Greg Thompson, Dick was from Seattle. Dick made his home and headquarters on Whidbey Island.

For Christmas in 1990 we went to Seattle, where I have family, for two weeks. For Christmas week-end we decided to go to Langley on Whidbey Island, and stay at the waterfront Inn at Langley, near a restaurant Dick owned, Francisco's Fine Dining.

The night before we took the morning ferry from Seattle to Langley, it had snowed, heavily. A small town of about a thousand permanent residents, Langley was a summer tourist destination, so we weren't surprised to see shops closed for the holidays.

The inn had no restaurant, and on the dark Christmas morning we found ourselves breakfasting in the room on the complimentary fruit basket. Days in the northwest are notoriously short. In the winter, it's not uncommon for daylight to begin at nine a.m. and end at three-thirty p.m.

Afterwards we bundled ourselves against the cold and ventured out to find a real restaurant. We found the town snow-shrouded, silent, here and there a holiday decoration and a light in a window. It reminded me of an old-time English picture postcard, except for the vision on one side of a cold, winter-gray Puget Sound.

In the half-darkness we trudged down a street full of snow that would not be plowed until the following day, if at all, and met a woman coming up the street. In a parka with fur-lined hood, a long, flower-printed skirt, she carried a wicker basket. We Christmas-greetinged one another, and Cork inquired about restaurants in Langley.

"Oh, my goodness, no," the woman said. "Everything's closed. Lots of people go to Seattle for the holiday."

"Do you know Dick Francisco?" Cork asked.

"Of course," she replied. "He lives over there." She pointed a mittened-hand in the direction of another street. "The third house down, on the left."

Cork thanked her and began to walk in that direction.

"What are we doing?" I asked.

"Let's see if he's home."

"Don't you think you should call first?"

"Naw. We're old friends. We'll just say hello."

We approached Dick's house, a single-story, white clapboard in a neighborhood of similar houses. Bright lights indicated someone was home.

"Wait. Let's have some fun," Cork said. I dutifully followed him to the side of the house where through a large picture window we could see into the living room. A Christmas tree of multi-colored lights dominated the room.

"Do this," Cork said. He pressed his face against the cold glass and raised his hands, one on each side of his face, flat against the window. I followed as instructed.

A woman entered the room, saw our grinning faces at the window, screamed and ran from the room. She returned, followed by Dick Francisco. He recognized Cork and erupted with laughter. He pointed to the front of the house.

We trudged through the snow to the front porch, where Dick beckoned us in.

When he had stopped laughing, he asked, "What are you doing here?"

"We're spending the week-end at your inn," Cork said. "We thought we'd surprise you by coming by to say hello."

"Well, you sure did," Dick said. "It's great to see you. What would you like to drink?"

We sat on the sofa by the Christmas tree and Dick introduced his girlfriend, the woman we had scared at the window. His mother, Brownie, greeted us from the kitchen, where she was preparing their Christmas dinner. Dick brought us drinks and his girlfriend brought us little bowls of mixed nuts.

For the next hour, Cork and Dick drank and exchanged show biz stories. Remember that time when...? What shows are you working on now... ? Whatever happened to that little pony dancer...? Would you believe...? No, Vegas/Reno/Atlantic City isn't like it used to be...

With only a bit of fruit on my stomach, I devoured most of the mixed nuts.

Second round of drinks, more mixed nuts, more show biz stories. The aroma from the kitchen of hot baked turkey made my stomach growl. I worried we would say goodbye, leave, and there would not be any restaurant open for dinner. This was turning into a risky Christmas.

Third round of drinks, no more mixed nuts. Dick interrupted a show biz story with, "Say, why don't you two stay for dinner? We've got plenty of food."

"My God," Cork said, "I thought you'd never ask."

The Roundabout Wedding Proposal

Not only did we walk residential ranch neighborhoods, we also bicycled them. The streets were wide and flat, with no sidewalks.

One day we biked past the ranch home of the owner of Walt Casey's Water Conditioning, an established bottled water company. The business manager, his son Steve Casey, had been a client when I sold radio time at KNUU.

Walt Casey himself puttered in the tree-shaded front yard, watering cactus and flowers and bushes. He and Cork greeted each other, and Cork introduced me as his "future ex-wife."

In the weeks that followed, this joke, in various forms, became a standard for Cork. My friends began to ask questions. "What's he mean by that?" "Are you getting married?" "When's the date?"

"You have to stop this," I told Cork. "I'm getting tired of trying to answer questions. They think you're serious."

Our conversation that followed was so convoluted I can't remember exactly how it went. But suddenly we were having a serious discussion about getting married. Cork never made a concrete proposal, just something like "Well, we could have a conversation about that…"

We agreed on the idea of a wedding—sort of—maybe—possibly—in November.

"You don't have to buy me a diamond," I said. I remembered my mother's platinum and diamond wedding ring. "I have one I can contribute." He said he had some old gold he could have melted down, and volunteered to "throw in" the heavy gold bracelet he had permanently soldered on his left wrist.

A few weeks later on a Tuesday he called me in my office and announced, "I'm going down to Gaudin Ford to look at new T-Birds. Want to go with me?"

"Thanks, but no," I said. "Got appointments all day."

On Wednesday he called and said, "I looked at a great new T-Bird, but I can't decide on blue or brown. You should come look at them."

Irritated by the interruption to my business day, I said, "Look, it's your car. You can decide what color you want by yourself. You don't need me to go down there with you."

On Thursday he called and said, "You might be driving this car some of the time... don't you want to take a test drive?"

"No."

On Friday he called and said, "You need to come down to Gaudin Ford and pick out the color you like...and drive the car...since this is going to be your car."

My attention shifted. "*My* car? What does that mean?"

"You need to get rid of that shitbox you're driving. I'm buying you a decent car as a wedding present."

Well, alright. I'll be right there to make my color choice!

I had long ago come to the conclusion that when a man can't find anything to complain about you, he attacks your car. The car is the last male bastion, the last stronghold of male strength and superior knowledge. My first husband had attacked my 1959 Nash Rambler with, "It's a dumb car." My second husband had attacked my 1964 Dodge Dart convertible as unsafe. Cork hated my Cadillac Cimarron.

"It's just a Chevy with a Cadillac body and a higher price. You'll get killed if you ever get in an accident with that shitbox," he declared.

For actual wedding plans, Cork's idea was, "How about we run away to the Caribbean to get married? Then afterwards we can throw a big party here to celebrate."

I laughed. "Do you have any idea how pissed all our friends will be to miss our wedding? And do you have any idea how much work it is to throw a big party? We need to get married right here at home. Same amount of work, less expense."

My Lutheran practicality kicking in, here.

* * *

Before I married Cork, I had been divorced from my second husband for fourteen years. I had always said—and believed—that "Great adventures do not happen to married ladies." As a child I could not answer when adults asked what I wanted to be when I grew up. But I knew I wanted to have adventures. I knew the word "adventuress" by the time I was ten.

Little did I know that marrying Cork would begin the greatest adventure of my life.

* * *

Our friend Fred "Mickey" Finn was appearing on the round center stage of Main Street Station Hotel Casino and Brewery in downtown Las Vegas. Florida developer and owner Bob Snow had designed Main Street Station after his then-highly successful Orlando attraction, Church Street Station.

Fred played ragtime piano and his wife was a banjo virtuoso. Dressed in Gay Nineties attire, they performed a long-time popular jazz and comedy revue.

We thought it would be fun to ask all our guests to dress in gay nineties/old western-themed attire and perform the wedding on the round center stage.

Between us Cork and I already owned two televisions, two crockpots, two toasters and five toilet brushes. What would anyone give us for a wedding present that we didn't already have? We decided to make our wedding a fund-raising event for Las Vegas'—and our—favorite charity, Opportunity Village. The organization, founded by former entertainer Linda Smith, mother to a Down syndrome son, served people in Las Vegas with intellectual disabilities.

We would ask each of our guests to donate twenty-five dollars to Opportunity Village in lieu of a wedding gift. We got some unusual responses to this idea.

Cork got a call from a friend who said, "Hey, I heard you're *charging* for your wedding."

"We're not charging anybody anything," Cork explained. "We're just asking people to make a donation to Opportunity Village instead of buying us a wedding present. You *were* planning to buy us a wedding present, weren't you?"

The guy stammered. "Well, uh, sure, I guess so."

"So, what kind of a decent wedding present can you get for twenty-five dollars?"

End of that conversation.

A comic friend called from LA to say he and his wife couldn't afford fifty dollars to come. I happened to answer the phone, and told him, "Quit smoking for a month and you'll have the fifty dollars."

He called Cork and complained: "When I told Carolyn we couldn't afford to come to your wedding, she copped an attitude."

Cork asked him what I said, and told him, "Well, she's right."

A girlfriend wrote me a letter explaining they couldn't afford the money, either. I called her and said, "That's what credit cards are for." She explained that her husband wouldn't let her charge anything. She and her husband had good jobs, and just the week before she had been excited to tell me about the new drapes she was having custom-made for her dining room. I'm sorry to say while no nasty words were spoken, that was the end of what I guess was not a strong friendship in the first place.

By this time both Cork and I were becoming disillusioned with some of our friends. One couple couldn't come because the cupboards were due to be installed that day in their new house. Another guy couldn't come from Florida because he had to entertain guys from Detroit so he could get another free Cadillac that year.

More than once I heard Cork on the phone say, "You know this is the only date I'm getting married. There is not going to be a repeat performance next year."

Cork's long-time friend Toni Hart, an ordained minister and mother of a former girlfriend, Linda Hart, would do the official nuptials.

Before we got married Cork and I did not have any exchanging of blood tests, still common in those days. We had the exchange of the TRW reports. Credit rating and financial responsibility were more important to both of us than political, religious, and other stuff combined.

Cork confided that he had been fortunate to never have contracted a venereal disease, though "I did get crabs from a dancer when I worked that strip club in Florida." He grinned and added, "But crabs are really easy to get rid of."

"Really?" I asked, thinking he was serious. "How?"

"Well, first you shave half your pussy. Then you pour kerosene on the hairy part and set it on fire. The crabs run from the fire to the shaved part, where you can smash them with a hammer."

The Fund-Raising Wedding

No wedding would be complete without a bachelor party for the groom. I worked with some of Cork's closest friends to arrange a surprise stag bachelor roast for him on Friday evening, November 1. The location was a popular Desert Inn Road bar called Pepper's Lounge.

I created a snappy flyer and mailed it to all of his guy friends. In addition to the surprise roast for Cork, I engaged six of my girlfriends to crash the party, dressed as men, with fake beards and mustaches.

* * *

It was Fred Finn's idea for Cork to enter the wedding ceremony by sliding down the firehouse-style pole in the middle of the center stage. During the rehearsal, with Cork wearing jeans, he found it easy and all went well. However, at the wedding he wore wool frontier pants with slash pockets, a type of fabric that slides differently from denim. He said it was so slippery, "I saw my life flash before my groin."

We had scheduled the wedding for noon on Sunday, to be followed by Mickey Finn's regular show. The previous Friday and Saturday nights, Cork did ten o'clock shows at Bally's comedy club, Catch a Rising Star.

Earlier Friday evening, we hosted a dinner for our wedding party at our favorite Mexican restaurant, El Sombrero, and earlier Saturday evening we hosted a dinner for our out-of-town guests at our favorite Italian restaurant, the Bootlegger. With all these exciting activities, culminating with getting married, by the end of the afternoon on Sunday Cork was exhausted, blotto, out-of-it. So, it was a good thing we had already consummated the deed.

I would not have thought anything at the wedding would move me emotionally, until Dr. Hart said the traditional words and Cork's eyes teared. I knew he was sensitive, but that did surprise me.

* * *

For my wedding dress I chose pink—halfway between virginal and scarlet woman. I designed and sewed the pink satin dress, made a matching hat dripping with pink ostrich feathers, and dyed lace stockings and shoes to match. Afterwards I sold the entire costume to San Francisco Sally's costume shop, for the same amount of money that I had invested in the materials.

Cork swears he saw Vegas hotel mogul Steve Wynn in the audience, and that he must have crashed our wedding, because he wasn't on the guest list and didn't pay the suggested twenty-five-dollar donation.

Because our wedding was a fund-raiser for Opportunity Village, we sent news releases to all the Vegas media—radio, tv, newspaper. The only one to respond by sending a reporter was the *Las Vegas Sun*.

They sent an Asian kid who, when we met him, we discovered hardly spoke English and seemed to have no idea what the event was about or why he had been told to show up. He took a lot of photos, but the single one they printed in the newspaper showed the only three people *not* in costume, with one-third of the shot blocked by the wide brim of a vintage, feathered hat.

As well-known as Cork was in town, he speculated someone at the *Sun* must have printed that photo to get back at him. "Must be for something I said somewhere."

The *Review-Journal* printed a picture of the entire wedding party, with me looking on as Cork kissed Dr. Hart. I honestly wondered from whom they got that photo, and if there was a local media conspiracy against us.

In any case, it was the best party I ever went to. I came home with a husband.

* * *

Monday morning after the wedding we drove to Temecula, inland from San Diego, California, where Cork had a week scheduled at Fats Johnson's comedy club, The Funny Farm. Fats, a singer comedian who had been with the New Christy Minstrels, had rented a bay in a shopping center for the club. Each week he featured another comic besides himself. One show a night.

He put us up for the week in a nice little condo, and during the day we explored the Temecula Valley, Southern California's Wine Country.

* * *

After the wedding I had the idea to submit an article to a bridal magazine about our fund-raising wedding. I queried eleven bridal magazines. One magazine responded after three months to tell me that while they were rejecting my article, the editor wanted me to know my submission had caused the greatest controversy ever within the magazine offices. It seemed the editorial people loved the concept of a fund-raising wedding, and the sales people were appalled at the idea of no gifts, fearing it would upset the magazine's advertisers. In the end, the salespeople (hense the money) had won.

No one accepted the full article, but *Bride's Magazine* paid me $100 for a mention in their Nuptial News column.

We raised over $6,000 for Opportunity Village.

* * *

The following year Main Street Station closed and one of the diamonds fell out of my wedding ring—omens for our future?

HELP! I Married ~~an Alien~~ A Comedian

PART TWO - THE EARLY YEARS

The Ranchita

For two and a half years, Cork had rented a little acre and a quarter *ranchita* he owned to a Sahara cocktail waitress/cowgirl, Cheryl. He had $20,000 saved, and in the spring of 1992, we began to look for a similar property in the southern end of the valley for a little ranch property to buy for our home. It was time to move our personal lives out of my warehouse office.

We enjoyed the search process, but eventually realized that every piece of rural horse property we looked at would eat the $20,000 as the down payment and require another $20,000 to bring it up to reasonable, modern living standards.

One day I said to Cork, "Why don't we move into your *ranchita* and use your twenty thousand to remodel. Then we'll have a low mortgage payment."

Cheryl had been wanting to buy her own property anyway, so the decision to kick out the cowgirl and move in made everyone happy.

In July Cork began to gut the house with the help of three construction workers referred to him by the owner of The Pasta Shop, our favorite Italian restaurant of the moment. When the owner showed Cork some cupboards the guys had built, Cork said he thought, *hey that looks like good work.*

The two brothers were coked up and wired like cheap toasters. Their partner must have smoked a lot of dope because "mellow" was his middle name. Nothing fazed him. One mistake soon became apparent: Cork gave them too much money up front.

Cork began to refer to them as "the Three Stooges Construction Company" because "They did a few things right and a lot of things wrong."

I knew Cork was a fix-it-yourself guy, and loved the remodeling process. I, on the other hand, didn't have time to get involved with that. My Graphic Communications clients kept me busy all day, and often in the evenings and on weekends. I handed Cork $1,000 and said, "Here's my contribution to the remodel. I don't tear things apart, sand, paint, or haul away debris, like maybe those other girls."

Several things about the property had never been permitted and weren't correct, but now could be fixed. He and the guys retro-fitted the windows, added skylights, took out a wall, rearranged and rebuilt the kitchen.

Cork and I took a home remodeling class. I won a fancy screwdriver set, and we learned what to look for so you don't make mistakes. But by that time, it was too late.

Cork told friends, "Here's what we learned from this experience: Always hire guys you just met who aren't licensed and have no experience, and always give them all the money up front."

It took longer than we'd expected, and we were excited about moving in. I decided the decor would be "Country Mexican" and had begun to paint electrical and switch plate covers in colorful Mexican designs.

In the midst of this Cork coined a new line: "Remodel is Latin for separation and ultimately divorce."

At one of the craft shows, we found a metal sign perfect for the front door: "Do you want to talk to the man in charge or the woman who knows what's going on?"

Puck

Each day we stopped by to see the remodeling progress. One Sunday afternoon when the workers were away, we drove into the driveway and saw a man running from the front door. Paradise township's zoned-for-horses properties were sparsely populated. Our rural property had not yet been fenced, so access to the house was easy. The guy had been trying to break into the front door and ran when he heard the truck approach.

"It's time to move in," Cork announced.

"But we have no kitchen," I said with dismay.

"The Berber carpet is down in the bedrooms. We can buy a bed and move it in tomorrow."

So that is what we did so we could be sleeping there at night.

Cork decided it was cheaper to get a dog than to invest right away in fencing. He asked a vet he liked if she knew of any "junk yard dog" we could adopt. As a matter of fact, she did, and gave us a phone number. We made arrangements to see a six-month-old border collie pup named, "Puck." The dog had been brought down from Oregon with a hippy girl now living with her parents, so she couldn't keep him.

In the foyer of the home Cork kneeled on the floor and knocked hard on the backside of the front door. Puck didn't hesitate with a ferocious bark.

"We'll take him."

Training Puck was a challenge in that Cork could not remember the commands. Puck, who I trained to answer to "Puck, come!" got confused when Cork commanded, "Get over here you little dickhead, before I send you back to doggie heaven."

We enrolled in inexpensive dog-training lessons at PetSmart. It should have been called "owner-training." The retired-canine-cop instructor said, "It's easier to train the dogs than it is the owners."

Since I was the one who took Puck to each lesson, he and I figured it out. I was the alpha dog, and Puck and Cork got to figure out who was the beta dog.

A few months later Cork left for Bermuda to appear for four weeks at the Southampton Princess. The day he left I drove Puck to our lady vet and had him neutered. I figured by the time Cork came home he'd be completely healed.

But Cork came home a week early. He walked into the house, and Puck rolled over on his back in greeting. Cork peered at the dog's stomach and said, "Did you have this dog neutered?"

"Yes."

"I thought we were going to talk about it first," he said.

"We did talk about it, and you couldn't make a decision. So, the alpha bitch did."

* * *

When we discovered mice chewing into the dog food bag, Cork got the idea to pour the food into a metal garbage can. While doing so, his reading glasses fell from his pocket in the can. He didn't see them fall, and found them weeks later when the food level got low.

Cork came home one day from a visit to Opportunity Village's thrift store with a surprise for both me and Puck: a box containing 500 frisbees.

"I got a great deal," he said. "The whole box for five dollars!"

Before we finally bought Puck a proper bed, he slept on a woolly purple blanket. One afternoon when Mack and Gene were visiting, I came into the living room to see what was causing so much laughter. The guys were sitting on the couch watching Puck, who had pulled his blanket into a ball and was busy humping it.

Landlords

Shortly after we were married Cork's ninety-two-year-old mother, in a rest home in Reno, passed. There had been no will, and Cork had to go to Reno to a probate hearing. Since he was an only child, and the only bill his mother had owed at the time of her death was a $29 utility bill, he planned to protest the $5000 probate fee.

Since his father's death, his parents' investments had been managed by First Independent Bank. Amy, the young, pretty brunette woman at the bank who handled the account, would be present at the hearing.

Cork and I walked into the courtroom and seated ourselves to wait. When Amy appeared, we saw warm "how's-the-family" greetings between her and the judge and the probate attorney.

"You no longer live in Reno," I whispered to Cork. "Even though they all know you, you are now an outsider from

Vegas. And remember, that San Francisco-LA rivalry thing is alive and well here between Reno and Vegas. You're fucked."

Indeed, he received no understanding from the court and had to agree to pay the five grand before he could claim his inheritance.

* * *

We paid off the balance of the mortgage on the *ranchita*. When our elderly neighbors decided to sell their property next door so they could retire to Utah, Cork decided to buy it.

As can happen in rural areas, while his wife planted beautiful rosebushes, Darrell tinkered and collected. Crates and rusting machinery parts and oil drums and pieces of corrugated tin and odd slices of lumber and assorted detritus filled the ground around the house. Even the wide oval horse corral had not been spared.

We went into escrow, during which time Darrell agreed to remove all that junk from the property. His wife, anxious to move on, had already moved to St. George, Utah.

One day Darrell approached Cork and asked if he could have $13,000 released early from the escrow so they could buy a trailer for their Utah property.

"No problem," Cork said. I was not consulted.

By the day we met with the escrow officer to close the escrow and officially take ownership of the property, Darrell had made little progress in cleaning up his junk.

The escrow officer slid the papers across the desk.

"I am really not comfortable signing this," I said. "Darrell has hardly cleaned off the property like he was supposed to."

Irritated, Cork said, "He promised me he would get it finished in the next thirty days. He gave me his word."

"But where's the motivation?" I asked. "He will have all his money, they have a new trailer in Utah, and they've already moved..."

"Oh, for God's sake," Cork said, his voice rising. "He gave me his *word*."

Feeling frozen inside, I turned to the escrow officer and in my calmest voice asked, "What would be the normal step in this kind of situation?"

I could see visible embarrassment on his face. "Well, normally you could close escrow but hold back the amount of money you think it would cost should you have to finish the work yourself, maybe a couple of thousand dollars."

"Makes sense," I said, looking hopefully at Cork.

"Oh, for God's sake," Cork repeated, angry and glaring at me. "Just *sign the goddamn papers!*"

Embarrassed and numb, I signed the papers without another word. Later I wondered, *why do I feel more embarrassed when he snaps at me in front of strangers than I do when he snaps at me in front of friends?*

After the escrow closed, we never saw or heard from Darrell again. It took six weeks and over a thousand dollars to clear the rest of the debris from the property, and we lost a month's potential rental income.

* * *

When we were finally able to advertise the property as a rental, I had the idea to do it through my property rental company client, Terra West. I had been quite impressed with the management skills of the two women owners. I thought it would be a good idea, since the property was next door and the tenants would be neighbors, if they didn't know we were the owners. Terra West's fee was only ten percent of each month's rent, and we wouldn't have to do anything but look at monthly statements.

Cork agreed to this. But six months later he fired Terra West. "They make too much money for doing nothing." Never mind that they had swiftly responded with an eviction notice when the first tenant got behind in the rent.

By then, in conversation with our new neighbors, they had figured out Cork was the landlord. Bonding relationships were building. I didn't know much about real estate, but I knew it wasn't a good idea to be "friends" with tenants.

The Non-Contributing Member of the Household

Often, we are judged—and valued—by how much money we make. I grew up in a world where a woman who stayed home, took care of a household and children, and "didn't work" was not seen as much of a contributing member of society.

Because I married a man who came of age in the fifties, I fell victim to this way of thinking. Even though I had a graphic design business that kept me busy eight-plus hours a day. I guess he thought, as many people do, that being self-employed meant you only worked a few hours a day, if at all.

One day, having heard me say something different from what I had said, Cork said, "So says the non-contributing member of the household."

Incensed, I retorted, "Oh yeah? I'll show you *non-contributing member of the household.*"

That evening I did not cook dinner. I fished something from the refrigerator and took it to my office, where I ate it alone. That night I pulled blankets from a closet and the pillow from my side of the bed and settled myself for the night on the couch.

For the next three days I continued this behavior, and Cork and I did not speak to each other.

Puck stopped eating. "There's something wrong with this dog," Cork said. "I better take him to the vet."

I thought Puck was upset because of the tension in the house.

On the fourth day, I awakened to find Cork standing over me. When he realized I had awakened he said, "We can't go on like this. You're sleeping on the couch."

"So? I like it here. I wake up and my first view is out the window at the pine trees lit by the morning sunrise."

That day I returned to the role he saw for me of "housewife cooking and cleaning," and that night I returned to the marital bed.

Cork never apologized for calling me the "non-contributing member of the household," and he never got around to taking Puck to the vet.

Cork Turns Sixty

On July 22, 1992 Cork turned 60. Carme threw him a party at his *ranchita*, and Jac Hayden decorated with balloons and confetti.

So many old and dear friends were there: Peter & Bonny Anthony, Carme's daughter Samina, comedian David Ianacci, burlesque comedian Uncle Willie, comedian Bernie Allen, Mack, Tad and Priss, Katherine Engle, the Rebers, and more.

Carme had written a limerick for the cake frosting:
There once was a comic named Cork,
whose mind was a real piece of work.
He was quick with a quip,
and generous with a tip
and he never lacked ladies to pork.

Jac had set up a microphone and sound system, and everyone took a turn telling funny Cork stories. Katherine told about the time when she and Cork were dating, and he had fallen asleep while she was giving him head.

I was the last person to speak. Under a tailored jacket I had worn a black lace bustier. At the end of my comments, I flung open my jacket and leaned forward to display cleavage.

"Just remember," I said, grinning in Cork's direction, "tits will upstage comedy every time!"

Will Work For Laffs

One cold January week in 1992 before Cork was scheduled for another appearance at Bally's Catch a Rising Star, a hotel engineer working on the tall Strip marquee dropped a wrench that hit the transformer and burned out the entire south side of the sign.

That was where in big letters would have been: THIS WEEK at CATCH A RISING STAR: BERNIE ALLEN, FIELDING WEST, CORK PROCTOR.

"Let's have some fun," Cork said, "Let's march on the Strip and advertise ourselves." Bernie and Fielding were all for it. The three comics would spend the afternoons on the sidewalk "picketing" in front of Bally's.

I volunteered to paint the signs.

"BERNIE ALLEN – Appearing this week at CATCH A RISING STAR"

"FIELDING WEST – Appearing this week at CATCH A RISING STAR"

"CORK PROCTOR – Appearing this week at CATCH A RISING STAR"

"SEE the Vegas Veterans of Comedy!"

"Will Work For Laffs"

The day they were to open, the three of them carried the signs up and down the strip in front of Bally's. Cork looked especially dashing wearing his long denim Aussie outback coat we had bought on a trip to Virginia City.

"We look like picketers, shamefully marketing ourselves," Fielding said.

"What's going on here?" Tom Bruny, Bally's Director of Advertising, had appeared. "Has this been cleared through legal?"

Several TV camera crews from the local stations had also appeared. Since Cork and Bernie and Fielding were not on Bally's property, but on the sidewalk of the Strip, the hotel had no legal power to stop them.

"Hey, Tom," Cork said, "We're having some fun. It'll be great film at eleven."

A woman Cork called, "the pseudo entertainment director for Catch a Rising Star", had also appeared and began to scream at them, her frustration clear in the tone of her voice.

"What's all the bull about?" Cork asked. "They're going to do a nice piece on us tonight on the eleven o'clock news. It's funny, and it won't hurt anything. The sign is burned down, in case you haven't noticed, and it's been burned for six weeks. Why are you screaming at me?"

The comedy club manager, Don Lane, approached in a huff and demanded, "Who authorized this?" Frustrated with no answer he liked, he retreated in anger to his office.

Reporters interviewed Fielding, Bernie and Cork, who explained that they were advertising their show since their names could not appear on the burned marquee.

Footage with the interviews appeared on Channel 8's eleven o'clock news.

"Thousands of dollars-worth of free television advertising and the hotel was pissed," Cork said in disgust. "Those suits have no sense of humor."

The Yellow Trailer

Cork had bought a '41 Dodge to restore and a custom yellow trailer to carry it.

One day in September he was driving down Maryland Parkway in KHUEVOS pulling the custom yellow trailer. He decided he would make a quick trip through Pioneer Citizens Bank's ATM.

Any sense of spatial awareness eluded him. The custom yellow trailer got hung up between two expensive metal deposit stands in the ATM drive-through lanes.

Cork had to go into the bank to ask Nancy, the branch manager, to call Triple A to come and free the trailer. Nancy, bank employees and people from neighboring businesses in the corner shopping mall came out to laugh at the old comic's dilemma.

Diane's Dress Shop

One sunny summer afternoon we were driving west on Charleston Boulevard, an early Vegas street where office buildings and casino hotels are sometimes interrupted by vintage 1950s houses. Most of these were now small businesses: an accountant's office, a maid service, a wedding planner, Diane's Dress Shop.

Every day Diane hung dresses outside from the eves to flutter in the wind, their movements catching the attention of passing traffic.

"Have you ever been in there?" Cork asked.

"Nope."

"Well, todays the day. You should check it out. Looks like they have some nice things."

He made a right and pulled *Que Huevos* into a parking space. Inside I was charmed by an array of Laise Adzer Moroccan dresses and tops with matching slacks with elastic waistbands. All perfect for when you want to look fashionable in hot Vegas weather.

I selected a sage green top and slacks, a tie-dye black and grey fringed Moroccan dress, and two more dresses to try on in a tiny fitting room. I loved all the padded shoulders. I looked great in everything!

From the dressing room, with an armful of clothing, I headed for the cash register. So enchanted by the clothes, I hadn't paid any attention to what Cork was doing.

"We can go now." I heard Cork's voice behind me. "She doesn't want to sell that El Camino."

I laid the clothes across the counter, and the salesgirl began to ring them into her cash register. "What El Camino?"

"The white one out in the parking lot."

Four hundred dollars in clothes later, we left Diane's Dress Shop and I had to laugh. "That wasn't about me checking out Diane's Dress Shop. That was about a car you spotted in the parking lot and wanted to buy."

I Hate the Bahamas

In March 1994 I presented a workshop on direct marketing at the Conference on Hospitality Advertising in Alexandria, Virginia.

At the conference, a large exhibit of hotel and motel print articles filled one hall. *Hotel Sales & Marketing* magazine sponsored a contest where you filled out a form and selected what you thought were the best ads. The forms went into a hopper, and at the end of the conference one name would be pulled to win an all-expense-paid vacation for two in the Bahamas.

I supposed since I was a conference speaker, I wasn't eligible for the contest. Oh no, I was informed, I could enter just like all the attendees.

The contest catch was that you had to be present when the name was pulled to win. That meant attending the final wrap-up ballroom meeting. The ballroom looked full to me. The form with the winning name was pulled from the hopper. No response. The guy wasn't there! So, they pulled a second form. Carolyn Hamilton!

"Congratulations! You are the lucky winner of a 4-night/5-day vacation at our out-of-the-ordinary-resort, NASSAU-CABLE BEACH-PARADISE ISLAND, THE BAHAMAS." read the official winner's letter.

Excited, I came home and announced to Cork, "Guess what! I won an all-expenses-paid trip for two to the Bahamas! And guess what? I'm *not* taking you!"

Cork had always made it clear he was not a fan of the Bahamas. "I hate the Bahamas. The natives are surly and the service is terrible. Those island guys hate white people. They're rude to tourists, and they'll rip you off if they can. I hate the Bahamas."

Now he said, "Great. Get one of your girlfriends to go. How about Cam?"

Since my original introduction to Hospitality Sales and Marketing Association International, the sponsor of the conference, had been from Cam Usher, Director of Tourism at the Las Vegas Convention & Visitors Authority, I called and invited her to go.

"Frankly, it's not a very tourist-friendly island," she said. "I'm not fond of the Bahamas."

I called my friend Gertie, General Manager of KXTZ, Las Vegas' top easy listening radio station. Gertie had lived in the Bahamas during her first marriage, and one of her three daughters had been born there. She said, "I'd love to go, but I can't get away from the station."

I called my friend Carole in Seattle, who had retired young and didn't work. She said, "I dunno… it'll be hot and sticky… I've always wanted to go to Ireland."

"I didn't *win* a trip to Ireland!" I said in exasperation. In the end, she passed.

Back to Cork. "Look, I'll take you with me to the Bahamas," I said, "and I plan to have a great time, so the first negative remark out of your mouth, and we separate. and I'll see you at the airport for the flight home."

"Deal," he said.

Our December week in Nassau, as guests of the local tourism office, turned out to be magical. The white sand beaches were just as glorious as the brochure pictures, and our hotel couldn't have been more comfortable and accommodating.

We visited the Ardastra Gardens & Zoo and the famous straw market and took a boat to Paradise Island, where a massive hotel/casino complex called Atlantis was under construction. We scuba-dived, enjoyed international and island cuisine and took local busses around the island. Everyone we met from hotel and restaurant staff to people on the street was courteous and friendly and helpful.

"I can't believe it," Cork said. "Someone must have put the fear of lost tourist dollars into them."

The Panama Canal

In April 1995 Cork was hired to perform on Cunard's *Crown Dynasty* on a repositioning cruise from Fort Lauderdale to Acapulco, through the Panama Canal.

We made wonderful new friends on that cruise. A late-fifties, well-suntanned couple, Bill and Barbara Rizer from Bradenton, Florida, had smuggled onboard their own stash of their favorite vodka. Every cruise has religious services for the major religions, and Bill was the Lutheran minister.

Rayna and Richard Knighton were lovely Kiwis from Aukland, New Zealand. Rayna, with her charming accent and boundless energy, taught handwriting analysis on at-sea days, and later I wrote a story about her and handwriting analysis in an issue of *Nevada Woman* magazine.

Cork performed two shows in the Rhapsody Lounge with his usual comedic wit that astounded our new friends.

* * *

In the cruise port of George Town on Grand Cayman island, we went with Bill and Barb to visit the Cayman Turtle Center. A major tourist attraction, this turtle center is an important research and conservation facility. For a small donation you could adopt a turtle. With true tourist enthusiasm, we donated. "Adopt" meant we got to release a baby turtle into the ocean and receive an official "Certificate of Releaseship."

As we released it Cork said, "Godspeed and swim as fast as you can."

* * *

In Acapulco, after leaving the *Crown Dynasty*, Cork and I treated ourselves to Sunday brunch at the Acapulco Princess, overlooking Revolcadero Beach. This elaborate beachfront hotel featured a fifteen-story Aztec-style pyramid, lush tropical gardens, swimming pools with waterfalls, tennis courts and two golf courses.

At the brunch we wandered from station to station sampling garlic salad grilled squash carpaccio, grilled cactus leaves with balsamic vinegar, sea scallops, octopus, and beef carpaccio with creamy garlic sauce, quails *ajillo* style, grilled mahi-mahi marinated flank steak, and the usual chicken, salmon, and roast beef. There was a sauce described as "chipotle strawberry cream," and I had no idea what dish it was supposed to accompany.

All the food cards were in Spanish and English. I was amused to see prosciutto translated as "Santa's ham."

Cork decided we should experiment in the drink area. He mixed half chocolate milk, half Corona beer, with lime, and half of a Mimosa. Immediately the chocolate milk curdled but it tasted surprisingly acceptable, if indescribable.

As we left the Acapulco Princess, sated and ready for a siesta, an instrumental version of "La Cucaracha" wafted in the background. Cork said, "You gotta love a country whose unofficial anthem is about a dope-smoking cockroach."

The Big Orange Garage

In the summer of 1995, Cork decided he would build a large, two-car garage on a corner of the property so he could restore old cars, a long-time fantasy left over from his days with Mack and Jim at Las Vegas High.

We discussed making it large enough that we could later build out a small single apartment in the back if we chose. It would be 900 square feet, have six-inch walls, four double-paned skylights, split unit air conditioning and two motorized overhead doors. In the rafters between the roof and the outside he planned two feet of insulation (I learned you normally get six inches.)

"It's going to have load-bearing trusses, with a chain hoist to lift cars, motors or transmissions, and a 200-amp electrical panel." He said this in the same ecstatic tone of voice a man would use to talk about his new mistress.

He found all the right people to farm out work. Eighteen thousand dollars later, he had everyman's dream garage, a place where he could now display his collection of license plates, including his personal favorite from earlier decades, SATYR.

He painted the garage his favorite color, orange.

* * *

Old cars: those mysterious mechanical mistresses that make men moan with childish delight. They adore them when they're shiny and new and prize them when they're ancient and grungy.

As baby boomers hit fifty and have money in their pockets, the hobby of old car collecting was hotter than ever. Cork told me it's not uncommon for a guy to have $45,000 invested in a car worth $25,000, restored. "But hey, it was a labor of love."

The restoration of old cars also requires the ongoing hunt for old car *parts*. Forget "Tool Time." It's "Car Time."

"Let's go out for breakfast," Cork said one Saturday morning. On the way he thought to stop at the multi-acre auto parts junkyard, Nevada Pic-a-Part, located in Henderson behind the Skyline Club. This was his favorite junkyard because he liked the guys who worked there and "they have a lot of old iron you can buy cheap."

"I'll just run in and pick up what I need," he said.

I'm as gullible as the next woman. We fall for the darndest lines. But intuition told me I shouldn't wait in the hot car.

In the junkyard I followed him in amazement up and down the rows of strange metal objects that were completely foreign to me.

On a loudspeaker a page bellowed through the parts yard: "Kevin, you have a telephone call. Kevin, telephone call." I smiled. I couldn't guess which one of those burly, bearded, suntanned parts guys was named, "Kevin."

Cork never did buy me breakfast that morning.

* * *

After the big car-restoring garage was finished, one morning Cork suggested, "Why don't you paint a mural on the north side? Maybe a big bottle of Corona, some limes, an antique car…"

I smirked. "This from the man who doesn't want to attract the attention of the county."

Wild with Phyllis Diller

That summer I had become the Managing Editor of a new regional magazine, *Nevada Woman*. Cork had been, in musician-speak, "between gigs", and began to rag on me about how much time I was spending producing the magazine. Translation: how much time he thought I was *not* spending with him, even though these were Graphic Communications day-time hours.

When Greg Thompson called, I answered the phone. He wanted to talk to Cork about being the comedian in his new Harrah's show, *The Great Wild, Wild West Show* in Reno.

"When do you need him to be there?"

Greg laughed. "Don't you want to know how much it pays?"

"I don't care how much it pays. Just tell me where he needs to be and when."

* * *

Between Greg's 7:30 p.m. and 11:30 p.m. shows, Harrah's would bring in a headliner for a 9 p.m. show. This week it was Phyllis Diller. Her week started on Monday night, when *The Great Wild, Wild West Show* was dark, so Cork and I went to see her show. Afterwards we went backstage, and Cork introduced himself.

After everyone had left her dressing room except us and the tenor saxophonist in the house band, Gordon Anderson, Phyllis, in her mink coat, blue knit cap and bunny slippers, opened a bottle of Chivas. We proceeded to talk about the business, laugh and trade jokes while we drank. She shared poignant stories about her early years at the Purple Onion in San Francisco, when women just didn't become comedians and she had to develop "attitude," fast.

We would laugh, Cork would throw a line, and Phyllis would cackle and say, "Oh, that's sooooo funny. Do you do that in your act?"

"No. It just comes out."

After that happened a few times, she said, "Well, what the hell *do* you do in your act?"

Three and a half hours later, the Chivas bottle was empty. Gordon had been drinking O'Douls, so musta been just the three of us drank all that scotch… we were trashed and still laughing.

At four in the morning we helped Phyllis find a security guard who escorted her from backstage to her room.

We Repair What Your Husband Fixed

In the kitchen remodel we had designed a second sink, handy when you have guests who want to help in the kitchen and need sink access. Cork had gone off to Reno and the second sink still had not been installed.

I remembered a billboard I had seen that read "We repair what your husband fixed" and in the *Review Journal* classifieds I found an experienced sixty-ish freelance plumber and hired him to complete the job.

When I told Cork what I had done he said, "Well he damn well better have done a good job."

I said, "Done is better than perfect."

* * *

By now I was well aware of Cork's fix-it and finish-it record. When he bought a fancy onion dicer, he and Carme sat at the kitchen counter and took it apart to see how it worked. When Puck chewed a book apart, Cork drilled holes in the pages to twine them together.

When the stockpot disappeared from my kitchen, I discovered he had taken it outside and left it to drain in the garbage can. When my Pampered Chef scraper disappeared, I discovered he had given it "to Puck to lick."

One Sunday morning he removed everything from under the kitchen sink looking for WD-40. I was sitting at the table reading the Sunday paper and after several minutes realized he had taken it to the garage without putting everything back in the cupboard.

Hours later he returned to the house. I had decided I was not going to put everything away after him. That night I prepared dinner using the second sink. For the next two days, I continued to use the second sink and wait for him to put all the cleaning items back in the cupboard under the sink and close the doors.

When I could stand it no longer, I said, "Don't you think you ought to put those things away?"

"What?" He looked at me with his best innocent expression. "I didn't do that."

VIEWPOINTS:

As I mentioned in the introduction to this story, there is always a his-version and her-version of given events in a relationship.

The following is an example from our kitchen.
Cork: "Boy, there's a lot of shit in this refrigerator!"

Carolyn: "It's a well-stocked larder, for which we are grateful."

TBird Fender Bender

Eastbound traffic on Sahara Avenue snail-paced that morning. I was sitting in the curbside lane in front of Palace Station waiting for the light to change at Rancho. Out of the corner of my eye I saw a car leaving the parking lot. At the last minute he seemed to suddenly become aware there was traffic. He stepped on his brakes but not soon enough to avoid hitting the right front fender of my Tbird.

We both got out to look at the damage. My immediate thought was how Cork would tease me about this. It would become a comedy bit to use onstage. I would hear about it for months to come.

I didn't imagine the dent in the fender would cost too much to fix, so I let the other driver, an older man who was clearly rattled, off the hook.

Since I was already headed west and was able to change my errand plans, I drove straight to the Oldsmobile dealership on Boulder Highway where I knew Cork had friends in the repair department.

I explained to Butch, the department manager, what had happened, smiled a lot and fluttered my eyelashes.

Could they fix it right now? Could they fix it with no paperwork for a case of beer?

No problem.

Could we not ever tell Cork?

No problem, ha ha.

Thus, I was able to stall the blowback for ten months, until the insurance bill came for the following year. The rate had one up, Cork questioned it, and I had to 'fess up.

Our House From the Air

Our friend Mel Larson, well-known for his marketing expertise as a twenty-year vice-president of Circus Circus

Hotel Casino, owned a helicopter company and belonged to several National helicopter organizations. When he had purchased his Bell 222 helicopter, he had told the company, "I'll buy it if you teach my wife to fly." His wife, Marilyn, became one of the first three women to fly the Bell Jet Ranger.

To promote Circus Circus, Mel had created annual chili cookoffs, featuring celebrity guests and Cork as emcee.

Mel began to fly over our ranchita and take photos from the air. We would come home to find them in an envelope in our roadside mailbox.

Cork wanted to climb up on the roof and paint in white letters, "Hi Mel!" but he never got around to it.

Bingo

Mel's wife, Marilyn, who managed an animal foundation, called to say they had a six-month-old border collie available for adoption.

"You have such a nice ranch," she said, "and don't you think Puck would like a little friend? Why don't you come down and meet this little guy? See what you think."

"Why not?" Cork said. Busy with something else, he sent me to the animal shelter to see the dog. "If you like him bring him home."

I had never been to an animal shelter before, and I found the experience profoundly disturbing. All those cages full of helpless animals with uncertain futures. Now I understood why San Francisco Sally had a ranch full of dogs from which she commuted for an hour every day to her costume shop.

When the attendant showed me the little border collie in his cage, I noted the sign on the wire mesh: "Bingo. Warning! Nips Children."

"My kind of dog," I said.

"We have a greeting room," the attendant said. "Why don't I show you there and have Bingo brought in, and you two can spend a little time getting acquainted before you make your decision?"

What great salesmanship, I thought. This was the equivalent of a car salesman suggesting a test drive.

I agreed. When Bingo was brought into the room the attendant said, "Now he might be a little energetic. He just had a bath."

What salesman would show you a dirty car?

Bingo and I adored each other immediately, and I hadn't even brought dog cookies. The deed was done, the paperwork completed.

In the parking lot, when I opened the door to our Taurus stationwagon, he couldn't have jumped in faster.

Backyard Tenants

It was not uncommon in Enterprise Township, with these large land parcels, for houses to have a series of outbuildings, one of which might be an unregistered "grandmother" house. Since we had a spacious area of land around our house, Cork thought it would be great to rent some space to somebody with a trailer. We invited Jac Hayden, who had to move since Carme had sold his acreage.

"Nope," Jac said. "I don't trust that Cork won't change his mind and sell the place one day. I need longer-term security." Nothing I could say would change his mind.

So began a series of unusual tenants, most notably the Vegas Vampire and Biff.

A popular local Vegas TV personality in the sixties and seventies, the Vegas Vampire had hosted a late-night, B-movie horror flick Friday nights on channel five and driven around town in a hearse. For the show he had worn a cape tied with a fat gold cord. His thick, dark hair had been cut in a page-boy, accented with a fat moustache. The Vegas Vampire was Cork's old friend Jim Parker, who still had the moustache.

When Jim moved his trailer into our backyard, he had a girlfriend from the Midwest he had enticed to Vegas to live with him. I think she was shocked by Vegas—and Cork's humor—and perhaps had expected something more substantial from Jim. She didn't stay long. Soon Jim also moved on.

Biff Jones, who owned a large friendly but fat Dalmation, worked as a baggage handler at Southwest Airlines. We had cut a hole in the back wall of the house for a doggie door for Puck and Bingo. On the outside wall we backed up a big wooden doghouse with the back wall removed. So, from the outside, the doggie door was hidden from view and it looked like a simple doghouse next to the house. The Dalmation got along well with our dogs, following them everywhere. But because of his extra weight, he struggled to go in and out of the dog house/doggie door.

Biff was a friend's brother-in-law. Biff had been living in a trailer parked in the driveway at his sister's house and had just been kicked off the property. Cork, accommodating soul that he is, said, "Hey, you can move over with us."

All was fine for a few months. Then on a quiet—Cork was still in the show in Reno—Saturday evening at eleven p.m. my cell phone rang.

"Help," rasped Biff. "Call 911! My lover stabbed me!"

While I dialed 911, I thought, *I didn't even know Biff had a girlfriend.*

The police arrived. Cops and Biff and his lover—a guy— stood in the middle of the yard discussing the situation. Biff refused to press charges. The cops said they would take him to emergency, but Biff insisted, "It's only a scratch," and he'd manage it. The cops shrugged and left, and Biff and his lover retreated to his trailer.

Our neighbor, Doug Trenner, appeared in my driveway. He and his wife Tina, who managed KNUU Radio, lived on the horse property on the corner. Tina had taken to referring to Cork as "Crock Pot."

"Is everything okay?" Doug wanted to know. "What are the cops doing here?"

I explained what had happened with Biff. Doug laughed. "Tina sent me over to find out. She was sure you'd finally banged Cork on the head with a cast-iron skillet!"

Gunshot

Mack and his car buddy Dana had come up from San Diego for the weekend and were sleeping in the big orange garage. On Saturday afternoon Cork's friend Gene came by in his vintage '51 Ford flathead truck, "Judy."

They had phoned a mutual friend, Ed Hillenbrand, to come by as well. In a previous life Ed had managed comedy clubs in Chicago where he had picked up the annoying habit of attempting to answer every question with a joke—stupid or stolen from comics—so that it was impossible to have a normal conversation with him.

When Ed drove into the driveway in his convertible, Puck began to bark and run circles around the vehicle. Ed waved a gun above his head and yelled, "Get that dog away from my car!"

"Jesus, Ed, is that a *real gun*?" I asked, alarmed.

I jumped at the deafening gunshot that followed. Guys' heads jerked up from where they were examining Judy's engine. Dana banged his head on the hood and swore.

"Wadda *you* think?" Ed snarled.

"Ed, that's *dangerous*!" I said in disbelief. "You're *never* supposed to shoot a gun straight up into the air. What's wrong with you?" I don't recall his smart answer, only that it pissed me off. "That behavior is unacceptable. I want you to turn this car around and leave now. You are no longer welcome on this property." I couldn't believe how rational my voice sounded under the circumstances.

Without another word, he backed out of the driveway and was gone.

Inside the house, I called Cork in Reno and said, "Let me tell you what just happened before you hear some crazy version from one of your friends."

In a calm voice I recounted the details, and what I had said to Ed.

"It's not my place to tell you who you can be friends with," I said, "but I don't ever want that man on this property again. If you want to continue to be friends with him, I am going to ask you to meet him for lunch in a restaurant or somewhere away from here."

I expected Cork to argue with me, but he agreed. When he was a child, his father, cleaning a shotgun, had shot a hole through the living room roof that really pissed off his mother, so Cork was not a gun guy. He honored my request and I never saw Ed Hillenbrand again.

Raul, the Gardener

With Cork, I was learning that it didn't work to be subtle and politically polite in our communications. You couldn't phrase things like, "Gee, I really wish you wouldn't …" It worked better to say, "That really pisses me off. *Don't do it again.*"

Cork began to make jokes about the ranch, the fact that he was older than me, and I would most likely outlive him.

"I know what'll happen," he said in a dismissive tone. "You'll run off with Raul, the Gardener and lose everything."

We didn't have a gardener named Raul. This was a metaphor he created to illustrate some point that totally escaped me.

References to "Raul, the gardener" began to increase. And with that, so did my annoyance. What was this all about? Did he think I was just waiting for him to die so I could run off with some other guy?

I tried to ask him, but he dismissed it as "just kidding."

Finally, I'd had enough.

"Listen," I said. "Your comment implies that I'm not smart enough to manage an inheritance, and that I'm vulnerable to whatever man comes along."

"Oh, you're too sensitive," he said.

My voice rose, and I almost screamed, "It makes me feel stupid, and I don't like it."

Now I had his attention.

"So that's enough with 'Raul, the gardener.' Don't you *ever* say that to me again."

Whatever he had been thinking, I never knew, because I never heard it again, and we never discussed it.

Visiting the Cosmetic Surgeon

Dr. Don Dombrowski, a cosmetic surgeon, was a long-time friend of Cork's. In the course of his career, Don had done a lot of boob jobs, reconstructed faces to look like Elvis, and performed coronary bypass surgery on a three-hundred-pound man. He had arranged for Cork to watch some of these operations.

Cork had referred past girlfriends to Don, and now he referred me when I wanted to have removed several crusty, mole-like growths that had begun to appear on my body at age fifty-two.

I made an appointment to get the job done. Because there would be anesthesia involved, Don recommended I not drive myself home from the appointment. Cork would drop me off and pick me up two hours later.

Don's entire staff knew Cork, of course, and took this opportunity to play a joke.

At 3:45 p.m. Cork called the office to see if it was time pick me up.

Don's receptionist, in a bright voice, said, "Oh yes, the doctor has just finished, and right now she is giving him head."

Jazz on the Sea of Galilee

In *West Coast Rag*, a jazz newspaper Cork subscribed to, I read an ad for a tour in December to Israel. Musician David Poe had organized it so a bunch of jazz friends from Las Vegas could go visit their friends in Israel, the Jerusalem Jazz Band, whom they had met at the Sacramento Jazz Festival.

"I know David Poe," Cork said. "He plays all the horns. Sign us up." One thing I have always appreciated about Cork is his ongoing curiosity about new restaurants, new countries, new adventures.

The tour company David had contracted to organize the trip was a Catholic company in the Midwest. With the confirmation paperwork, they sent each of us a blue carry-on bag with big white letters on the side: 1-800-Catholic. When we gathered at McCarran airport for departure, I noticed a lot of the musicians had used blue paint to paint out the white letters on their complimentary bags.

We flew to Tel-Aviv on Israel's flagship carrier, El Al, whose motto is, "Your home in the sky." We settled into our seats in the back of the plane. A stewardess came down the aisle carrying an immense clear plastic bag full of bagels. Across the aisle she opened an overhead compartment and with some effort managed to stuff the big bag of bagels inside.

While I noted the bagels, Cork noted the security. "El Al has the best airport security system I'd ever seen," he said. "The guy came up in a coat, tie and suit, spoke slowly, precise with his questions. He had eyes like a wolf."

* * *

Other than sitting in with the Jerusalem Jazz band, no specific playing had been planned. Our tour members just set up and played when they felt like it. On an open boat on the Sea of Galilee, they erupted into "When the Saints Go Marching In."

We traveled through Israel in a big tour bus. It picked us up at the Tel Aviv airport, drove us to Nazareth, the Dead Sea, Masala, Bethlehem and Jerusalem.

Our guide was a charming young French Jewish girl, Chantal. Everywhere she took us, her descriptions were selective. Nothing was definitive.

"Here Jesus is said to have…"

"Here it is believed that Jesus…"

"Here is where Jesus may have…"

"Here is where some people think that Jesus…."

"Here archeologists have discovered… and think maybe Jesus…"

Along the way we made some interesting bathroom stops. Even if it was a concrete structure by the side of the road, everything was spotless. Until we arrived at McDonald's in Jerusalem. Cork came out of the men's room and declared, "That is the dirtiest bathroom I've seen in all of Israel."

At McDonald's we marveled at the sight of four young people—two guys, two girls—in full camouflage, munching hamburgers with their Israeli-made semi-automatic rifles propped against their table.

One night, traveling through the dark, we saw ahead some sort of check point. Big lights lit the place like a mall in daylight. As our bus approached, we saw uniformed men carrying big guns.

Our bus slowed. The driver opened the door. I wondered if we were going to stop and have to get off the bus. Chantal held onto a hand grip, leaned out from the doorway with a big smile and a display of young cleavage and a hearty wave. The big gun guys grinned at her in greeting, and we breezed right through that check point, the bus never coming to a full stop.

After our jazz vacation in Israel, Cork said, "I'm more confused now about organized religion than I ever was. And where *is* God, anyway?"

The County Commission

More developers and individual homeowners had their eyes on Paradise Township, our area south of McCarran Airport. As a friend from San Francisco exclaimed as we drove him around our neighborhood, "Wow! Look at all this open space!"

Even with the completion of the I-15 freeway, built to connect with San Diego and facilitate tourism access to Las Vegas, traffic was increasing on the part of Las Vegas Boulevard South that extended south of the famous Las Vegas Strip. The Strip—actually US Route 91—had previously been the main highway between Salt Lake City and Los Angeles.

The county now decided to widen two-lane Las Vegas Boulevard South.

Besides horse people, most folks who had lived in Paradise Township for a long time had moved there to get away from city rules and regulations and the CC&Rs of planned housing communities. These folks wanted to do things their way, pile junk on their property if they so chose (like our former neighbor, Darrell), and not be bothered. A lot of these folks had a kind of loner, hoarder, feisty, independent bent. The one thing that could bring them together was the county coming in and messing with the neighborhood.

Paradise Township had regular meetings that not many of these people normally bothered to attend. The meeting at the small, neighborhood library to discuss the widening of Las Vegas Boulevard South attracted neighbors we'd never seen before.

It was decided all of us would attend the next County Commission meeting and protest the widening of the road. And who best to speak on behalf of the community but the resident comedian?

As the resident artist, I created flipcharts showing traffic patterns from the freeway off ramps and where potential traffic bottlenecks could appear.

The day of the County Commission meeting Cork looked professional in a suit and tie. I was proud of my visual flip charts. Paradise Township was on the agenda, and neighbors filled the audience.

The County Commissioners sat with their microphones on a raised dais. I wondered if it had been designed that way to intimidate the unwashed public who would be seated on the main floor.

Cork was introduced and called to speak at a center microphone on the floor. Commissioner Chairman Paul Christianson peered over his glasses at Cork and said, "I remember you when you were *Corky* Proctor."

"And I remember you when you had hair," Cork said.

At that moment I knew our little protest was doomed. Cork made his speech, I flipped my charts, the neighbors were satisfied with our presentation and—nothing happened. To our dismay, the widening of Las Vegas Boulevard South went forward as planned by Clark County.

The Orleans Opens

Michael Gaughan opened his new hotel/casino, The Orleans, on December 13th, 1996.

That night the movie *Titanic* debuted in the Orleans movie theaters. This was a coup for the Orleans opening because it would be two weeks before the film opened nationwide.

Michael and Cork had a longtime business friendship, so when Michael offered Cork the position of Entertainment Director, Cork accepted. He saw it as a chance to "get off the road and spend more time at home."

Cork hired four musicians—trumpet player Dick Greene, guitarist Tommy Rich, trombonist Jimmy Dell, tenor saxophone Charlie McClain—to play in the theater lobby. He had a sign made for the band that read, "This *is* the band from the *Titanic*."

For the hotel lounge, Cork assembled a new band he called, "Deja Blues." The four musicians from the opening, plus Bob Pierson on tenor sax and Kenny Harkins on Hammond B3 organ. The band appeared only in the afternoons, and Cork played drums.

He had custom brocaded vests made for the guys to wear over dress shirts I dyed in pastel colors. Black string ties completed their snappy look.

A huge fan of the Hammond B3 organ, Cork had discovered Circus Circus was going to an electronic piano and had two of the organs for sale at $1,000 each. He bought them both, and installed one in the Orleans lounge. The other sat in the big orange garage.

"Why did you buy *two*?" I wondered out loud.

"Because they were on sale," he said. "They were a *steal*."

By the following March managing—babysitting—the entertainment and the band in the afternoon became too much, and he disbanded Deja Blues.

Boys Paint the Dining Room

I left to go to my friend Kara's house in Malibu for a few days. I had been helping Kara photograph, number, tag and list over 2000 pieces of her extensive collection of celestial-themed jewelry for an exhibition at the opening of the new Griffith Observatory, which had been closed for renovation for five years.

Cork had agreed while I was gone, he would paint our dining room white. For this project, he enlisted the help of his friend, Gene Paulson.

I returned from Malibu to discover my dining room a bright royal blue, with white graffiti-style lettering saying, "*Viva Zapata*" and "*Baño*" with an arrow pointing to the bathroom. While I was shocked to see bright blue walls where I expected white walls, I thought it did seem to complement our *ranchita* décor theme of turn-of-the-century Mexican Country. So why make a big deal over something that turned out other than what was agreed and what I expected?

Gene confessed relief. "When Cork decided on the blue instead of the white, I thought, oh boy, what if she doesn't like it?"

* * *

Another surprise greeted me on the dining room table. I had a stuffed bear that stood on four feet and looked like a baby black bear.

A few months before my trip to Malibu the daughters had come for a week-end visit and we had visited The Secret Garden, Siegfried and Roy's dolphin and white tiger exhibit at The Mirage Resort & Casino. In the gift shop I had bought a stuffed white tiger cub, about the same size, that also stood on four feet.

Now Gene and Cork had cleared the top of the dining room table and placed the two stuffed animals so the bear was affixed atop the white tiger at a forty-five-degree angle. The effect was clear that the little bear was humping the little white tiger.

Only guys would think of this, I thought. But it was funny. I wish I had a picture of that for this book.

Cork, the Story-teller

Our friend Toni, who often traveled with her mother to exotic, foreign lands, had just returned from a fabulous trip and Cork wanted to share it.

At lunch one day with friends, he excitedly related how Toni had just returned from Madagascar, where she and her mother had a great time. At first, I wasn't sure what he was talking about, since the details were unclear. But that has never stopped him from telling a story.

Later, I said, "You know, I don't think she went to Madagascar. I could swear she said they'd gone to Morocco."

Cork waved a dismissive hand. "Oh, Madagascar, Morocco. What difference does it make? They both start with an 'M'."

The Jimmy Buffet Concert

When Jimmy Buffet came to town he appeared at the largest venue, The MGM Grand Garden Arena—17,157 seats.

One evening Cork came home with two tickets to the Jimmy Buffet Concert. In Las Vegas, complimentary show tickets flow around town among those in the know. Since Cork was now Entertainment Director for three major Gaughan hotels, I figured someone gave them to him.

"Who gave you those?" I asked.

"Nobody. I bought them for $300 from Rick." Rick White was the Orleans Marketing Director. I didn't ask where Rick got them. I was too impressed that Cork paid that much for tickets to a concert by an artist who didn't fit into Cork's preferred jazz, swing mode.

The Saturday evening of the concert we were to meet Rick in the bar nearest the Arena. We arrived before Rick to find the bar standing-room-only, in the back. Corked yelled an order for a margarita for me and a Corona for him.

"Sorry, no Corona." The message was relayed to us in the back near the entrance to the room.

Okay, two margaritas. Soon they were passed over heads to us. Thirty dollars was passed back, $15 for each margarita.

"Corona's the official sponsor of this concert," Cork muttered. "Where's the Corona?"

A nearby patron said, "They ran out. The parrotheads started tailgate-drinking in the parking lot at ten this morning." We were surrounded by parrotheads, questionably-sane people wearing grass skirts over jeans, island shirts and straw hats hung with faux parrots and plastic hamburgers.

Rick arrived and we ordered a $25 platter of Hawaiian *pupus*, which again was passed to us over the heads of other patrons. We devoured the appetizers a half hour before the concert was scheduled to begin.

In the spacious outside corridor to the Arena, along one wall booths had been set up selling all things Jimmy Buffet: mugs, stickers, license plate frames, ball caps, tee shirts, posters, fridge magnets, golf balls, beer glasses. Cork spotted a tee shirt he liked, and I said, "Why don't you go over there and find out how much it is?"

He returned a few minutes later with a disgusted look on his face. "Thirty-five dollars," he said, "for a *tee* shirt. With *short* sleeves."

I laughed. "Wait a minute, you're telling me you paid three hundred dollars for tickets, ten dollars for special event valet parking, fifty-five dollars for two margaritas and a few *pupus*, and now you won't spend thirty-five for a tee shirt you like?"

"I don't like it thirty-five dollars much," he said.

The Sacramento Jazz Festival

We were now attending a lot of jazz festivals, including the 25th annual Playboy Jazz Festival in the Hollywood Bowl.

As Entertainment Director for the Orleans, Cork brought in Zydeco bands like violinist Tom Rigny and Al Rapone's Zydeco Express. He found these people through the agent Louisiana Sue. Aka Susan Ramon, from New Orleans, she lived in Sacramento and managed zydeco bands. (She would later produce the The Crawfish & Catfish and the Gumbo Ya Ya Food Festivals). She also sang with one of the bands, and Cork had hired them all for the lounge in the Orleans.

Louisiana Sue invited us to be her guests at the Sacramento Jazz Festival over Memorial Day week-end. This music festival had been organized in 1974 by the Sacramento

Traditional Jazz Society and at its height attracted 85,000 people. (Sadly, by 2017 its popularity declined, and it ended.)

That week-end, we hung out with Cork's friend Jim Fitzgerald and his Sorta Dixie Jazz Band (resident entertainers in the lounge at the Gold Coast), Louisiana Sue and Al Rapone and his wife, Alice. We became huge fans of Igor's Jazz Cowboys and Avalon Swing, whose singer Shelley Burns looked like Olive Oyl, dressed like a 1920s flapper and did a campy rendition of "Hernando's Hideaway."

* * *

Al Rapone had partnered previously with his sister Ida Guillory and his brother Willie Lewis, and had been the vocalist, guitarist, arranger and a Grammy winner for Queen Ida's Bon Temps Zydeco Band.

Al had a raspy voice and always answered the phone, "Hello, this is Al Ra*pone* on the tele*phone*." Al gifted us often with homemade *boudin blanc* from New Orleans, a seasoned white sausage of pork, pork liver, pork heart and a rice dressing.

After the festival Al insisted on coming with Alice to cook us a traditional Cajun dinner—in our kitchen.

We provided the wine and invited a few friends to join us. Al and Alice brought the food and several large pots and pans and took over my kitchen to prepare from scratch Jambalaya, Crawfish and Shrimp Etouffee, Cajun Boudin and other dishes. They wouldn't take any money for any of the supplies. Our house smelled divine, and we drank and laughed like Mardi Gras fools, and ate till we were stuffed like the big *boudin* sausages.

After everyone had left and I was cleaning my kitchen, I noticed the big jambalaya pot had been so heavy it had broken one of the stovetop's electrical elements. When I pointed it out to Cork, he said, "Goddamn—that Cajun can *cook*."

* * *

The frenzied and exciting Zydeco music in the Orleans lounge eventually led the casino dealers and floormen to complain about the sound of the rugboard, and Cork was directed to tell the bands, "no rugboards."

Kakadu

The summer of 1997 Cork wanted to return to and show me Australia. Ann Geno had told him about Kakadu National Park, a huge—everything in Australia seemed huge—nature reserve in the Northern Territory where you could camp, or "go caravanning" as the Australians called it. The area included wetlands, rivers, saltwater crocodiles, sandstone escarpments, and aboriginal rock paintings dated from prehistoric times.

Ann insisted I had to see Sydney, and made arrangements for us to fly there first.

Quantas, what a civilized airline! Free movies, free booze, choice of entree, no shortage of pillows and blankets like El Al, and a free packet containing a comb, socks, toothpaste, toothbrush and eyeshade, which I drew in my new travel art journal.

Sydney in winter: COLD COLD COLD. After a healthy breakfast at the Gemini Hotel with dark, strong coffee and cream in a steamed pot, and determined not to be deterred by gray and drizzle, we spent the day walking an area called The Rocks. We visited the Ken Done Art Museum, and lunched on grilled calamari salad at Eliza Blue. From the restaurant we enjoyed an expansive view of the Sydney Opera House, looking unremarkable in the gloom.

People seemed to all be dressed in black, blank clothing—no logos and messages. Cork thought a lot of them looked "sneezy," adding, "This must be the red runny nose run."

Every person we spoke to said, "You should have been here yesterday."

That evening, after a fine dinner at Ummarin Thai restaurant, we left for the Capitol Theater in Chinatown, where we had tickets to see the play, *Miss Saigon*. I assumed we'd take a taxi.

"We'll take the bus," Cork announced.

Was he kidding? We're tourists! What do we know about Sydney's bus system? I also worried that this would take a lot longer than a taxi to get to the theater.

Cork ignored my concerns, and we boarded a bus with a driver who assured us he went "near" the Capitol Theater.

"Why are we doing this?" I couldn't let it go.

Cork said, "I feel safer on the bus."

"We'll be late for the play," I protested.

"No, we won't. We have plenty of time."

The bus inched through traffic and unfamiliar streets. I looked at my watch. We arrived at the Capitol Theater exactly at eight o'clock. Three minutes later the play began.

Later I told Cork, who has never liked "to be rushed," "You should have been born a King. Then the entertainment would begin not at eight o'clock, but when you arrived."

* * *

The following morning at 7 a.m. we flew on Qantas to Darwin, where we were met by ATT King's tour guides Steven and Robyn.

At the Museum and Art Gallery of the Northern Territory, they introduced us to aborigine art, paints, tools and themes. I discovered twelve poisonous snakes indigenous to the area. *Is it too late to get our money back?*

Kakadu is known for its biodiversity. This area of rivers, wetlands, sandstone escarpments with prehistoric Aboriginal rock paintings, diverse wildlife and over 2,000 plant species makes up the National Park.

Steven and Robyn introduced us to the bus that would be our transportation and rolling supply coach during our camping trip in Kakadu. The forest green of this Mercedes tour bus, dubbed "Huey", made me think of a big jungle land rover. The back third of the bus stored tents, tools, provisions and cooking supplies, and our fuchsia-colored sleeping bags. Steve drove and Robyn cooked.

The first evening we camped in a caravan park on the edge of Darwin, just inside the southern entrance to the Park. One entire side of the bus folded down to create a prep and cooking "kitchen." Those German Mercedes people understand space-efficiency.

On the Daly River we camped at a mango farm. The owner, Alan, took us all for a ride on the river in a canopied flat boat to see crocodiles as long as the boat.

"Keep your hands inside the boat," he advised.

We erected our tents under massive eighty-year-old mango trees and enjoyed a colorful sunset over an open field at the edge of which a group of wallaroos munched on the grass.

I had just fallen asleep when I was startled awake by the *thunk* of a large ripe mango that fell from a tree. The first of many that night.

"Oh well," Cork said, "you didn't need that sleep anyway."

After a cool night we were up at 5:30 a.m. in the dark of a damp morning. At sunrise we saw a dozen straw-necked ibis on the lawn, digging with their beaks for grubs at the tree bases. We packed everything, had our hot "brekkie" and left the mango farm at 8 a.m. Those Aussies were punctual.

We rolled through flat country with forests of tall skinny trees—and lots of mosquitoes and flies.

"The trick is to talk like a Queenslander," Steve said, "with your teeth shut, only moving your lips, guaranteed you'll never swallow a fly.

After a hot, strenuous hike to some small waterfalls and fresh-water pools and streams, we camped one night at Peterick Rainforest. Nearby was a hidden pool three to four feet deep with a sand bottom, rimmed with pandanus roots. We splashed and floated and relaxed from our hike.

Cork wanted to leave after everyone else, so we could have sex in the water. I declined.

In Litchfield National Park we made another swim stop at Wangi Falls, where parts of *Crocodile Dundee* had been filmed. Swimming there, I closed my eyes and confess I imagined Paul Hogan, as the Legendary Mike Dundee, swimming beside me.

Robyn showed us how to make billy-tea in a bucket hanging from a makeshift tripod of branches. On a low, grated iron, table-like frame set over a campfire, she prepared beef stroganoff and steamed vegetables. At dusk, for a half an hour a great, seemingly endless, hoard of fruit bats flew over the high treetops.

On the low-land plains of this arid Northwest Territory we saw fields of seventy-to eighty-year old Cathedral termite mounds. Cathedral termites are the largest grazer of these plains, consuming more grass than any other herbivore. Amazing how teeny ants could build a skyscraper-like structure six times my height.

Cork said, "Wow! An ant high-rise with no elevator!"

* * *

Perhaps the most famous, internationally known aborigine rock art gallery is located at Ubirr in the East Alligator region. Kakadu National Park itself is known to have the largest number of and best preserved and oldest rock art sites in the world, some dating back 20,000 years.

The people made the paintings and—and still paint today—to express their connection to nature and the world as well as to express their cultural identity.

We learned that Aborigines, who call themselves *bininj*, consider the *act* of painting more important than the painting itself, so on the rocks you sometimes see a newer painting covering an older one. I marveled at how similar this idea is to the Zen Buddhist idea that art is a form of meditation, so when you have finished creating the art you have gotten everything out of it you were meant to, and it doesn't matter what happens to the painting after it has been completed.

We climbed a winding trail, surrounded on all sides by spectacular views of colorful escarpments and scrubby landscape. At one point we faced, under a massive overhanging rock shelter, a wall of paintings. Here we stopped, and our local guide told us more about the history of the *bininj*. While he spoke, I felt moved in an almost spiritual way. Here I stood, three feet from paintings that had been made so many thousands of years ago. In this wild lonely and mostly silent place I could raise my hand and touch this rock art. What a contrast to standing in front of the glass-protected and security-monitored Mona Lisa in the Louvre.

Today the *bininj* continue to share their stories in paintings on canvas, paper and bark. Their themes still depict animal they hunt, activities they do, and even objects they still use.

Of course, at one of their modern galleries we bought several pieces. Two bark paintings, one framed with woven grasses, a carved saltwater crocodile, and we even carted home of full-size didgeridoo.

* * *

When it came time to erect the tents for the nights, you could tell Cork and I were the long-time married couple.

"This pin goes here."

"No, it doesn't."

"Then where does it go? And where does that one go?"

"Over here? No, maybe right there."

"I told you, the pin goes *here*. Hand me that thingamajig."

"What?"

"I said, hand me that *thingamajig*." He pointed to a small pile of posts and pegs and tools lying next to the mound that was the crumpled tent.

"You need to be more specific. I don't know what you want."

"Well, you're standing right next to it! Oh, never mind." He walked to the pile, gave me an annoyed look, and picked up what he wanted.

Between these heated debates we were always the last people on the tour to get our tent erected for the night.

I rested well after I noted the sides and floor of the tent were connected all the way around so nothing could crawl inside in the dark of the night. Australia has ten of the most poisonous spiders in the world and is infamous for more deadly snakes than any other country in the world. I remembered my thoughts about the Milford Track: *and you want me to go where and what?*

I was glad Cork didn't bump the center pole and bring the tent down around us, and he felt the same about me.

* * *

It seemed all of a sudden, our amazing camping trip had come to an end, and I felt reluctant to leave this wild, mystical place. We had seen so many amazing things, and I knew there were even more to see and experience.

A few days before we returned to Darwin, feeling rushed from place to place, I asked Steve, "Why don't we spend more time in any one spot?"

With a serious and perhaps a bit sad look on his face, he said, "Tourists want to see as much as possible. They want to feel they got a lot for their money."

Kuranda, Tjapukai, and the Great Barrier Reef

From Darwin and the Kakadu National Park we headed for Cairns in the territory of Queensland, where we planned to book a dive in the Great Barrier Reef.

We discovered a day trip on the Kuranda Scenic Railway up to the village of Kuranda in the rain forest. Kuranda had been settled in 1885 as a mining village. The railway had been built to bring needed supplies from civilization to the miners and to transport supplies from the jungle mining area down to the sea.

It was only twenty-three miles from Cairns up a thousand feet to this little mountain town, but this slow train took a couple of hours. It snaked through Barron Gorge National Park and made a photo stop at Barron Falls so people could get off the train, admire the falls and marvel at the view of Cairns and to the Coral Sea.

The rail line had so many curves that I spent most of the trip leaning out the window to take photos of the front end or the back end of the train as it crossed the trestles of the Stony Creek Bridge, ninety feet above the creek bed.

With all the cliffs and waterfalls and gullies and precipices and dense forests, I couldn't even imagine how they constructed this railway line, but I was glad they did.

"Wonder how many guys died digging and dynamiting this thing," Cork mused out loud, always the cheery observer.

103

Back in Cairns we bought tickets to see the Tjapukai Theater performance, celebrating the Tjapukai, the world's oldest living culture, which dates back over 40,000 years.

In 1987 three international theater artists and an Australian aborigine man and his wife, who had grown up in the Tjapukai culture, teamed up to create a one-hour play focusing on this dance-rich culture. Their performances became so popular that they were able to move in 1996 to this larger site in Cairns, build a real theater, the cultural village, a restaurant and gift shop gallery.

I loved the music and singing and chanting and thumping sounds of the dance, accompanied by the haunting didgeridoo. The elaborate body painting and decoration of the almost-naked dancers and musicians appealed to the artist in me.

Cork mused that they would do well in Vegas.

Our tickets to the performance included a visit to the Tjapukai "village," called the Tjapukai Cultural Park, that had been created behind the theater to showcase how aborigines had lived. Their "kitchen," though a primitive cooking area, looked practical and functional to me. I could easily see myself working in it. We learned about Bush food and medicine, and how to make fire without a matchstick.

Interactive demonstrations included how to throw a boomerang and how to throw a spear. We passed on the boomerang throwing. I have no idea how we decided spear throwing would be easier, but I think Cork and I shared a fear the boomerang would come back to hit us in the head.

Young people in native attire and painted bodies demonstrated the different activities. A sixteen-year-old boy showed us how to throw a spear. Under his guidance, I felt quite proud that my spear went further than Cork's.

Curious, I asked the kid, "Doesn't all that mud on your face harm your skin?"

"Are you kidding, lady?" he said in perfect English. "It's the best thing for your skin."

I thought, *I suppose it could cure acne, and if not, it would hide it well.*

Two nights in a row we dined at the Red Ocre Grill in Cairns, we liked it so much. This Australian restaurant famously served native game food like grilled kangaroo, red dear venison steaks, barramundi spring rolls, wallaby filets and crocodile burgers, plus fresh fish and oysters. Our favorite dish was the emu paté.

From Cairns we booked our scuba-diving trip in the Great Barrier Reef, the world's largest—and now endangered—coral reef in the Coral Sea off Queensland. One of the seven wonders of the natural world, it's the only living thing on the planet visible from space.

At the Cod Hole, one of the best-known dive sites in the world, we encountered a giant cod, over five feet long, that approached the divers in expectation of a food handout. We didn't have any food but the thing was so big it made me think if it wasn't a good sport about *not* getting a handout, it could smack us around a bit.

Afterwards, stripping out of our extensive dive gear, Cork looked at my chest and said, "You are lucky to have your own floatation devices."

The Flaming Napkin

Back home, across the road from our little *ranchita* lived our bachelor neighbor, Ike. For years Ike had worked as a maître d' at the Tropicana Hotel Casino and now worked, through the culinary union, independent gigs in catering. His Swiss girlfriend worked at UNLV.

On a summer Saturday afternoon, they threw a barbecue and invited her friends from the university and Cork and me. Around sixty people filled his spacious backyard, a grassy area surrounded by Chinese elm trees and massive oleander bushes. Looking around Ike's yard you'd never guess you were in the desert. Places were set at long picnic tables with checkered tablecloths and centerpiece candles, with the food served buffet style.

Cork and I found ourselves sitting among a group of university people, all engaged in university-world conversation. It occurred to me later that perhaps Cork had felt out of place among such academic people. I have no clue what he was thinking, but he took his paper napkin, waved it over the candle flame and said, "Watch this!"

I knew he hadn't thought this through when his face registered sudden surprise. The napkin flared into flames. With a deep, fast breath he blew them out. Ashes and tiny embers exploded in front of us. Many landed on the white blouse of the woman sitting across from us, who jumped from her seat with a horrified scream.

Others rose and rushed to brush off her chest while Cork and I sat silent, dumb-founded.

How could this happen? I thought. *What was he thinking?*

While attention was focused on the screaming woman, we rose and slunk away to throw our paper plates into a big garbage can.

"We'd better say, good-bye," Cork murmured. We found Ike and thanked him for a wonderful party.

"You're leaving?" he exclaimed. "Why so soon?"

Before Cork could open his mouth, I said, "We accidentally caused an incident with one of your guests. I'm sure you'll hear all the details later."

And we were outta there.

Cork Recycles

The rural area of Enterprise Township was subject to Clark County sanitation regulations.

For recycling purposes, they issued to each homeowner plastic recycling baskets. Red for paper, white for plastic and blue for aluminum cans. We placed them between the fence and the big orange garage.

I had noticed when I took things to dump that each plastic basket contained a mish-mash of papers, bottles and cans.

When the baskets were full, they were to be placed on the street for pick up. One morning I came out and Cork had dumped each basket's contents in the driveway. He was now busy sorting it, magazines and newspapers in the red basket, et cetera.

"Everything has to be separated for recycling," he said.

Duh. Those instructions came with the recycling baskets. Most people would set things in the appropriate basket along the way. Not Cork.

I concluded my husband was not opposed to doing things the easy way—he just wanted to be sure he had tried all the other (hard) ways first.

Christmas in Tahiti

My timeshare company had a travel booking department and had sent a lovely color flyer on December air fare specials to the island of Tahiti. Yes! We were able to book a room at Cook's Bay Hotel on the neighboring Island of Moorea, spending a few days in Pape'ete on the front and back ends of the week.

After an eight-hour flight from LA. we arrived in Pape'ete at 4:30 a.m. on Monday, December 15 and found our transfer to the dock to catch a 5:30 a.m. catamaran to Moorea. However, too busy enjoying French coffee and croissants at a café, we missed it.

We caught the 6:30 a.m. catamaran, checked into Cook's Bay Hotel, showered and napped and read until noon.

Cook's Bay Hotel proved to be a graceful, white eighty-five-year-old colonial house surrounded by red Ginger flowers, vanilla plants and pine trees imported from New Zealand. While the amenities were basic—no air-conditioning—they were spotless and the surroundings were everything colorful you would imagine on a tropical island.

The next day, in a Jeep with our French/German driver who had lived on the island for twenty-four years, we explored Moorea. From a high viewpoint we could have seen Bali Hai of *South Pacific* fame if it hadn't been raining. As tropical downpours are known to do, the rain magically disappeared by the time we reached the pineapple plantation, and tourist-hungry mosquitoes attacked. How good it felt the next day to sit in shallow water at the ocean's edge and scratch our arms and legs in the salt water!

We lazed through the days, eating and sleeping and reading and taking a bus tour circling the thirty-eight kilometers around the island. I painted in my art journal and found a local jeweler where I spent more than our week's accommodation on naturally-cultured black pearls.

At dawn one morning I sat on the bed next to Cork who was gazing out the window at fisherman readying their boats. I assumed his contemplative posture and said quietly, "We're in cosmic tune."

"Yeah," he laughed. "You're my soul slut."

On one island safari in an another four-by-four jeep, our guide gave a detailed lecture on island government, religion of the people, and a personal viewpoint that the Tahitians came from Egypt with Jewish slaves from Israel. He cited similarities to support this, including circumcision on the eighth day.

Cork could not help himself and said one of his often-used comedy lines: "I admire the Jews because they cut off the end before they know how big it's going to get."

* * *

Too soon, our week-long South Pacific island idyll ended, and we returned to Pape'ete. The capital of French Polynesia was a stark contrast to our experience on Moorea. Pape'ete was a city of about 30,000 people. The few sidewalks were dirty with the oily dust that comes from diesel fumes. Pedestrians did seem to have the right-of-way because drivers appeared to be polite. There was a huge central outdoor fresh food market. Palm trees were girded with metal as a protection against rats and coconut crabs, both of which eat young coconuts.

Our afternoon walk became stalled by a sudden tropical rainstorm. We stopped in the sheltered outdoor area of a local restaurant for a few local Tiaporo beers.

A young man entered the restaurant alone and Cork recognized him as another tourist at the pineapple fields the same day we had been there. Cork hailed him and invited him to join us for a beer.

He introduced himself as a professor from Tucson, Arizona's Pima College on a three-month sabbatical traveling all over the South Pacific. He was a training advisor for the U.S. Peace Corps.

"The Peace Corps is still around?" Cork asked.

Oh yes, it was the organization's thirty-sixth year.

After we had chatted a bit, the young man said we'd make perfect Peace Corps volunteers.

"Aren't we too old?" I asked.

"Oh no. The oldest volunteer ever is Jimmy Carter's mother, Lillian Carter. She served as a health volunteer in India, at sixty-eight."

"We'd like to go to the island of Dominica," Cork joked. "The diving is supposed to be really good."

"Actually, a good friend of mine is the Country Director on Dominica."

Incredulous, I asked, "You mean the Peace Corps is in the Caribbean?"

We were surprised, since you normally think of the Caribbean as a vacation paradise. But of course, there's a lot of poverty in the Caribbean.

How cool would that be, I thought, *to serve for two years in the tropical Caribbean?*

In the sixties, fresh from commercial art school I had worked for the Los Angeles advertising agency, Keye/Donna/Pearlstein, that had just taken the Peace Corps account away from New York's Young and Rubicam. The week I began work there as a paste-up artist, there had been an article about the agency in *Newsweek*. It alleged KDP had been awarded the account as a payoff for their pro bono political work in the Nixon campaign. Full of sixties righteousness, I'd thought, *oh, that would never happen.* In the eighties I had learned from Paul Keye that indeed, that had been the case.

My job had been to create the camera-ready art (paste-ups) for the printing plates for the full-page ads Mario Donna designed for *Newsweek* and *Time*. I was enamored of the idea of serving in Sargent Shriver's Peace Corps, but in the sixties, you had to have a Bachelor's Degree (which I did not have) and I'd heard you had to be able to repell (I wasn't even sure what that was). So, no Peace Corps service for me.

The man from Pima College brought back for me all that nostalgic yearning. I didn't entertain the idea out loud, certain Cork would never want to do anything as radical as join the Peace Corps.

Bryn Hartman Goes Berzerk

In the afternoon of May 28, 1998, I came home to find Cork standing in front of the television, staring at a news story.

As soon as he heard me enter the living room, he exclaimed, "Oh My God, it's awful! *It's just awful.*"

No-hi-honey-how-was-your-day. Straight into Hollywood high drama. Startled by the intensity in his voice, I asked, "What's awful? What happened?"

"Jeez, it's just *awful*." His voice shook. "She killed him— it's AWFUL!"

"Who killed who?"

"His wife. Phil Hartman's wife."

"Who's Phil Hartman?"

"You don't know who Phil Hartman is? *Saturday Night Live*?"

"I told you. I never watched *Saturday Night Live* because it came on late and I was already out on a date, or in bed asleep."

"And you don't know who Phil Hartman is? Boy, you gotta get out more."

Brynn Hartman had shot and killed her husband while he slept in their Los Angeles home. Some hours later, she killed herself. I thought, *boy, he must have really pissed her off.* (Later, I learned she had serious mental health and cocaine issues.)

It occurred to me then that Cork really was terribly upset about this. Being in show business he knew a lot of other show business people, so I figured this Phil Hartman must have been a friend.

"I'm sorry," I said. "I can see you're really upset. Did you know him well?"

"*Know* him? No, I didn't *know* him. I never even met him." Cork turned his attention back to the TV screen. "God, I can't believe   he's   *dead*,   and   his   *wife*   killed   him!"

Anniversary at Ocho Rios

Our seventh wedding anniversary in 1998 coincided with a gig for Cork on an NCL Jazz cruise on the *SS Norway* that would visit Jamaica—of Harry Belafonte fame! How romantic! Cork raved about the famous waterfall tourist attraction in Ocho Rios, Dunn's River Falls, which he couldn't wait to show me.

Jammin at Sea, the 16th annual floating jazz festival, carried some of the greatest musicians in the jazz world: Drummers Max Roach, who founded the jazz "be-bop" style, and Louie Bellson, who had been married to Pearl Bailey; tenor saxophonist Houston Person and his jazz singer wife Etta Jones; trumpet virtuoso Dizzy Gillespie; "the great guitars"— Mundell Lowe, Herb Ellis, and Charlie Byrd; and the University of Miami Jazz Band. And singer Ruth Brown, who had been seated next to me on the flight from Vegas to Miami.

"If that ship sunk, it would be the end of jazz as we know it in the world today," Cork said.

Ralph Sutton hated the piano he was playing and kept calling for the tuner, who he told, when he finally showed up, "I've played better pianos in whorehouses." He told me he actually had grown up in a whorehouse.

I love "high tea" and made a note to attend what was described as "Elegant Tea in the Club International." When I asked the server, "What tea are we serving this afternoon?" he answered, "Lipton."

In a shop on Front Street in St. John, the smallest of the U.S. Virgin Islands, Cork bought a wooden carved and painted flying frog made in Indonesia. Later, when we got home to Las Vegas, he hung it over the dining room table and dubbed the ranch, *la villita de sapo volado*, the closest he could translate into Spanish "the little house of the flying frog."

* * *

November 3rd, our wedding anniversary, the *SS Norway* arrived in the Jamaican port, Ocho Rios, and we taxied to Dunn's River Falls.

I looked at the wide, terrace-like, cascading water and couldn't wait to join the other tourists climbing them.

At the ticket booth, Cork said, "You go. I'll stay here with our bags."

Startled, I asked, "You're not coming, too?"

He shook his head. "I've already climbed the falls lots of times. I don't need to go. You go, and I'll stay here and take your picture."

I looked at all the Dunn's River attendants out there in the falls helping awkward tourists climb over the rocks, holding their cameras for them. All handsome, young, well-buffed, dark-skinned Jamaican boys.

"Oh great," I said, "Then we get home and I show my girlfriends pictures of me climbing Dunn's River Falls on our anniversary and they'll ask, 'Who's the black guy?'"

Who Do You Have to Fuck to Get Out of Here?

By spring 1999 Cork would come home at the end of his day at the Orleans fed up and disillusioned. Somehow, his official title had gone from Entertainment Director to Entertainment Manager to Lounge Manager, as Michael Gaughan hired a few other guys and gave them pieces of Cork's job.

In frustration Cork was buying Stoli Vanilla by the case. He had also taken to mumbling the classic bad-gig comedy line, "Who do you have to fuck to get out of here?"

One day for the third time he came home and announced, "You wouldn't *believe* what happened there today. It was so stupid it made the *Peace Corps* look good."

We joked about chucking it all and running away to join the Peace Corps, until finally he said, "If we're going to joke about it, why don't you call somebody and get some information?"

Why does the wife always get the secretarial duties?

Online I found an email for the nearest Peace Corps office, in San Francisco, and emailed a request for more information.

112

A large packet of colorful brochures and forms soon arrived in our mailbox.

In continued secretarial mode, I filled out my—and his—applications in neat block letters, and wrote my—and his—required essay about why we wanted to serve in the Peace Corps.

* * *

A Peace Corps recruiter, May Ng, came from San Francisco to interview us. On the application we had filled out there had been an option to note if there was a region of the world where you didn't want to go. We had noted Africa and the Middle East. Cork was wary of AIDS, and I refused to go to any country where a woman couldn't leave the house without her husband or her husband's permission.

"And we don't want to be cold," Cork told May. "I have arthritis."

She smiled. "No problem. Believe me, there are plenty of warm countries."

She returned to San Francisco and I made arrangements for us to get the required medical check-ups. We were taking it one step at a time, to see what would happen next. Neither of us were yet fully committed to this idea of taking two years away from our Las Vegas life.

We received a letter that we were accepted and could choose between Eastern Europe or Inter-America. The latter included the Caribbean, Central and South America. Eastern Europe sounded *cold*. We chose Inter-America because we thought it would be great to learn Spanish in the Peace Corps. Imagine our surprise when May called and offered us Suriname, one of only two Peace Corps countries in South America that didn't speak Spanish.

We had never heard of Suriname, but hey, why not? We figured we'd go down there, and if we didn't like it, we'd come home.

* * *

As Cork's job title and responsibilities had morphed downward, Michael hadn't messed with Cork's salary, and now Cork saw a few months of continued employment at the Orleans as a way to pay to build a single free-standing apartment in our backyard, next to the big orange garage. "In case we go into the Peace Corps and don't like it and come home early," he said. We had already talked about leasing the *ranchita* for two years if this Peace Corps idea came to fruition.

He designed a 600-square-foot, free-standing, single guest house and began construction in our backyard.

Our friends Karen and JD Huffer wanted to sell their condo and use the money to build straw bale homes. We made arrangements with them to stay rent-free in the house with the dogs for two years, and began to pack our personal belongings.

From Machu Picchu to the Amazon

Cork decided if we were going away for two years, we should see the Amazon rainforest "before they tear it all down."

In continued secretarial mode, I searched online and found Explorations, Inc., a tour company in Bonita Springs, Florida that specialized in vacations in Peru. I emailed the owner, Charlie Strader, and learned we could combine a week to Machu Picchu and a week in the Amazon at the Explorama lodges. The price was right, and it looked like an amazing experience.

In a phone conversation with Charlie I asked about the kind of beds in the rooms of the Explorama lodges.

"For this price, you want beds?" Charlie said. He turned out to have a great sense of humor and made all the arrangements easy for us.

No way we could know that in six months we'd be living in a tiny cabin in Suriname on the northeastern edge of the vast Amazon basin.

I'm so glad we visited the Peruvian National Park of Machu Picchu when we did, because I understand now there are so many visitors the grounds are crowded, and there is a visitor limit of 2,000 people a day.

Our experience was quiet and mystical. Because we stayed one night at the only hotel at the entrance to the park, we were able to rise at dawn and experience the Inca ruins in the misty morning light before the tour busses from Aguas Calientes arrived at 9 a.m.

That evening at the end of dinner, Cork began to entertain our group with a long story, one I had heard many times. For me, hearing the words felt like knowing all the lines to a favorite song, and without thinking I blurted out the punchline as he was ending the story.

Furious, he turned on me with a nasty remark that left the table silent and me mortified and embarrassed. I knew what I had done was the worst thing you could do to a comic—or any storyteller for that matter—but it had just slipped out.

On the tour bus a few days later, two women in our group approached me, and in all seriousness one whispered, "That is terrible, the way he talks to you. You shouldn't let him do that."

Their words made me feel even worse. How could I stop Cork from being who he is? I was torn between consciously knowing you cannot change another person, and feeling responsible for his behavior, as I'd always believed wives were sometimes expected to be. So often I would think, *if only I could find the right words to say to him that would make him understand how his flippant words hurt me.*

There is a fine line between comedy and cruelty and I blamed myself because I had stepped over it.

PART THREE - THE PEACE CORPS

Bon Voyage From Our Garage

Cork left the Orleans the last Friday in August, 1999 so we could go do "Rural Community Development" in the Peace Corps in Suriname.

After a year of paperwork that included copies of military records, our marriage certificate, medical reports and sealed references, we were scheduled to depart at the end of August. With the Huffers moving in, we had to pack all of our personal stuff, which for the following two years would be stacked in boxes in the big orange garage.

"What are you *thinking?*" exclaimed comedian Sandy Hackett when Cork told him we were leaving to join the Peace Corps.

One week-end Mack came up from San Diego to visit, sleeping on a cot in said garage. In the bedroom, Mack and I were pulling things out of a stuffed closet and deciding what should be kept and how to pack them. In one of Cork's never-unpacked-since-we-moved-in boxes was something fabric I had never seen. I unrolled it to display it full-length. It appeared to be a long, hand-appliquéd vest.

Cork walked into the room.

"What *is* this?" I asked.

In a sad tone Cork said, "Oh... a girl made that for me thirty years ago, and then she died."

Mack busted up. I couldn't help laughing, either. "So, do we keep it or what?"

"Just give it to me," Cork snapped. I don't know what he did with it, but I never saw it again.

* * *

We couldn't leave without a little help from our friends, who demanded a going-away party. That orange, 900-square-foot air-conditioned garage—Cork's pride in which he had intended to restore old cars—turned out to be a great place to throw parties.

The flyer/invitation/mailer headlined, "Bon Voyage From Our Garage, a Festival & Celebration of Cork & Carolyn's Departure for the Peace Corps." Dress was "Casual jungle attire" and it announced, "Cork & Carolyn are off to the tropical South American country of Suriname, where they will be supported for the next 27 months by your tax $$$!"

Suriname (formerly Dutch Guyana), is an equatorial South American country on the northeast corner of the Amazon basin. Think half-way between Devil's Island and Jonestown. Not that Americans are necessarily geographically challenged, but one friend thought the Amazon River was in Africa…

Our assignment, "Rural Community Development," was a broad title that could cover any number of projects. We were off on this adventure without any clear picture of what we would be doing.

Privately we talked about whether or not we would last the whole two years of service. Peace Corps isn't like the military; if you don't like it, you have the option to leave. But we made a good show of being committed. I had cut my hair really short for the humid jungle, bought a simple gold wedding band to replace the diamonds I would leave behind in the safety deposit box, closed Graphic Communications and sold my new Mac—a surprise gift six months earlier from Cork—to my former ad agency partner, Rich Newman.

Jac Hayden knocked himself out to decorate the garage in a "Suriname" motif. He discovered the country flag colors, the capitol is Paramaribo, and somehow, he'd even run across a few words in Sranan Tongo, the *lingua franca* of the country.

Along one wall he created an almost life-size backdrop of how he imagined a Paramaribo city bus looked.

Friends gifted us with their ideas of jungle necessities: hand-sanitizer, blank journals, fanny packs—even a machete!

There was a lot of love and laughter in that garage that made me pause to reflect, "Indeed, to leave all this behind? What *are* we thinking?"

The Last Hot Shower

From Miami we did not fly directly to Suriname. We spent two nights at a Marriott so we could spend one day participating in what Peace Corps called, "staging."

There we met our country director, Eddie Stice, and twenty-four fellow volunteers. They were mostly young and said "um," "like," and "you know" way too much for Cork's taste. We learned we were the two oldest volunteers ever to serve in Suriname.

We were part of "Sur 5." This Peace Corps designation meant that we were the fifth group of volunteers to serve in the country. The PC program in Suriname was just five years old. Each year a new group was brought in, and because the service commitment was two years, this meant we would be working in-country for our first year with the group from Sur 4.

In a series of meetings, we were given an overview of this developing country. Located at the top of South America just above the equator, the country's total population was 422,000.

Because for four centuries the country was known as Dutch Guiana, the official language is Dutch. The *lingua franca* is Sranan Tongo, a mixture of Dutch, English, and French, peppered with words from the Gullah language of West Africa. In addition, several of the different cultural groups of the country each speak their own language.

Oh great, I thought, *so what language will we have to learn?*

At the airport the day we departed for Suriname, Country Director Eddie Stice looked at our group standing in line surrounded by our luggage and remarked, "I have never seen new volunteers arrive with so much luggage."

Cork regarded the expansive Miami International Airport's rows of shops and restaurants and remarked, "This is not an airport. This is a mall with parking for cars and airplanes."

Later we would remember it was at that Marriott we had our last hot showers for a year.

Naks Volkshoge School

Our two months of in-country training began on Wednesday, September 22, 1999. Not yet real Peace Corps volunteers, our official government designation was, "Peace Corps Trainee."

In Lelydorp, a suburb of the capital, Paramaribo, we were housed in a military/meeting compound called Naks Volkshoge School, with sleeping rooms, meeting rooms and dining room. There we learned a few women would be assigned to health organizations in the city. The rest of us would be split up between Amerindian villages and Maroon villages, inhabitants of the latter being descendants of African slaves who worked the sugar plantations in the 18th and 19th centuries.

It seemed to me Suriname had just celebrated twenty-five years of independent development—but in the wrong direction. After gaining independence, the country had plunged into civil war, and many educated people had fled the country and never returned. The infrastructure had never recovered.

We learned Suriname has four seasons: the big rainy season and the big dry season, and the little rainy season and the little dry season. We learned that the entire population of the country celebrated the holidays of each of the five cultures (Hindi, Javanese, Maroon, Amerindian, and Dutch), and the local beer was called Parbo. We learned that the capital was referred to as *foto*, the Sranan word for "fort," since it was the location of the seventeenth century founding fort.

Cork and I would go to an Amerindian village, so our language training began in Sranan Tongo, originally a slave contact language during plantation times, when all the slaves from West Africa did not speak the same languages. Today Sranan Tongo is spoken by everyone in the country. This is a simple language, not a language in which one would discuss the agricultural merits of planting different varieties of cassava.

119

"Thank God we don't have to learn Dutch," Cork said. "Such long words. So many syllables. All those *kchk* sounds."

In-Village Training

After a week at Naks Volkshoge School, our group of volunteers for Amerindian villages were moved to the village of Powaka, where PC had just completed construction of a new training center. Our group would be the first volunteers to experience "in-village" training. We were given rooms to live in village houses with families for the duration of our training.

Peace Corps trainers Stephan and Eric helped Cork and I hang our hammocks in our room, while our new host mother, Sylvia, watched.

Sylvia's house was a typical Amerindian structure of horizontal weathered wooden slats with a corrugated metal roof. Inside, the three bedrooms and sitting room were separated by thin sheets of pressed wood nailed to two-by-four frames. Outside, a wooden lean-to sheltered the cooking area, a few hand-built wooden chairs and an iron framework to support pots over an open fire on a floor of savannah sand. Several yards away was an outhouse and a bathhouse. The house had electricity and (cold) water from a hose connection. It sat three feet above the sandy ground and chickens and dogs could be heard prowling about beneath the floor.

One morning Sylvia killed a tarantula the size of her hand. It was in the corner by the door where a lot of old clothes were piled. A dark brownish thing, it had pink toes. Sylvia took it outside on the end of a long stick, set it in the sand and squashed its head.

I couldn't believe Cork asked her, straight-faced, "How did it get in?"

Meanwhile Eddie had last minute frantic meetings with the village captain. There were a few construction details not yet completed on the building, and a discrepancy had arisen over who would actually own the completed building, the village or Peace Corps.

Sleeping in hammocks was an adjustment. One night I was awakened by a resounding thud on the wooden floor.

Cork had rolled over and fallen out of his hammock.

Bad Day in Powaka

One morning the downside of this new Peace Corps experience hit me full force. I felt like I was living out of a suitcase in a sandbox with no beach in sight. In the middle of class I started to cry and fled to the toilet stall, next to the shower stall where one of the volunteers had recently encountered a deadly fer-de-lance snake. The humidity, the so-much-wasted time, the unstructured instruction, the noise of Sylvia's household, the classroom—and nowhere to go to be alone—all got to me at once.

The following day my black moment had passed, and I could again appreciate the absurd humor of what we were doing. Paramaribo, which I had first viewed as dirty and shabby, had begun to look quaint.

"Human urine is sterile," said Mr. Vlugman, the Dutch civil engineer with PAHO, the Pan American Health Organization, who lectured us one morning on "Public Health Aspects of Waste Water and Excreta Disposal."

"Excreta" became our new favorite Scrabble word.

I learned way more about latrines and shit management than could possibly be useful. But Mr. Vlugman told a great story about getting an ant in his ear in Africa and flushing it out with a child's urine. I had already decided I wanted to write novels and imagined that scenario as an intriguing story for one of them.

In one class session, we broke into pairs and each pair selected a different American nursery song to translate into Sranan Tongo. Cork and I chose "Itsy-bitsy Spider." *Chin-chin anansi...* This was the most insane fun we'd had so far. Everybody was ditzy from living with the uncertainty of food, electricity, and lack of sleep. Eric recorded our songs, and when he played them back our laughter bordered on maniacal.

Peace Corps—or "Peace Corpse" as the locals pronounced it—preservice training had now taken on the aura of summer camp.

Vegetarians Versus Meat-Eaters

Food for the volunteers became an issue in Powaka. Each host family had been given a stipend from the Peace Corps of 35,000 Suriname gilders a week per volunteer to offset the cost of feeding their guests. Maybe there was a little extra rice for us, but mostly I noticed children with new toys and women with colorful new tee-shirts. Things like eggs and fruit and green vegetables were rare. Breakfast, if you could call it that, consisted of a quarter of a hot dog bun and a cup of tea. No butter, jam or jelly. The main meal was fish and rice, or meat and rice.

One day I asked Sylvia's eight-year-old son what kind of meat we were eating. "Jungle meat," he said.

Sylvia said she was told, "Americans don't eat rice." She also thought we ate canned sardines—a Dutch staple—and had never heard of tuna fish. By our reckoning, Sylvia was making out like the proverbial bandit with those 70,000 guilders. We declined the morning hot dog bun and often declined the evening meal of rice and the common creek fish, *kwekkweki*, a six- to eight-inch long fish with sweet white meat inside hard, crustacean-like scales. Too much work for spoiled Americans—not yet hungry enough—to eat.

The Peace Corps had hired three village women to prepare lunch for us five days a week when we were in class. Served buffet style, the dishes were tasty, but there was barely enough for all of us.

When one of the women spotted me taking a portion of the meat dish and a portion of the vegetable dish, she became agitated and exclaimed, "No no, that dish is for the vegetarians." I guess she thought if there were Americans who only ate vegetables, the rest of the Americans only ate meat.

This prompted a meeting between Eddie and our trainers with the three women to explain that those of us who were not vegetarians ate vegetables as well as meat. It was another week before there was a change and enough vegetables were served for all of us.

Meanwhile, when we were in town, we bought our own fruit, eggs and vegetables and snuck them into the training center at the end of the day and on week-ends to boil the vegetables and hard-boil the eggs.

In all my imaginings of what being in the Peace Corps would be like it had never occurred to me that any village in the world would not have a nearby market. Powaka only had a tiny store, *winkri* in Sranan Tongo, that sold basic staples: sugar, margarine, Candy, cigarettes, rice, milk, Coca-Cola and Parbo beer. For fruits and vegetables villagers took the bus into Paramaribo and shopped at the Central Market on Waterkant street, at the riverside.

* * *

One day during training when Cork complained about this and that—little things he thought "should be" different—I said with impatience, "Look, there isn't anything that's here or that's happened to us that wasn't in all that material they sent from DC."

He gave me a blank look. "I never read any of that."

"Of course, you didn't. That's why you're bitching now."

Captain Clive Kelly

Sylvia informed us we were invited to go with them to an exhibition of Amerindian photos at the village of Pierrekondre, on the other side of the Suriname river.

Cork and I had already been told that this was the village that would be our site for the next two years. Our rural community development assignment would actually encompass two villages beyond Pierrekondre, Redidoti and Casipora. While those were larger villages, we would live in little Pierrekondre because that was where the captain for all three villages resided.

Around 10:30 a.m. Cork and I hopped into a blue pickup with a bad clutch that began picking up others. Soon twenty men, women and children were crowded into it—silly us, thinking we few Peace Corps volunteers would be the only passengers—and we bounced our way from Powaka to Pierrekondre, on the other side of the river.

Arranged in the central recreation *kampu* (a thatch-covered cement patio) in Pierrekondre were fifty of about 3,000 photos taken by Captain Clive Kelly, an Englishman who had spent the past thirty years campaigning to save the rainforest of the Amazon basin. Each photo had been printed on a color copier and laminated. A forty-ish Dutchman named Eric, who spoke English, narrated the exhibit to the villagers.

After an hour, our group decided to return to Powaka. Cork was determined to meet the captain who Eric said would arrive "soon" and probably would be more than willing to show us his trimaran, reputed to be a veritable floating museum of Amerindian artifacts.

"If we stay," I said to Cork, "how are we going to get back?"

Nonchalant and adventurous as usual, Cork replied, "Oh, it'll work out. So, we might have to walk back. So what?"

The idea of walking four kilometers in hot humid weather did not appeal to me, but my own curiosity to meet the captain prevailed.

We watched as the blue truck, which had to be pushed to get started, left without us. We would trust to luck our way back to Powaka…

Not long after, the captain indeed arrived with his two dogs, a wolf named "Kelly's Eye" and a Chihuahua named "Tintin," a Brazilian deckhand, and a beautiful young Brazilian mistress, Jessie. Eric made the introductions.

At the same time, we met the Pierrekondre village captain, Martinus, who shared some melon juice and chatted. No one had offered us any food, and I was hungry.

Captain Clive Kelly was about my height, five-foot-ten, with a square jaw and shoulder-length hair that, at age 58, he was dying jet black. Over the years he had gone native. Each arm and leg, as well as his chest, was decorated with detailed tattoos. He wore floral print shorts and shirt (not matching) and a painted bark headband and facial markings. Across his shoulder he carried a colorful, square, cloth bag.

You couldn't help but immediately like this outgoing and outspoken and flamboyant man.

The only other language he spoke besides English was Portuguese, which was a good thing because that was all the mistress spoke.

Jessie was a striking Brazilian beauty of perhaps twenty with long brown legs and thick black hair pulled back and secured at the nape of her neck. She wore black shorts and a white tank top that perfectly encompassed the curves of her breasts. Around her neck she wore a shell necklace similar to the Captain's, feather earrings, and no makeup. Her Julia Roberts smile revealed perfect white teeth.

Eric took us all to Martinus' house where we met his wife and also the village *dresiman* (shaman), Robbie Sabayo. Martinus' wife, Lucia, brought out a big plastic bottle containing a brownish liquid and a cassava gourd. This was the infamous *cassiri* we had heard about. It was an alcoholic drink made from cassava juice that had been fermented by spitting into it. Every Amerindian woman had her own secret family recipe. Lucia filled the gourd, it was passed around, and everyone took a drink. I didn't expect to, but I liked it. It tasted like a chocolate raspberry liqueur.

Robbie invited us into a small windowless hut, no more than six-feet square with a five-foot-high door. There he showed us the spiritual articles he had inherited from his father, the previous shaman, who had died the year before. Crammed into the little hut were Robbie, Eric, Captain Kelly, Cork and I. Jesse had found herself a spot in a hammock in a nearby *kampu*.

One of the most sacred things Robbie showed us was a woven bracelet, quite old, that he used in calling the *winti* (spirits) to ask for blessings and sometimes help in determining the illness and appropriate treatment for a particular patient. Reverently he dangled the bracelet from a string in one hand, took a swig of rum from a newly-opened bottle, spit the rum onto the bracelet and began a prayer. The bracelet swung, seemingly by itself, first in one direction, then in the other. It stopped, swung in a circle. Another rum swig, other spit, more movement, and another prayer in Sranan Tongo, some of which I actually understood. The whole thing reminded me of a séance.

He showed us a small bottle of clear liquid, "For going to work." He poured a bit into Cork's hand and showed him how to splash it over his face, head, neck and arms, explaining that you do this before you go to work in the fields "so you can work strong and safe." We all followed Cork's example. The liquid had the smell and consistency of white crème de menthe.

I asked Robbie if women can become shamans.

"Yes, but not until after menopause."

Back under Martinus' *kampu*, we sat and visited. Captain Kelly's Brazilian deckhand brought out a one-string instrument called a *"bahia"* in Portuguese, and an old village man played it. He balanced the long wooden shaft against his forehead, hugged the gourd at the bottom to his belly and played the string with a stick in one hand and a stone in the other. He positioned the stones between the string and the shaft to change the tones. The rhythm was lively. He showed Eric how to do it, and Eric toyed with it while the village captain's wife brought out cassava bread and a bowl of chicken broth to dunk it in. Delicious, but as hungry as I was, I couldn't be greedy.

When these villagers discovered Cork and I were soon to be Peace Corps volunteers, they began to question us about getting a trainee in the village. Martinus explained they had a house ready for a volunteer, but had heard nothing from the Peace Corps in months.

Did we know Judith? Yes. Would we give Judith a message from the village? Yes. Would we like to see the house? Oh well, if you insist!

Like obedient Peace Corps trainees, we said nothing, as we had been advised, about our assignment to Pierrekondre, but it was a challenge to hide our excitement to see the very house we would be living in for the next two years.

A thatched roof covered three connecting rooms. We were shown the latrine, the nearby creek, and the large attached *kampu* under which today village women were making cassava bread. We assured Martinus Peace Corps had not forgotten the village of Pierrekondre, but they were very busy after the recent office move. And yes, we would give Judith their message.

Back at the exhibit area, the Brazilian was showing Jessie how to play the *bahia*. While she played a simple rhythem, he performed a traditional acrobatic Brazilian dance, *Capoeira*. It had been developed in Brazil by African slaves in the 16th century, later outlawed as a martial art, and had become a traditional "dance."

In the middle of a song, Captain Kelly stood and beckoned us to come to see the trimaran. "This will go on forever," he said, with a loose gesture.

We left Marinus' *kampu* and trudged down the road behind this Englishman who looked like something out of a sixties Coppola movie and his two dogs. At the river's edge we climbed into an inflatable Zodiac and motored to where his trimaran was anchored in the middle of the Suriname river.

Clive Kelly had had this custom fiberglass trimaran built in Bristol twenty-five years earlier and christened it *Survival*. Painted bright yellow, its interior was a primary-colored melange of Amazon Indian artifacts, from elaborate feathered headdresses to blowguns, woven cloth pillows, purses and mats and even a turtle skull the size of a football. Every nook and space was painted, adorned, or displayed some tiny surprise. Clive Kelly was also a scrimshanger and showed us several whales' teeth he had carved. His objects reminded me of Seattle's waterfront Ye Old Curiosity shop.

In several albums, he had collected over 6,000 names, signatures and locks of hair from everyone who has ever visited his floating museum/home. He explained the reason many pictures of his friends were nude was because he believed "Clothing separates us from mother Earth."

A full-frontal nude photo of rock star Sting prompted Kelly's tale of how he had introduced Sting to several important village chiefs and helped the singer set up his Rainforest Foundation. However, in the past year he said a third associate had absconded with $70 million in foundation funds, so he is no longer involved "in any way" with the singer.

"My father was Irish, and my mother was a gypsy, and I was born in Liverpool, England," he told us. He also said he had been an early manager of the Beatles and the Rolling Stones—he had photos to seemingly prove it—and had at one time owned a string of rhythm and blues clubs, first in Manchester, and later in Bahia, Brazil.

"Sea-cide" was the word Captain Clive Kelly coined to denote the killing of the earth's seas.

"The Sea is the heart of mother earth," he said, clasping his fists passionately over his heart to emphasize his words. "And rivers are the veins that float to and from the heart. By poisoning the rivers, we will kill the heart."

Probably Kelly's most well-known declaration of his beliefs was the documentary he filmed in the seventies, *Raoni*, about an Amazon chieftain he knew by that name. The film won the "Palme d'Or" at the 1977 Cannes film Festival, and was nominated for an Academy award the same year. In the photos he showed us, Kelly was younger, tanned and blonde.

He railed against the Catholic Church. "Their teachings are single-handedly responsible for the fact that the Amerindians no longer care for the forest, the earth, and their natural resources."

Raised Catholic himself, he ran away at fourteen. His message was that the natives don't want civilization. "They want to be left alone to hunt and live as their ancestors did in the forest."

Well, maybe some Indians he knows. Certainly not the teenagers who live in Powaka. Kelly's views smacked of sixties idealism, but overall his stands against dynamite fishing and deforestation were worthy.

At first, I thought Clive Kelly was too flamboyant to be taken seriously, but I decided, perhaps, it was this flamboyant appearance that attracted the media and made people stand up and pay attention to his message.

Kelly served us Earl Grey tea. As we sipped from plastic mugs, he told us his version of the origin story of the Amazons:

"Once the women of a tribe noticed they were doing all the work while their husbands and sons and fathers laid around in hammocks all day and painted themselves. The women went to *watramamma*, the *winti* of the river and described their plight and asked her what they could do.

"*Watramama* told them to tell their men to come fishing the following day at a certain time and location. She told the women to tell them they must come or they would get no sex. When the men appeared, *watramama* turned them into snakes, spiders and scorpions, the lowest form of life, and they scattered in all directions into the jungle.

"From then on, the women continued to hunt and do all the work, and kept the men in cages to be used only for procreation. They were never allowed to become strong again, and each woman cut off one breast so they could more easily shoot bows and arrows. The word 'Amazon' means 'one breast.'"

Our afternoon ended with signing Kelly's latest log book, scotch-taping our snippets of hair to the page, and being ferried back to shore in the Zodiac. It was 6 p.m., the rain had stopped, and Jessie, Eric and the Brazilian were waiting to go back to *Survival*.

Cork was impressed that the trimaran had sailed all through the Caribbean, survived a hurricane off Yucatán, down the coast of South America and four times across the Atlantic to England.

* * *

We walked back over the Suriname river on the wooden Carolina bridge—the longest wooden bridge in South America—as the sun set and a beautiful rainbow crowned *Survival*.

We held out our thumbs to hitchhike and the third vehicle stopped. A Hindustani family of seventeen rearranged themselves even more tightly so we could squeeze into their van. The cassette of Indian Bollywood music had been cracked up to the highest volume possible, and we began to bounce our way back to Powaka.

During the ride the family wanted to talk with us—they spoke excellent English—and there was much gesticulating along with the music. From the back of the van, over heads,

129

was passed popcorn, cups of *Stroop* (a Dutch kind of Kool-Aid) and finally a deliciously welcome *roti* plate!

When they dropped us off in Powaka, Cork tried to give the driver money for gas. He refused to accept it, and from his adamant shaking head I wondered if he might have felt a little insulted.

Our Kind of Commitment

We were never completely committed to twenty-seven months in the Peace Corps. At first, we agreed, "Let's just apply and see what they offer us." When we were offered Suriname, we agreed, "Let's just go there and see what it's like. If we don't like it, we can come home." Even though the Peace Corps is brought to you by the same folks who bring you the military and the IRS, volunteers do have the option of quitting, if for some reason it isn't working for them. When we got into training we agreed, "Let's just wait till we get to our village and see what that's like." And on it went.

This was a huge commitment for Cork, who declared it "harder than stand-up comedy and a whole lot less rewarding financially, but then we're not here for the money, or we'd really be crazy!"

Las Vegas' veteran comedian garnered his first laughs in Suriname when he told the native Amerindians his name. They immediately called him *Opa Corku*, which meant "grandfather" in Dutch and "cork" in Sranan Tongo. Each time he was introduced, the word "Corku" got a big laugh.

"Hope it doesn't mean something else that no one's telling us," Cork said, "like, maybe, butt plug."

After two months we were becoming accustomed to getting around Paramaribo, finding our favorite little bars, restaurants, the art store, etc. Cork and I tended to prefer the places other volunteers didn't frequent.

Between Peace Corps' living allowance and *Opa Corku's* social security we began to survive in grand style, enjoying the peppery native cuisine, wild "bush meat," and two-dollar bottles of imported French wine.

The Host Volunteer Visit

Part of the Peace Corps training included a field trip to the sites of currently-serving volunteers to see what it will be like firsthand to live at a similar site, in our case an Amerindian village.

The trainees came into *foto* and overnighted at another military-like compound for a series of meetings before the HVV (like any US government organization, things are abbreviated).

The next morning, half the group had bed bug bites and we had to sit through a boring safety presentation, distracted by a skinny orange kitten under everyone's feet. In the afternoon we went to the markets to provision for our trips and had another round of meetings with PC office staff at what Cork now called "Bedbug Manor."

Cork and I were scheduled to take a bus across the country to the western border, the river Corantyne. At the town of Nickerie, where the river flowed into the ocean, we would take a boat upriver to visit Jessie Longacre at the Amerindian village of Apoera.

At 8 a.m. the following morning Cork and I and another couple, Bobby and Susy, boarded a bus for what the office staff, who had never traveled further than the city limits of Paramaribo, had told us it would be "about two hours."

PC trainer Gladys also accompanied us so she could finalize the arrangements at Nickerie for the boat to take us to Apoera.

Four hours later, at Nickerie, Gladys said we would have to wait till 2 p.m. to leave with the upriver tide. I looked at the boat, surrounded by four or five guys, and suspected they were working on the motors.

"Well, if we have to wait, let's get some Parbos," Cork said.

The market at Nickerie was nicer than the Waterkant market in Paramaribo. Smaller, cleaner, more variety and everyone spoke English! Many vendors were from British Guyana on the other side of the Corantyne River.

The boatman informed Gladys "oil went up" and the cost was now 275,000 Suriname guilders, about fifty dollars more than the Peace Corps HVV budget. Gladys called the office for approval, and went to the bank for more money.

At the dock, we crawled down a single pole with two nailed cross boards, spaced two feet apart, from the dock to the boat. Then a big leap/step across the mud bank to the bow.

"If one of us falls into the mud," Cork said, "it's back to a motel in Nickerie." I agreed—no long, mud-soaked boat trip for me.

This open boat resembled a giant dugout canoe with an outboard motor hanging off the rear. On the river the sun was hot but it began to be an enjoyable afternoon ride.

The Corantijn river is brown and sometimes as much as a mile wide, like the Amazon. Everything went smoothly until the stupid Rasta-haired motor guy ran the boat into a mud bank. Now we were stuck with no oars, no long pole to push off with, no lights and no form of communication. But hey–we were wearing our Peace Corps-issued lifejackets!

"This gives new meaning," Cork said, "to the phrase, 'up the creek without a paddle.'"

In his attempt to free us from the mud the guy revved up the motor, risking damage to the sheer pin.

In exasperation Cork stood to his full height in the boat and yelled, "WHAT THE *FUCK* ARE YOU *DOING*?"

Eventually we were free and continued on to Orealla, an Amerindian village of thatched houses on the Guyana side, where at dusk we stopped to pee. Technically, we four Americans were not supposed to be on "foreign soil" without Peace Corps permission and certainly not without passports and ID, none of which we had. But happy to be out of that boat, even momentarily, we didn't care.

Dusk darkened to night and now it had been five hours since we had left Nickerie. Gladys, who had planned to leave us at Nickerie and return to the capital, had changed her mind and had decided to come up the river with us, announcing her husband was in Apoera. Visiting? Working? Unclear.

With tropical clouds blocking the moon, it was dark at 9:30 p.m when the boat approached the bank. Gladys and one of the boatmen began to call Jessie's name. How they knew this was Apoera was another mystery of Suriname. All we could see was blackness water line to skyline. A flashlight appeared high above the riverbank and Jesse appeared. He showed us where hard dirt stairs have been constructed in the jungle on the bank. We got out our flashlights. From across the river we must have looked like a group of ascending fireflies.

Gladys announced it was too dark now to go looking for her husband, so she would ride back to Nickerie in the boat that night with the rasta guys. Because Gladys had not told her husband she was coming, Cork suspected at the last minute she feared an unpleasant surprise "like her husband sleeping in a hut in the arms of another woman."

Luggage was passed hand-to-hand, and somehow we took everything but one forgotten life preserver. Our flashlight beams bounced as we walked to Jessie's house.

The office had told Jesse via the Amerindian radio that one couple was coming. Instead here were four of us. Jesse, who lived with his Amerindian girlfriend Yolanda and her two-year-old daughter, was a good sport, giving up his double bed to Bobby and Susy and the living room/porch to Cork's and my hammocks. This left their daughter's single bed for Jessie and Yolanda, and that night the baby slept on the floor.

Apoera was a clean village of traditional palm-thatch-roof houses and Dutch-influenced raised wooden houses with the occasional car parked underneath. Most of these homes were on Dutch-built cobblestone streets, remnants of Apoera life before the interior wars.

"Apoera is a very commercial village," Jesse said, "because of its dual position on both a river and a border. Everybody speaks English, the language of Guyana." He waved a hand. "People here have stuff, so they're fairly comfortable." This status quo, he added, had made it difficult for him to interest them in any development projects.

The next day Yolanda, a great cook, made us barbecue chicken and homemade French fries with her fancy industrial French fry cutter, and a native soup of fruits, potato, chicken broth and coconut milk.

Jesse spent the day looking for someone with a boat to take us back to Nickerie the following day. A stone barge, from a quarry upriver, came around about two in the afternoon, but made a quick stop at the pier. The barge captain didn't want to wait for us to get our stuff. By the time we grabbed everything and schlepped it to the pier, the stone barge was gone.

"I would have really liked to ride on that," Cork murmured, disappointed.

Jesse finally found a man leaving at midnight, who had room on his boat for the four of us. Cork, in his OC way, continued to grouse because he thought the stone barge would have made much more interesting travel.

We played cards by hurricane lamp light until midnight when it was time to go to the riverbank. I laid on the hard, wooden floor in Jessie's house in a vain attempt to nap. At a quarter to twelve we schlepped the bags, hammocks, mosquito nets and life preservers through the dark to the waiting boat and the beginning of a nightmare trip.

Approximately fifty feet long and ten feet wide with a large, covered bow, this was basically a cargo boat of a common river design. Under the bow—the only structural protection from the rain—people had already settled. No room for us.

This boat was nothing more than an oversized rowboat, with three cross seats and two motors. The bottom was covered with tarps, and loose tarps were provided to protect us from the rain. With no thought for anyone else, Bobby and Susy spread out prone on the bottom of the boat, leaving only the last seat, backed up by the gas cans, for Cork and I to sit with barely enough room in front of us for our feet. They had placed their bags as pillows, with their heads comfortably positioned against them, and immediately fell asleep.

Cork and I pulled a tarp over our heads. I leaned into his shoulder and, both physically and mentally exhausted, began to cry.

"Maybe this Peace Corps thing wasn't such a cool idea after all," Cork murmured to comfort me. I could not find any way to rest my back against something. I could never get even close to comfortable. Poor Cork sat up all night on the hard, wooden seat with no back support at all. I was alternately angry, exhausted and frustrated. All night rain would start and stop and start again.

Eventually I needed to pee. We jockeyed around to find our plastic bucket. I figured with Cork's help I could position our space blanket behind me so the two men at the rudder couldn't see me with my pants down. In Sranan the older man, Edwin, protested, trying to get us to put the space blanket in front of our bodies, thinking we were trying to protect ourselves from the rain. I snapped at him in such a vehement tone he backed off. Afterwards, Cork dumped the bucket over the side and rinsed it in the river.

I thought, *seven-and-a-half hours up the river, seven-and-a-half hours down, so we'll arrive soon.*

Wrong.

The sun came up. Beautiful pale light behind the gray of voluminous rainclouds. People in the front of the boat began to wake, pee in various containers, break out their breakfasts and feed their children.

Hours passed. We reached the mouth of the river, and the boat ran out of gas. With the outgoing tide, we began to drift out into the open ocean.

"Jeez," Cork muttered. "No oars, no communication, no common sense."

Cork helped Edwin and the other boatman—a burning cigarette hanging from his lips—marry the last remaining drops of gas from each plastic can into the gas tank. They pooled just enough to counter the outgoing tide and carry us back towards shore, where the boat made it to the dock a little after 11 a.m.

Bobby and Susy wanted to hurry and catch the bus to Paramaribo. I no longer hurried anywhere. They left and Cork and I wandered the market, munched on snacks, had coffee, and rejoiced in being off the damned boat and alone for a while.

We returned to Bedbug Manor by mid-afternoon, the last of the group to arrive. Bobby and Susy only beat us by half an hour.

A new surprise—no water. Cork and I were given our same tiny, cramped room as before with the two twin, metal frame beds. We looked at each other and made a pact that we would wait one hour, and if the water did not come on, we would go find decent accommodations elsewhere. With Cork's social security in addition to our Peace Corps stipend, we had options, and the best hotel in town, Torarica, with that beautiful swimming pool, beckoned.

Half an hour later the water came on. We showered, put on clean clothes and went out alone in search of a good dinner. We had had enough of young Peace Corps trainees for a while.

Later we heard the boat with Gladys and the two boatmen ran out of gas shortly after leaving Apoera and the three of them had drifted on the Corantijn river all night, until a boat had picked them up at dawn.

The Kerosene Lantern

We ordered a kerosene lantern from the Peace Corps office and carried it carefully on the bouncing bus to our little room in Sylvia's house in Powaka. Now we would have light in the evenings.

That night I lit it while Cork fussed and worried that we would burn down Sylvia's wooden house. I loved his vivid imagination, but it had begun to make me crazy. When the lantern began to sputter from some air issue, Cork insisted I turn it off.

"Just let me see it," he said. He messed with it and lowered the wick so far that it disappeared into the kerosene reservoir and in the darkness, he couldn't get it out.

The next morning, I had to take it apart to fix it, getting kerosene all over my not-a-happy-camper hands.

The Training Evaluations

In our Powaka Training Center classroom we were handed "training evaluation" forms to fill out.

I couldn't in all honesty say all was wonderful, but how far did I want to go to be truthful? I decided to include words like "unstructured, confusing, not clearly defined, and minimally informative." I left out one phrase I wanted to write, "You can't teach what you don't know."

I decided to omit the following personal thoughts: With so much emphasis on learning about Suriname culture, I have yet to meet one Suriname person who had shown the slightest interest in learning anything from us. Many of our voiced concerns as volunteers were met with a shrug and "that's Suriname." *So, if nobody cares,* I asked myself, *why are we here?*

Comedy on the Bus

City busses in Paramaribo were mini vans, each one colorfully painted and appliquéd, most owned by Hindi or Javanese drivers. The seats were tiny, with drop-down seats in the aisle to accommodate more passengers. This meant that if the bus was full, and you were sitting at the back, when you got to your stop, each person sitting in the drop-down aisle seat had to get up and get off the bus so you could exit. They then reboarded and resumed their drop-down aisle seat.

Suriname being a lively country, each bus driver would play at full volume a cassette of his favorite music.

One morning we boarded a bus and heard a comedy cassette in English. By the voice we could identify the comedian as Afro-American, but we didn't recognize who it was. Passengers normally did not talk to each other on the busses, so we weren't surprised to hear only the comedy routine.

It went something like this: "Da trouble wi' de bitches is de mamas. De mamas be tellin' de bitches, get a man wid a big job, get a man wid money, get a man wid a fancy car. What ever happened to fallin' in love wid a nigger wid a bus pass?"

Cork and I, unable to contain ourselves, hooted. The passengers stared at us. I wish we had thought to ask the driver the name of that comedian.

Lafu Lafu

So much of what we'd done in the previous six weeks seemed ludicrous. Disorganized. Totally without reason. We had traveled all over the country with no ID, no phone card—which you must have to call anything, including emergency—and minimal money. I felt like I'd been in some sort of Chinese mental torture experiment.

Everything was now funny. One morning Cork and I designed a tongue-in-cheek T-shirt line, "Lafu lafu, then you die." Seemed to me to sum up the attitude of the population of Suriname. *Laugh laugh, and then you die.*

Brownsberg

On the last day of our last week in our village-based training we threw a party in the training center, complete with simply-made paper decorations and chocolate milk for the kids. When it disappeared in the first twenty minutes, we learned they had never tasted chocolate milk.

The last weekend of our training, before we would be sworn in as official Peace Corps volunteers, the office decided we deserved a "celebration" vacation.

The Saturday morning after the party we loaded baggage, hammocks, water purifiers, etc. onto a bus to take us for two days at the thousand-foot mountain retreat called Brownsburg.

Located on a plateau, this former corporate retreat for the Suriname aluminum company, Suralco—a subsidiary of Alcoa—was now a national reserve. It overlooked an expansive body of water called Afobaka Lake, formed in 1964 when the Afobaka dam had been built to generate hydroelectric power for Suralco. Seventy-five percent of the power generated supported the aluminum smelter, and the rest provided power for the capital.

Several Maroon villages along this part of the Suriname River and several hundred miles of tropical rainforest had been submerged, and more than five thousand people had been displaced. Some of the older people had refused to leave

138

the nearby burial grounds of their ancestors and had chosen to drown.

At the same time the ISPA (International Society for the Protection of Animals) and a professional animal protection officer, John Walsh, had established Operation Gwamba to rescue about 10,000 animals that would have been trapped by the fast-rising waters.

Midday we arrived at Brownsberg, and some of the kids jaunted off on a hike to a waterfall. I settled on a bench with the current paperback I was reading and enjoyed a view of the lake's surface, spotted with dark twiggy-looking structures that were the remains of treetops.

Cork and I bunked in a room with two young women, again no privacy. Eddie and his wife, Debbie, and some of the office staff had come so we could "mix" with them on a social basis. Debbie made popcorn with butter and sugar, and dinner was welcomed barbecued chicken.

Eddie and Judith, the Peace Corps program director, took Cork and I aside and told us they had struck a deal with the village of Pierrekondre to build us a new house, since now they'd been told the one we saw the day we met Captain Kelly was "no longer available."

"What will the new house be like?" I asked.

"Standard Peace Corps issue," Eddie said.

Like we would know what that was. He did not elaborate and we did not ask.

"But before we send the materials out today, we need to know that you're in. You've made a lot of comments during your training that have made us wonder if you're still committed."

I guess we had scared him with our pointed, cryptic, detailed responses to the preservice training assessment survey.

"Eddie, we are too old," I said, "and have experienced too much by which to compare, to not be forthright. You'll always know where we stand."

Cork assured him that, yes, we were critical but still committed and were excited about a new house in Pierrekondre.

* * *

At dawn we heard our first howler monkeys. My spine chilled—the eeriest sound I've ever heard. At first, I thought it was wind in the trees, but the sound became louder and moved around us.

"Sounds like a spoon stuck in the garbage disposal," Cork said.

It became deafening, then subsided as the troop moved away.

At 6 a.m. the electricity went off, so no coffee maker. Breakfast looked like it had not been planned—the Brownsberg Nature Park lodge staff was not sure what to do with all the ingredients that have arrived with us. I managed to grab one thick, tasteless pancake—no honey, syrup or jelly– a hard-boiled egg, and some *pamplemous*, a kind of giant sweet pink grapefruit the size of a soccer ball.

Afterwards Debbie led a game called, "You might be surprised to know that I…" Each of us had to finish this sentence, revealing something "personal," and drop it unsigned into a bowl. One by one they were drawn and read and we all tried to guess whose "secret" was being revealed.

I wrote that I had been a Playboy Bunny—"before many of you were born"—and Cork wrote that he had acted in *The Gauntlet* with Clint Eastwood. Great fun.

* * *

On Sunday we were moved from Brownsburg to Naks where we would stay while we were sworn in as official Peace Corps Volunteers and prepared to move to our individual sites.

On Tuesday of this memorable week, in preparation for Wednesday's big ceremony, Cork got his hair cut.

At Tushar's barber shop the price was about the equivalent of a US dollar. The young Maroon barber, snipping away with the scissors, clipped Cork's ear. Who knew an earlobe could bleed so much? When Cork protested, Tushar, the Hindustani owner, said, "What do you want for a hundred guilders?"

Tushar sent the barber next door with money to buy some band-aids. Cork told the barber, "Young man, you are the only black man in Suriname with a job where you can get paid to cut a white man."

Polite laughter, but I'm not sure the barber spoke English.

It's Official—We Swear In

Cork zinged his way through pre-service language training in Sranan Tongo to graduate with the lowest score. No matter who he was speaking to, he continued to bastardize a mixture of Sranan and English that continued to get laughs.

Wednesday, October 28 was the big government suits-attended ceremony, held in the meeting hall at Naks. While all the Peace Corps advertising described volunteer training as a three-month process,

our training had lasted only two months. I guessed there just wasn't that much to learn about serving in Suriname.

By this point Cork and I had had enough of listening to idealized young people spout about how things "should be." We couldn't wait to get to our new cabin in our Amerindian village where we could experience quiet and look forward to coming into town at least once a month to check our e-mail, shop and enjoy fine dining. We already had our favorite bar, where other volunteers did not hang out.

While over 200 government dignitaries and VIPs had been invited to the ceremony, only about seventy-five people attended.

During the ceremony, each of us lined up to swear allegiance to the United States and shake the hand of the American Ambassador, Dennis K. Hayes. (I learned that his full official US title was Ambassador Extraordinary and Plenipotentiary.)

I must admit to becoming teary-eyed when I shook Ambassador Hayes' hand and was handed my certificate and pin. Cork said it hit him during the "Oath of Allegiance."

The ceremony lasted an hour and was followed by a reception where we snacked on hors d'oeuvres and drank soft drinks.

We asked Ambassador Hayes if he knew our former Nevada Republican Senator Chic Hecht. who had been appointed US Ambassador to the Bahamas. (This after losing his Senate seat when he became known for his verbal slip-ups, including a vow to never permit a "nuclear suppository" in Nevada.) We also asked if he knew our Vegas marketing contemporary and former US ambassador to Iceland, Sig Rogish. Indeed, he knew them both.

The next day Eddie would be leaving for a country directors conference in Washington DC, and Ambassador Hayes would be on the same plane headed to a conference of American ambassadors.

"Please do say 'hello' to Sig from Cork and Carolyn Proctor," I said. I wished I could have seen the look on Sig's face when he heard we were in the Peace Corps!

As I shook Eddie's hand I murmured, "We're still here."

After the ceremony, Cork and I had a quiet dinner in the Naks cafeteria. Many of the volunteers went to the Roof Bar to drink, party and celebrate. We had not been invited and were not disappointed. Many of us had already had enough of each other.

After swearing in I wrote this in an email to family and friends: "The PC pre-service training is over! What a strange experience it was! Alternately boring and a little dangerous. Living in a not-very-healthy environment, I'm amazed we didn't get sick! Our clothes are loose, so we must be losing weight. Otherwise, our bowels are tight, and we are still in love!"

Moving to Site

The day after swearing-in we were all taken to Hakrinbank where Eddie and the Peace Corps Administrative Officer, Devon, helped us signed up for bank accounts and ATM cards, with which we would be able to access our monthly living allowances. In addition, Peace Corps gave us a lump sum "settling-in allowance," deposited that day into Hakrinbank.

142

In a furniture store Cork negotiated with the owner for a discount on mattresses for us and Rolf and Pam, who would be living near us in Powaka.

And one last check for email. At that time Carib Computers was the only public internet service in the capital, located in a room in the same building as the Jewish synagogue. By the time I left two years later, it seemed there was an internet cafe on every corner.

On Friday we were all free to shop for our settling-in household goods. But that morning we discovered Hakrinbank's ATM was at that moment out of money.

Welcome to our next two years in Suriname.

Daf trucks began to arrive at 6 a.m. Saturday morning to move all the new volunteers to their respective sites. Mattresses, gas cylinders (called "gas bombs"), bicycles, building materials, large quantities of food and personal belongings filled the central recreation house at Naks.

When our vehicle came, it was not big enough for all the stuff of four volunteers. I told Devon it was unacceptable for any of our household goods to be separated. We compromised by leaving the bicycles behind—to be delivered, we were assured, to our site on Monday.

Our first stop was Powaka, to move Rolf and Pam into the building that had been the village school library, where they would live until the village completed the construction of their house.

"Our House Is A Very Fine House"

"Standard Peace Corps issue" turned out to be two rooms and a slanting roof. About fifteen by twenty, it smelled of freshly cut wood. In the four outer walls were six windows with hinged shutters that swung upward to be held in open position with poles, and two doors.

"US building standards require that any house construction must have two doors for escape," Eddie explained. "As a fire precaution."

The slanted corrugated tin—*zinkplaat*—roof had a gutter along the lower side to channel rainwater into a 200-gallon black Durotank. The floor was two feet above the sandy ground. Think rustic cabin. The area between the top of the walls and the roof on three sides was screened. The inside "wall" that divided it into two rooms looked like a thin sheet of Melamine plywood. It seemed silly to have it, and Cork tore it out and threw it away.

Looking out of our doorway towards the creek, we could see the three-room house and *kampu* we had been shown "for the volunteers" when we visited with Captain Kelly. In comparison to what we had now it was a hovel. Its only saving grace was its attached *kampu*.

Away from our house we had a new outhouse and a separate wash house, a simple shed built on a cement slab with a bench along one inside wall. Lucia, Martinus's wife, gifted me with half a casaba gourd to use in our wash house. After Sylvia's we felt like we were living in the lap of luxury. The new outhouse smelled like a healthy barn, that wonderful combination of wood, vegetation and animals.

Our new Amerindian neighbors told us to be sure to close our shutters at night to keep out the *fufuruman*—a combination bad spirit, ghost and bogeyman. Lucia and my neighbor on the other side, Woni, got into an argument about how best to advise me to position the stick in the ground to grow *kosbanti*, the long Chinese bean. I discovered later this didn't matter—the thing will sprout from the moisture in the air.

* * *

Wednesday, November 3 was our eighth wedding anniversary. Who knew, when I said, "I do," that this was one of the things I would be doing? And to think, for fourteen single years I had always said, "Great adventures do not happen to married ladies."

Of course, with Sranan time, the bicycles and the mandatory bike helmets—failure to wear your helmet was grounds for immediate volunteer termination—were not delivered by the Peace Corps office on Monday as promised. We didn't care, as we didn't see ourselves biking much on the rough dirt roads.

After some deliberation and an increasing need for fresh food we decided to make the journey into *foto*. The noon bus got us there at two. I went to Caribe Computers, and Cork went to shop for tools and secure us a room for the night. He checked out Lisa's guesthouse, a cheap Peace Corps recommendation and reported, "I would not board my dog there." He got us into Stadszending, a gospel mission run by a Dutch Church. Peace Corps got a special room rate there. The rooms were small, with two single beds, a sink, cupboard, and louvered glass windows. On opposite sides of the second floor—all the rooms faced an open outdoor garden—were men's and women's bathrooms and showers.

In Stadszending's large, comfortable recreation room with huge color TV and remote, we found four Sur 4 volunteers couch-potatoed. They were in town for quarterly Peace Corps medical/dental checks.

The following day Cork and I shopped, had a nice Chinese lunch, and visited Fubar, where we had a long conversation with the American owner, Martin. A transplanted south Floridian, Martin was thirtyish, dark-haired and married to a Suriname girl he met in Florida when she was attending university there. He had a snappy, "with it" personality he had probably developed when he had managed a bar/disco chain in south Florida. Besides the bar, he owned a construction company, and talked avidly of flying into the interior by helicopter with his buddies "to do some hunting and fishing and just get away from it all."

He was also quite outspoken on "what's wrong with Suriname."

Cork and I had finished our drinks and were about to leave when another American came in and Martin introduced him as "my helicopter pilot."

Later we heard Peace Corps volunteers avoid Fubar in general, suspicious of Martin's exuberant, hip demeanor. One thing Peace Corps stressed was avoiding anything that might look like military or drug-related activities.

"A young American male with money and indiscriminate use of helicopters certainly falls within one of those categories," Cork remarked.

Building Materials

Early one morning a large, brown spider dropped from the ceiling onto the top of the mosquito net that cocooned our bed. Already dead, it still made me feel glad for the netting. I was so paranoid about our bed—one of the volunteers had found a scorpion in his hammock—that I kept the net tucked in under the mattress, all the way around, even during the day. The Amerindians pulled theirs out, gathered the sides to the center and tied it into a big loose knot above their beds. Not *my* style.

We battled our share of mosquito bites, and my hairbrush, with its little rubber bristles, became my erotic tool of choice.

Another day an even larger black spider scuttled across the floor boards when I moved a suitcase to sweep. I called for Cork, and we
moved a lot of other stuff—rubber boots, tools, gardening gloves, books—until we chased it down. Cork skewered it with the machete. We embarked on a cleaning frenzy. We hammered more nails into posts and walls, suspending shoes, gloves, clothes and plastic sacks.

We desperately needed shelves for clothes. Before we had arrived, Eddie had told us there would be a lot of lumber left from our house construction that we could use to build furniture. In fact, there were barely enough scraps left to build a table.

Cork soon became frustrated and angry that repeated requests to Martinus for information on where we could buy wood had been met with his frequent comment, *"Wakti, wakti."* Wait. wait. Wait for what? Lumber to fall from the sky?

We placed the table in the shade under the trees on the west side of the house and had our midday meal—tomato/rice bisque with garlic bread—there. It felt so spacious to be eating outdoors.

Cork did little things to make us more comfortable: repositioning the hole in the latrine and adding a comfortable white authentic toilet seat; lowering the wood steps in front of the wash house so we could leave our sandals there and still open and close the door; hang the longer hammock in the house; trim the corners of the boards supporting the Durotank so one wouldn't walk into them and bang one's leg.

While he was adding a snazzy reading rack to an inside wall of the outhouse, I heard loud, angry words. "Goddam-cheap-fucking-Chinese-*junk*!"

I rushed outside. "What happened?"

He held the wooden handle in his hand. "The head fell off."

"Can you fix it?"

"No." He threw the handle into the bushes. "I swear they send the Chinese shit to the US and the even *cheaper* Chinese shit to Suriname."

Spending Time

We discovered that, unlike the colorful, boisterous Maroon people, Amerindians are quiet, shy people with a simple cultural heritage and no interest among young people in learning or preserving it. They were not ambitious, but they were nice, and we began to enjoy a quiet life among them.

Mostly they wanted to go swimming with us. I hung out with Woni, her husband Billy, and their three curious little girls.

The rest of the time—we had a LOT of time on our hands—was spent planning to get to and from the capital to buy food and wine, and lying in our hammocks reading a LOT of books. On each trip into town we were able to exchange books from the extensive paperback collection in the office's volunteer lounge.

Since we had no electricity, nights were looooong. Cork and I played gin rummy and drank martinis, and I decided to learn to make manhattans.

"Do you think this is a dangerous time for us?" I asked Cork. "Do you think we could become alcoholics?"

"Naw," he said. "If it didn't happen to us in Vegas, it won't happen to us here."

That logic was lost on me, but okay, I could go with it.

We began to feel guilty for not working. When our neighbors discovered we did not bring money, they could not understand why we were there. The idea of creating a project, for instance to get electricity to the village, garnered little interest. We learned a new Sranan Tongo phrase, *"Winti wai, Lanti pai."* The wind blows and the government pays. The prevailing idea that we can wait and eventually the government will provide.

When I mentioned our guilt to Eddie, he said, "No one expects you to have a project during this first six months of your service. It takes time for the village to get to know and trust you." He paused and laughed. "Of course, if we hear you never come out of your house, then we will have a talk."

Our village neighbors found it hard to understand why anyone would leave a rich, cushy, American lifestyle to go to another country and help people they don't know, and are not related to, for no money.

I believe you can find stereotypical thinking everywhere in the world. In Suriname, many people believed the Maroons (descendants of African slaves) will steal, the Amerindians are lazy, the Dutch and Americans are rich, and the Hindustanis are successful in business because they can change themselves into snakes at night and steal money from the banks.

Billy Shoots A Monkey

Woni's husband, Billy, shot a capuchin monkey. I don't know if he knew it had a baby before he shot it. I didn't ask—I didn't want to know.

The mama was destined for the stew pot and Billy's adult son, Brian, planned to keep the baby for a pet. The little male looked awfully young to be without his mother's milk, but Woni said, "No no, he has teeth." In the beginning the baby hid out in the peak of their *tasi* roof, and usually squealed when Brian held him. Yet he laid quietly on his back in Brian's arms and let us apply Neosporin to the few scrapes and cuts he had received in the foray that had killed his mother. The family named this baby capuchin monkey "Danny."

Now that Amerindians and Maroons have guns and no longer hunt with blowguns, they have to forage further into the jungle to find food. The noise of gunshots has driven game away from villages.

Woni skinned and gutted the monkey and boiled the hell out of it until the meat fell off the bones. She proudly served Cork and I this "stew" in half-gourd bowls with white plastic spoons.

"Never again," Cork said later. "Tasted like a steel-belted radial tire."

Health and Wellness

We tried to get into town each week or so to buy food and check e-mail. We were still in the dry season, and from Pierrekondre to *foto* on the government bus took about two hours.

I began to suffer from intense pain in my boobs because they bounced every time the bus hit a pothole or deep ridge in the dirt road. The bus never went fast because there were so many potholes and the driver had to maneuver around or over them as best he could.

When I mentioned this pain to Dr. Legiman, the Peace Corps doctor, he said it was in my chest muscles, and the only thing he could advise was for me to bind my breasts as tightly as possible each time before I boarded the bus. For this I found and bought a long strip of soft fabric.

Cork grew a snow-white beard to match his silver-turning hair. It was easy to fantasize that I was sleeping under the mosquito net with Ernest Hemingway.

Taking an independent, free-form creative like Cork and making him a US government "representative" opened the door for interesting situations.

"I can't even *spell* 'protocol'", he told the Peace Corps administrative officer, Devon.

Most of our time was spent in our village, away from Peace Corps' watchful eye. When we did have to go to the PC office for mail or a meeting, Cork would become antsy and easily agitated. He could smell rules and regulations. The only attraction the office held for him was the volunteers' washing machine in the downstairs storage area. It provided him with both clothes not washed in the river and the chance to grouse about youthful volunteers who ("like young Vegas dancers") were not taught by their parents to clean up after themselves.

One afternoon, while I went to Carib to send my latest "Suriname report" to friends, Cork went in search of the ultimate laundromat, that is, one that was open. He got a taxi to drive him around and collected the names, telephone numbers and hours of three places, all with hot waters and dryers. "But they look like Russian prisons," he said.

Besides cleanliness, there was ample opportunity in this equatorial country for Cork to obsess on his other concern, health and wellness. His first battle had been with a staph infection contracted when we had gone swimming in the cola-colored water of the Powaka swimming creek, and he had an overly-scratched mosquito bite on his ankle. Dr. Legiman prescribed antibiotics and no swimming in the *kreki* for a while.

When the savanna sand around our house became infested with *sekas*—minute sand-flies that lay their eggs under the skin—he contracted a record forty in one foot alone. These must be dug out with a sterilized needle and this activity, not unlike popping zits, can become addictive. For several mornings in a row we spent the first hour drinking coffee and picking at each other's feet like monkeys. This is a questionable level of intimacy I believe is not reached in the average marriage.

Cork milked a three-day bout with dengue for a month, announcing to everyone he met, "I've got dengue fever," until—finally—he tired of talking about it. The only time we suffered from *loosi beri* (diarrea) was the day I didn't cook some brown beans sufficiently.

The following morning, we needed to take the bus to *foto* for a meeting and worried about how we would make such a long trip without a bathroom stop.

We mentioned this to Martinus. "*Wakti.*" He went into his house and returned with two glasses of water with sticks in them. "Drink," he said.

We already had the runs so bad we figured wherever the water came from and whatever the sticks were couldn't possibly make us worse.

Amazingly, thirty minutes later we felt much better and another trip to the latrine produced nothing. We made it to the bus and our meeting on time, with no further bowel disturbances.

Martinus refused to tell us what the sticks were, as if it were some secret bush medicine.

(The following year I would have the opportunity to meet Dr. Mark Plotkin, who had spent years in the jungle with a knowledgeable shaman, Fritz Von Troon, whom I would also meet and spend my own time in the rainforest with, studying rainforest plants and medicines. Plotkin is the author of *Tales of the Shaman's Apprentice* and *Medicine Quest*. He told me most likely the "sticks" had actually been bark from a common rainforest tree.)

* * *

It looked like a prehistoric fugitive from Jurassic Park. I had just stepped up into our cabin when I saw it on the back of one of the cement block steps, close to the top. Eight inches long, with an inch-wide brown hardshell body, it had black legs and orange antenna waving menacingly.

"Cork, I need you," I said urgently.

"What is it? I have a hoe in my hand."

"Good. you're going to need it."

With the hoe he brushed it off the step into the sand. He chopped it into methodical pieces, each of which continued to wriggle. I had movie-morphing visions of each squirming piece springing into a whole one, forming for attack. I could see the headlines, "Peace Corps couple Succumb to Killer Suriname centipede."

The multi-legged critters of Suriname kept life interesting. We discovered large white patterns on one side of a black duffel bag. I photographed them and showed them to a Dutch biologist friend, but he could not identify what kind of creature had created them.

When Cork yelled, *"Holy Shit!"* I knew he'd seen something impressive. In this case it was a seven-inch centipede on the wall behind some shirts.

Another day he yelled, "Holy Shit!" and I asked. "What is it, this time?"

"You don't want to see."

"Yes, I do."

With its legs, the wolf spider spanned at least five to six inches, the biggest spider we'd ever seen—so far. Suriname is technically home to the largest spider in the world.

The creature eluded our flapping and yelling. At last Cork brushed it from the house into the sand, where it met its end when I hacked it several times with my machete. As soon as I turned away, a chicken came running to investigate. It's all about the food chain.

One morning, enjoying his coffee, Cork jumped suddenly when a fat, pink-toed tarantula emerged from under the table to greet the day. This creature, too, met death by machete.

Dramatic as these events were, I preferred them to the daily endurance of the smaller creatures, namely mosquitoes, chiggers, *sekas*, gnats and ants. There seemed to be tiny ants everywhere, all the time. At dawn and desk the gnats and mosquitoes drove us dottie. They were no worse in the Midwest, I supposed, but that thought was no comfort. I much preferred to deal with an occasional monster bug than the myriad minute ones. A big bug was easier to see and whack once and for all.

When Cork began cutting his blood pressure pills in half, ants came and ate the sugar coating off the half he left out on the table for the next day.

One morning Cork opened the jar of peanut butter and announced, "It's moving."

"What's moving?"

"The inside of the peanut butter jar." He grabbed his reading glasses and peered inside the jar.

"Ants!" he exclaimed. "The smallest ants in the world!"

"Did you leave the lid unscrewed?" I asked.

He looked at me as if I'd just asked the stupidest question in the universe. "No. Of course not."

These ants were so tiny they could crawl under the lid and follow the swirling glass ridges in the top of the jar to get into the peanut butter. From then on, we wrapped a little square of plastic wrap over the top of the jar before we screwed on the lid.

Hoeing persistent jungle weeds from around our house, Cork discovered a tiny spider that was a fluorescent lime green. We had never seen one like this before. Because it was in the yard and would probably meet death by chicken, we admired it and let it be.

Cork said, "It's either innocuous, or it'll kill ya."

Living on the edge of the Amazon jungle put us more closely in touch with nature than one would normally want to be. At night we could hear the soft sound of little, leathery fruit bat wings flapping about outside our tented bed. One morning I discovered a large brown toad in the wash house. One afternoon another wolf spider—we began to see them often in the house—gave me a merry chase. I crushed it underfoot at the bottom of the steps and the whole experience left me adrenaline-pumped and covered with goose bumps. The body knows....

Our First Peace Corps Project

It seemed to be the custom among Amerindians to wait one year after a relative dies and then to erect a headstone. To make sure they're really dead and not coming back?

We volunteered to help with the construction of a cement cross and headstone for a man who had died one year earlier: Frederick Josef Sabayo, the shaman who had been Robbie and Billie's father.

Cork, Martinus, Billy and Robby planned to pour the cement. I could write the letters on the monument.

Actually, Cork mixed and poured the cement and Martinus, Billy and Robby watched.

Billy commented, "I don't like that kind of work."

Cork gave him a sarcastic look and said, "Me either, pal."

I thought I would do the lettering and that would be the end of it, but no, they wanted the entire cement monument to be painted white with black painted letters. Plus, a cross and a rose on the headstone. It turned into a week-long project. Since no one had red paint, I painted the rose with red nail polish.

When we told Eddie we were building a monument, he said, "Sounds like a good village project."

I laughed to myself to remember he had commented in training, "We don't want you to think you have to *build any monuments* to count your Peace Corps service as successful."

Jodensavanne

Part of our "rural community development" assignment meant Cork and I would be working with a village foundation—*stichting* in Dutch—to help promote the destination of Blakawatra.

Along the wide red dirt road on our side of the river were three Amerindian villages. Pierrekondre was closest to the river. Four kilometers further was Redidoti and a few kilometers farther was Cassipora, where the government bus that serviced the area turned around and returned to Paramaribo.

The creek that ran next to Cassipora widened at one point so much that the area had become a popular swimming and picnic destination for people who would bus or drive all the way from the capital. No part was more than about four feet deep, large flat boulders made perfect sunning spots and massive rainforest trees enclosed the area. This destination was Blakawatra. This was where the Hindi family had been coming from the day they picked us up after meeting Clive Kelly.

The Blakawatra *Stichting* had been formed to enhance the area with picnic tables, *kampus*, and little wooden sheds the size of our wash house for bathing suit changing. The year before we arrived the organization had asked Peace Corps for volunteers to help publicize the destination.

So here came advertising experts Cork and Carolyn from Las Vegas.

One might think logic would dictate we would have been housed right there in Cassipora. But no, we were several kilometers away in the smallest of the three villages, Pierrekondre, because, of course, that is where the captain of the three villages lived.

We had spoken to Martinus about what we could do for the *stichting*, and received the same where-can-we-buy-wood response. *"Wakti wakti."* When we mentioned to anyone else that we might be able to help them promote Blakawatra, we received similar vague responses.

Judith, the head of the Peace Corps programming office, couldn't get any definitive answers from Martinus either. Since the Peace Corps now had the investment of a house in Pierrekondre and support of two American citizens, and no one there seemed interested in talking about promoting Blakawatra, they had to find something else for us to do.

A meeting was arranged with Guido Robles, the handsome Jewish owner of the two Galaxy clothing boutiques in *foto* and head of the Jodensavanne *stichting*.

Next to Redidoti was a vast half-wooded area that extended from the road to the bank of the Suriname river. The area contained the brick ruins of Jodensavanne, the New World's only autonomous Jewish agrarian community.

In the 1600s European Sephardic Jews had migrated to Brazil to escape the Inquisition. As the Jesuits became more powerful in Brazil, hundreds of these Jewish people moved up the coast to the Guyanas. The first governor of Suriname, when it was still a British colony, recognized the industrious nature of these Jewish people and saw an opportunity to establish sugar plantations. Basically, he told them, "If you come here you can have all the land you want and practice your religion with no outside intervention, but oh, by the way, not here near the capital. We have this great land way upriver you can have."

This settlement of sugar plantations became Jodensavanne, or in English *"Jewish Savanna."*

It was not long after that the Dutch won the second Anglo-Dutch war and gave the British, as a sort of consolation prize, the island of Manhattan in exchange for the British colony of Suriname. The Dutch saw the rich agricultural potential of

Suriname and after all, what could you grow on Manhattan Island?

Jodensavanne is noted for its Dutch-influenced geometrical town plan with open roads and ample access from all four sides to the synagogue, surprising in a time of perilous threats from rival European powers, runaway slaves and local Amerindians. The central brick ruin is of the ninety-foot long synagogue itself, Bracha ve Shalom (Blessing and Peace) and its surrounding plaza where the people gathered from their neighboring plantations.

Two overgrown cemeteries remain, each containing hundreds of European-made marble and bluestone (shipped from Europe) graves, some elaborately illustrated despite prohibition by Jewish law. A third "freeholders cemetery" of artistically-crafted wood and concrete grave markers was rapidly decaying.

Jodensavanne had survived until the mid-1700s, when the decrease in value of cane sugar caused by the introduction of beet sugar in Europe, bankruptcy of the major business house in Amsterdam, and local political upheaval caused its decline. A major fire caused its eventual abandonment.

With Guido we discussed what could be done to promote Jodensavanne, a UNESCO World Heritage destination.

Bicycle Ride

Told the bus wouldn't run again until Thursday, we decided to try out our bikes on a trip to Redidoti. We left our house at 8 a.m., helmeted according to Peace Corps mandates. I felt nervous with these teensy bikes and skinny tires on the dirt road.

Just before we reached Redidoti we turned off the main road where a sign read "Jodesavanne" and showed a map of the site. We biked through a leafy glen of trees and wild ground vegetation.

An open area on the right revealed the slave cemetery, with five-foot-high weathered wooden crosses. The next open area, on the left, was the larger cemetery of roughly two-by-five-foot flat carved headstones. The ground and many of the headstones had been heaved and broken with time so that walking on the uneven ground was precarious.

There was no one else around, not even on the road, and the entire tree-shrouded place was cool and eerily quiet.

The narrow road ended at a grassy, expansive area distinguished by the crumbling ruins of narrow brickwork that once formed the stairs, walls, floors and pillars of the synagogue. To our right was also a newer structure with the sign—in Dutch of course—indicating Jodensavanne was being maintained by a Paramaribo Jewish organization and the interior was a small museum. We couldn't enter because the door and shuttered windows were closed and locked.

The far side of this open meadow-like area sloped downward, with well-maintained stairs leading further down to a sturdy peer and boat ramp. Part of the pier, painted white, was covered and sported long benches. A truly magical, quiet place for relaxing, reading, and reflecting.

In Redidoti, we parked our bikes and seated ourselves in the wooden chairs in the covered patio in front of the *winkri* (village market). We chatted with the owner, Mena, a low-energy young Amerindian woman with a wardrobe of shiny, fluorescent-colored tights. Today she wore fluorescent orange. I wondered how a woman could wear latex tights every day in such a humid climate without experiencing repeating vaginal infections.

We didn't linger, since Mena was out of beer *and* soft drinks.

We bicycled on to the school, where the children were outside on a break, so we were encouraged to approach. We met the three school teachers, and Cork made them laugh, even in his broken Sranan and English mix.

Back in Pierrekondre before noon, we congratulated ourselves on our accomplishment, and agreed we wouldn't be biking there often, and certainly not in the rainy season.

My misgivings about these bicycles had been confirmed. The tires were way too narrow for dirt roads, I'd already taken two spills, and the bikes would be useless in the rainy season. I'm not an athletic person, and I had been no marathon bike rider at home, even with the eighteen-speed mountain bike Cork had bought me. I was mad at myself that

157

I hadn't been more vocal to the Peace Corps regarding my physical limitations.

Billy Shoots a *Tigre*

Early one morning Brian came to our house to tell us "Billy shot a *tigre*. Come to see."

The beautiful cat was hanging by his head from the corner of their chicken coop's corrugated tin roof. I recognized it as an ocelot. Endangered species? How do you explain this to an Amerindian family whose tradition is to eat from the land?

Woni said she would cook it, but admitted they have never eaten *tigre* before. Have I? *No*—! And after the monkey, the idea did not tempt me.

"When Billy saw it," Woni said, "he thought it was a deer."

Billy insisted I take the ocelot skin as a gift. Cork was adamant he did not want it in our house. "Who knows what kind of bugs it will attract?"

Of course, we would never be able to take it back with us into the US. What to do? We nailed it to a side of our washhouse, where over time and weather that beautiful ocelot hide rotted and fell away.

Life on the Bus to the Interior

Cork continued to speak to people in his bastard Sranan/English. When asked to tell a bit about himself before the Paramaribo camera club, he did thirty minutes in two languages that put those educated, tri-lingual professionals on the floor. In restaurants and shops, he would tell every pretty young girl—and there are plenty of them in Paramaribo—that she should run for Miss Suriname, and they would blush and giggle.

Even on the rural bus, he was a hit. People in a four-village radius from our little cabin in Pierrekondre knew *Opa Corku*. Sometimes cars containing people we didn't even know would pass on the main road, see the American flag on our door, lean out their windows, wave and yell, "Opa Corku!"

* * *

One day Cork went to *foto* to shop without me. I had a full quiet day with nothing to do but lie in my hammock and read my book and enjoy the chirps and chatters of the surrounding jungle.

That morning while we had been drinking coffee at our outdoor table a flock of colorful toucans had settled in the dark branches of a dead tree on the far side of the clearing. After Cork left, I continued to enjoy their noisy presence. I enjoyed the usual visits from neighboring children and later in the afternoon a quiet nap.

Just before dusk I heard the hollow rattle of the bus as it crossed the Carolina bridge and the sounds of tires on dirt and potholes as the bus climbed the hill from the river. I heard it stop and left my hammock to meet Cork.

He saw me before he got off the bus, leaned his head through the open window and called, "Hey! *Joe jepi mi, mi sribi nanga joe!*" You help me, I sleep with you.

Our neighbors on the bus laughed and repeated that line to the rest of the village for days.

* * *

To go south into the interior, we took a big lumbering bus that looked like a used yellow school bus from the US. The city departure point was on a commercial street on the southern side of town called Saramaccastraat. The early morning busses that left from there served all of the Amerindian and Maroon villages in the south along the Suriname River, as far as the Afobaka the dam.

After leaving town the busses made one last stop on the road at a rural market called Robbie's. There you had one last chance to buy fruits and vegetables and eggs and toilet paper and anything else you might have forgotten to buy in *foto*.

Robbie's was a good-sized market with only one checkout stand, and there were often several busses stopped at the same time. So, we had plenty of time to wander the aisles and make a real indoor bathroom visit.

This particular morning everyone on our bus had completed their business and were back on the bus seated and ready to go—except for Cork.

"Pe Opa Corku?" Where is Grandfather Cork? Our neighbors asked.

"I have no idea. I last saw him by the cheese and eggs."

Since busses to the interior had no particular time schedule, our driver could wait for the last passenger to reboard.

We waited. And waited.

I had begun to worry that something unusual had happened to him, when Cork appeared at the door and climbed the steps inside, a perplexed look on his face.

"I got on the wrong bus," he announced. "I got on, sat down, looked around, and realized I didn't know anybody. I didn't see any familiar faces." Luckily that bus was still waiting for a few people so it didn't depart with him on it. "It was the bus to Bronsweg."

Bronsweg was a Maroon village just south of the Afobaka dam.

Our neighbors laughed, and our driver said, "Don't you look at the color of the people when you get on a bus?"

Close Encounter of the Snake Kind

When we first moved into our newly-constructed cabin, we battled a few bugs with ferocious intensity. *Whack!* with the machete. Whenever Cork saw something new, my first question was, "How big *is* it?"

We discovered black centipedes an inch wide and six inches long and wolf spiders the width of an open hand. Most everything moved slowly enough that it was easy to dispatch with the machete.

One evening at dusk I heated some hot water for a warm wash. I was headed for the washhouse, hot pan in my pot-holdered hand, when I nearly stepped on a snake in the sand near the Durotank. I was proud of myself that I didn't scream.

The half-light of dusk washes out colors, and I had no idea what it was. At my call, Cork armed himself with a shovel and appeared with the kerosene lantern. We cornered the two-foot long thing at the entrance to the washhouse, snaking along the cement lip of the entry.

While I hissed, "Kill it. Hurry! *Kill it now!*" Cork hesitated.

"It could be a common garden snake."

"So *what?* Just kill it!"

"Do you think it's living under the washhouse?"

"I don't *care* where it's living. Just get rid of it! *Now!*"

"Well… maybe it has a family…"

"Oh, for God's sake…"

While Cork debated, the snake slithered under the wooden steps and disappeared into a hole under the concrete slab.

Even though in the light of dusk I couldn't determine bright colors that could signify deadly, I thought maybe it didn't have any, that it was brown or gray, darker in value than the sand.

"Do you think it could have been a bushmaster?"

This is the longest—as long as ten feet—venomous pit viper found in South America, with the largest fangs of its kind.

Cork said, "Oh no, they're *really* big."

I thought, *How does he think they get that way? They don't emerge from their snake egg fully grown.*

After that I never went to the washhouse after five p.m., while it was still daylight. I learned snake sightings are more prevalent during the rainy season, and the correct Sranan phrase for what one should say, "go away snake," is *sneki gwe.*

One-Room Marriage

We tried to stay up later in the evening so we wouldn't spend eleven hours in bed, but there wasn't a lot you can do by kerosene lantern. My experiment was to put tin foil behind the flame of the kerosene lantern to see if the reflection would double the strength of the light. Not.

161

Many nights we played a little gin rummy—the only card game we knew. Sometimes I would journal, and Cork would make popcorn. We began to associate making popcorn with making martinis and playing gin rummy, and Cork developed a popcorn-perfection obsession.

"Making popcorn is a delicate art. Too much oil, it doesn't pop, too little oil, it burns the pan."

We also played Scrabble, and one night a lizard fell from the wooden roof supports onto the scrabble board. Startled, Cork and I leaped back from the table. Letter tiles flew. The lizard scampered off into the darkness. A traumatic experience for all of us.

It seemed like we were tired most of the time, but Cork did a lot of physical yard labor. I was just bored. I even read the PC manual on "Non-formal Education" which we should have studied in training. (Instead, at the end, they had just signed us out for a huge stack of reference books and sent us on our way.)

One afternoon we got into a ludicrous argument over whether or not I had placed the nail on which I hung the "It's-full-of-germs" flyswatter too close to the inside table where we ate. It was time for one of us to take a long walk to the river, and I began to refer to our living situation as "one-room marriage."

And what if we bought a cell phone? If we charged it when we were in the city, how many days would it last in the village? Could we find a solar panel and put it on top of a pole so we could charge the phone in the village? This was an exciting new project for Cork to obsess on, and we fantasized about it for days.

We had too much time on our hands.

"Watch out!"

Cork developed a bad habit that annoyed me to no end. We would be walking in Paramaribo and pause to cross the street, of course looking both ways as we were all taught as children.

With no warning Cork would grab me and yell, "LOOK OUT!"

162

I would respond in alarm. "WHAT?"

"There's a truck coming."

"Where?"

"There!" He would point farther down the street. The vehicle he pointed out was so far down the street and moving so slowly that we had plenty of time to cross.

After he did this a few times, I said, "Look, I understand you care about me and you don't want anything to happen to me, but you startle me to death when you do that. So, here's the thing, you can grab me *or* you can yell at me, but you can't do both. You choose."

One of the questions that had been on a form in the initial Peace Corps packet had been, "How comfortable are you walking on uneven surfaces?" Between ancient cobblestones and cement uprooted and broken by massive Mahogany trees, the streets themselves were far more dangerous than any approaching vehicle.

Seka dog

Dr. Legiman told us *sekas* live in the sand and have nothing to do with dog shit. They are simply spread by dogs.

Rolf told us an incredible story about Sylvia and the little black dog with burns on its back from sleeping under her cooking fire table. One of the dog's legs got terribly infected from *sekas*. With her machete Sylvia cut the leg off. Now the dog is hopping around on three legs.

"But he's doing fine," Rolf said.

Last September we would have been horrified to hear the story—now we just say, "How 'bout that!?"

Spies for the CIA

Eddie had told us about a new restaurant across the street from Torarica that we decided to try. Indeed, the filet, the smoked salmon, and the shrimps in curry sauce made us feel that for the moment we had stepped away in a time machine to a more developed culture.

Afterwards we walked back to our room at Stadszending. A few doors from where we had dined was another restaurant with outside umbrellas and tables. We waved to a group of man enjoying drinks. We recognized one of them as the Galaxy shop owner and head of the Jodensavanne *stichting*, Guido Robles.

As we passed by the tables I swear I heard one of the men whisper, "They are spies for the CIA."

We had heard the ridiculous rumor that in some countries Peace Corps volunteers were considered to be spies for the CIA. No one we knew took this seriously. It was a common joke. And now, here was a supposedly educated, intelligent businessman who believed it.

Cork said, "Doesn't he know CIA spies look like Steven Seagal and Bruce Willis?"

Bad Husband

I was so mad at Cork I was speechless and numb. That afternoon we had gotten kicked out of our room at Stadszending.

Mrs. Dotts, the manager, said Cork had told her the previous week that we were "coming back on Thursday but (he) would call" her. When he hadn't called, she only reserved a room for us for one night.

And now Stadszending was full.

Fortunately, the girl in the office got us a room at another cheap hotel, Zinzendorf. The regular afternoon monsoon-like rain had hit, so we had to get a taxi to move our things.

Zinzendorf was a dilapidated two-story building on a main street, Gravenstraat. The interior was just as tired as the exterior, with unpadded, wrinkly, gray carpet and the same institutional iron single beds featured at Stadszending. But at Zinz, the ceilings were high, with Casablanca-style ceiling fans (no air-con), the rooms much larger. The tall windows had no glass, only wooden shutters. No cable in the TV room and cacophonous traffic morning, noon, and night. Its saving graces were that there was no curfew and was half the price of a room at Stadszending.

I felt like I was traveling with a two-year-old. I berated myself, telling myself I should have known by now he wasn't good with detail-type communications, so why did I trust him to make a clear room arrangement with Mrs. Dotts?

Cork redeemed himself by admitting his fault, apologizing, and behaving in a newly submissive manner. He was really sweet the rest of the day, and by evening when it was time to find a new restaurant for dinner, my conniption had passed.

Thanksgiving at the Ambassador's

Our American Ambassador hosted Thanksgiving dinner for the Peace Corps volunteers. This might not have been feasible in other countries due to the size of the volunteer groups, but in little Suriname, where some of our volunteers had already ET'd, our group consisted of about twenty people, including Eddy and his wife.

In our room at Stadszending I showered, gelled and blow-dried my hair, even put on makeup. With my new equatorial suntan, I hardly recognized myself, and I felt good. I was going to dinner at the ambassador's! It sounded so international. I made me *feel* so international, like I could have been one of those James Bond girls.

At 3:30 p.m. we took a cab to the ambassador's residence for the big dinner.

Ambassador Dennis Hayes lived in a tropical, two-story, white home situated on the Suriname River in a long line of ambassadorial residences. Cork and I had our pictures taken in front of the guard gate with its American seal. Later someone remarked, "They don't like to have you take too many pictures. Someone might locate the home of the American ambassador." Yeah—pretty hard to spot the big American flag flapping in the front yard.

The grounds consisted of spacious lawns, a swimming pool, volleyball sand court and airy gazebo bar, dotted with potted greens and bougainvillea. The whole compound was encased in serious fencing and guarded by gun-toting men in snappy uniforms. The "guard dog" was a Lhasa Apso.

Dinner was served buffet style in a large central dining area where we sat at table rounds of ten. The China was gold-edged and bore, along with the crystal wine glasses, the ambassadorial seal.

In Hayes' absence—he had gone to the US for the holiday—Deputy ambassador Arnie Campbell welcomed us. Eddie said a few words, and then we hit the buffet. Needless to say, we ate like the American Thanksgiving pigs we were.

Though one glass of wine was served, Cork and I had brought a plastic water bottle full of a fine French red. Eddie was sitting next to Cork, and the look on his face was pure astonishment when I pulled out the bottle and offered to refill his wine glass.

One of the embassy staff members, Robin, had served in the Peace Corps in Africa. At the dessert end of the buffet, Robin, a woman of ample proportions, positioned herself between me and the majority of the people in the room and whispered, "I know what it's like to miss food. If there's anything you'd like to slip into your pocket or bag for later, do it now."

During dinner we chatted with another embassy employee, David, and the subject of emergency evacuation arose. One of the first things we learned in training was what to do in case Peace Corps needed to suddenly evacuate volunteers from the country.

David explained that even in the Embassy everyone is assigned an emergency situation job.

"What is yours?" I asked.

"Mine is to break the china," he said, "and bury the silver." He said once somewhere in the Caribbean there had been an emergency and all the Embassy staff had to flee the island. When they returned months later, they discovered a high-up military guy on the island had confiscated the china and silver and crystal glassware for his own personal use. Hence a new US governmental procedure to prevent that embarrassing situation from ever happening again.

After the First Six Months

Friends at home wondered what sort of work we—and Cork in particular—were doing in this developing country. Things moved slowly. Suriname gave new meaning to the word, "*mañana.*"

Guido Robles asked us to man the information center on week-ends at Jodensavanne. We passed out to the occasional visitor literature printed in Dutch, telling the story of the restoration and history, answered questions in English and surveyed where the tourists came from.

"We should get the foundation to do a Jodensavanne magazine," Cork said. "They could call it *Good News For Jews.*"

Since we hadn't been able to interest our village adults in any development projects, Cork got the idea to create an educational field trip for children to Paramaribo. His idea was that they could visit various businesses and see what kind of jobs they would stay in school and graduate. The current school system for village children only provided education through sixth grade. If they wanted to continue, they had to move to *foto*, where they could live with relatives who were okay with extra mouths to feed.

We got permission from the programming office to create this project, arranged with several business owners and managers we had met to let the children visit, and presented our project to Martinus. Everyone was quite enthusiastic about the idea.

The glitch came when, according to Peace Corps project funding requirements, the village was required to provide twenty-five percent of the project cost. This could be in money or in-kind goods and services. We did the numbers and even with the village providing sack lunches and adult supervisors, they couldn't meet the twenty-five percent requirement. Cork told Judith he would pay the difference for the village end, but no, "That is not allowed because it sends the wrong message."

End of project. Cork felt devastated, and for weeks I had to listen to him rant bitterly about the Peace Corps.

* * *

Dr. Legiman weighed us, and Cork had lost twenty pounds and I had lost eight.

"How did this happen?" I asked. "We eat everything we can get our hands on, and we drink a lot of Parbo and wine."

He said, "You are doing a lot of walking and sweating."

And to think people in America paid money to go to a gym and sweat!

* * *

Frank, a driver for the Peace Corps office, made an interesting cultural observation. "The first things men in Suriname want after getting a job is a car and a gold chain."

One morning in a small Dutch bakery we frequented, we ordered coffee and my favorite almond cake.

A young Maroon man, wearing a muscle shirt and several heavy gold chains on his wrists and around his neck, stood next to Cork. As Cork passed guilders to the clerk, with no hesitation, the Maroon said, "You should buy me a coffee, too."

Cork gave him a direct stare and answered, "Young man, by the amount of gold you're wearing, *you* should be buying *me* coffee."

* * *

After the first six months, friends stopped writing, "What can we send you," and some friends stopped writing, period. Some even stopped responding to my e-essays.

The novelty of communicating with someone in a strange land, with whom you no longer have shopping/drinking/gossiping in common, had worn off.

The Letter

Cork had always loved to write letters, and in *foto* he found and bought an Omega 40 manual typewriter for $60.

On this he labored over a lengthy missive to Mack which he then put into an air mail envelope with the appropriate number of U.S. stamps. He planned to give it to a volunteer who had decided to leave the Peace Corps because her mother had been diagnosed with cancer.

A good plan soon gone awry.

The woman was staying at Stadszending for her last week, finishing PC paperwork. We went into *foto*, and Cork went to her room to give her the letter. She wasn't there, so he slipped it between the louvres above the door, thinking it would drop to the floor inside, and she would find it. He forgot that room had air conditioning, so the louvres were boarded up on the inside. Now the letter was stuck.

Nearby he found a screwdriver with which he was attempting to retrieve it when Mrs. Dotts appeared.

"*Meneer* Proctor, what are you doing?" Her tone indicated she was not pleased. Perhaps, Cork suggested later, she was still pissed off from having her establishment reported (by Cork) to Dr. Legiman as being infested with scabies.

"Breaking and entering," Cork quipped.

He couldn't get the letter with the screwdriver, so he returned the following night with a bent coat hanger. He poked the louvers again and was just about to give up in frustration when he noticed a tiny red and blue corner peeking out from the lowest louver, where it had slipped. He was able to simply pull the letter out with a thumb and forefinger. By now, the letter looked like it'd been well traveled through the postal system, and it hadn't even left the country.

When Mack finally got it, months later, it was so battered he got just the envelope and not the letter inside.

The Site Visit

Peace Corps policy requires a visit to each volunteer site within the first quarter of service, to see how the volunteer is living, talk with the village head, and discuss any problems or concerns.

Our first written notice of this said Judith and Stefan would come that day in the morning.

The Amerindian radio, a kind of shortwave system, was in Om John's cabin. The previous afternoon he had come to tell us Peace Corps had called on the radio and would not be showing up until the afternoon.

At 9 a.m. Om John came to tell us we "must call Peace Corps office immediately." He added, "All volunteers must go to town."

Cork's imagination fired up with visions of a countrywide military coup, with Americans being ransomed for four million dollars. He even envisioned the exact amount! Leaving me behind with instructions to prepare a "flee list" of critical things we should grab to pack in case we had to "leave in forty-five minutes, never to return."

An hour later Cork returned with the news that it was all a "fire drill" to see how fast volunteers could check-in.

The problem with our village's Amerindian radio was that we couldn't use it effectively to call because it only worked during certain hours, Om John was out hunting a lot, or he was drunk.

I had cut up my polyester muumuu—can't wear polyester in this climate—for a table cloth for our outside table. I had prepared Mexican chicken for our midday meal, and we were enjoying Parbos when Judith and Stefan arrived in their Peace Corps Jeep.

Though we offered them a beer, we happily did not have to share because Judith and Stephan were "working."

"How are you doing?" Judith inquired.

"We are doing what Eddie told us to do," Cork said. "We are living well."

Y2K

The third week in December when we visited our Peace Corps office mailbox our only mail were Y2K/New Year's Day advisory warnings.

We had been hearing that in the US the end of 1999 was being referred to as Y2K, and there was a lot of fear about electronic, internet, and computer meltdowns. I never understood how a date change, created by humans, could make that happen, but decided, perhaps, after four months of living in the jungle, I was out of touch.

Volunteers planning to be in the capital on New Year's Day were required to register in advance in the office and check in with Eddie, either in person or by telephone, before noon on New Year's Eve day. The DC office would call him at noon, and we all had to be accounted for.

Cork and I did not plan to be in town on New Year's Day, but we were advised to "stay away from crowds and maintain a low profile."

Cork shook his head and laughed. "Here we are, a foot taller than just about everybody else in the country, and *white*. And we're supposed to maintain a low profile?"

We spent Y2K quietly in our little house in Pierrekondre. "Quietly" because we had begun drinking, along with our neighbors, at noon on New Year's Eve day. They had set off all the fireworks, and by 6 p.m., when it got dark, we were all crashed in our beds or hammocks.

Cork had purchased a bottle of champagne with the romantic idea that at midnight we would take it to the bridge and drink it while watching the moon reflected on the Suriname river. Instead we drank it for breakfast on New Year's Day.

And I can report with certainty that animals and insects in the jungle had not been the least bit affected by Y2K.

The Peace Corps Annual Survey

In January each volunteer was given an annual survey paper with the option to fill it out about their Peace Corps experience. We could be free to express ourselves honestly as the papers would be sealed in a big manila envelope and sent directly to the DC office. We were assured no one in the Suriname office, including Eddie, would see what we had written.

In the pre-service materials sent from DC had been the statement, "You will have a better experience if you have no expectations." I thought that was a huge expectation on the part of the Peace Corps.

Along with my food-market-near-every-village expectation I had also assumed there would be a greater percentage of Americans working in the Suriname Peace Corps office. I had envisioned it similar to my imagining of a US Embassy. The reality was that everyone who worked in the Peace Corps Suriname office was a "host country national" except for the positions of Country Director (Eddie) and Administrative Officer (Devon).

Unless they were a trainer, none of them had ever traveled beyond the edge of the city. Their attitude was, why would you? There's nothing there but jungle and mosquitoes. One of the girls asked Cork, "What do you do for water?"

Appalled, he said, "And how long have you been working for the Peace Corps?"

Once during a casual conversation with fellow volunteers and the Peace Corps staff that included gossip and speculations, Cork had made a flippant remark. "Hey, I'm not taking any of this seriously."

He continued to rattle on, and on Judith's face I noticed a startled and concerned expression.

"Whoa," I said, interrupting. I turned to Judith and explained. "He doesn't mean he's not taking his Peace Corps service seriously. What he said is an American idiom, a kind of lighthearted joke, not meant to be taken seriously." One thing I had discovered was that in Suriname though many people spoke English, they did not understand our sense of humor.

Later we learned we were the only group ever in Peace Corps to have 100% completion of the optional annual surveys, and ours were rumored to be full of negative responses. Additional rumors were "people are coming from Washington to evaluate" our presence in the country.

The Business Card

Though we had continued to visit Jodesavanne on the weekends, often there were no other visitors, and it turned out to be just a peaceful picnic day for us. Guido Robles expressed his belief that Cork and I could not do anything to help the foundation.

"You live way out in the jungle," he said. "You don't have a car, and you don't have a phone."

He was right, in a sense. It got me to thinking about more than our cell phone fantasy. With my graphic design and printing background, it would be an easy matter to get a simple business card printed.

We made the mistake of mentioning this to a few of our fellow volunteers, upon whom the business side of the Peace Corps was lost.

They objected that we were "setting (ourselves) apart from Peace Corps." One even said she felt we were "setting (ourselves) above the common volunteer." These kids may have been knowledgeable in their areas of expertise, but they were naïve in the ways of business and networking.

I designed a simple card with a tasteful US flag rather than the Peace Corps logo, which I knew would come with all kinds of use determinations and restrictions. I used the office telephone number and my personal email address.

As soon as we had it printed, someone ran to Eddie to announce "Cork and Carolyn have made themselves a business card!"

Eddie didn't care. "Yes, I've seen it," he said. "I have one."

I think he had some respect for my business background since I had taught the native receptionist to answer the phone, "Suriname Peace Corps office. How can I help you?" instead of, "Hello?"

Mr. Peter's Wild Ride

That Monday morning in the village for me was calm and organized. I believed in doing no work on a day we went to *foto*. I needed to focus on eating and packing, and I hated to rush. Cork, of course, worked in the yard up to the last minute.

As we approached the bridge on time for the 12:30 p.m. bus Cork had just exclaimed, "I feel great", when a neighbor in his truck approached us from the direction of the river. He stopped to tell us *"bus no de."* (Bus is gone.)

Cork sputtered and swore, and I said loud and clear, "FUCK." Not exactly appropriate PC image, but certainly expressive of my feeling at the moment.

Indeed, the bus stop was deserted. We stood there, bewildered, frustrated and angry. A minute later we heard an engine. A bright red Mitsubishi King cab with tinted windows approached and stopped (everyone on a jungle road does) to visit. We told our sad tale and begged a ride to town. Without hesitation the two men inside agreed to take us. We threw our bags in the bed of the truck and climbed in the backseat before they could change their minds. They rolled up all their windows, turned on air conditioning and we were off in style.

The driver introduced himself as Peter, an import/exporter with a boutique next to his house in town. His companion, Morris, was the mechanic for all the Embassy cars. They were returning from a visit to Blakawatra.

Peter drove an average of 110 kilometers an hour. Each man had his own Nokia cell phone with portable antenna clamped to the roof on his side of the vehicle, making it look like a giant bug on speed. No pothole in the road was going to slow these two down.

In the Alcoa company town of Paranam, we flew by crowds of schoolchildren on both sides of the street. No sidewalks here. I prayed one of the children would not suddenly step out into the road. Peter didn't even slow down.

These two fine Dutchmen who chatted and took phone calls along the way, dropped us right in front of our favorite restaurant, a record hour and 45 minutes after leaving our village. As they sped away Cork and I looked at each other, laughed with relief and shook our heads.

Cork said, "I knew somehow when we got in that truck it would be a wild ride."

Dog in the Can

Our village was overrun with what Surinamers call "garbage dogs." These unspayed, short-haired, medium-sized, tan-colored, noisy creatures with large, pointed ears ate everything they could, including chicken bones.

According to Cork, "All the dogs in Suriname are sired by bats."

Toetie was no exception. A little short-haired beige puppy with long legs, a black face that ended in a pointy nose with one deformed nostril, and huge bat-shaped ears. Since she was a puppy and often slept or took refuge under our house, we assumed she was homeless.

When Woni saw me give Toetie an egg, she said, "No no. You give a dog an egg, it will grow up to chase the chickens and steal eggs."

Toetie also took refuge inside our latrine, where she could slip between the front face board of the toilet bench and the wall to disappear into the dark area around the top of the diesel oil drum that formed the pit of the latrine.

One afternoon Martinus saw her slip in there, got his long casaba stick, and in an attempt to drive her out began to poke it into the darkness around the base where the walls meet the sand. With no luck, he finally walked back to his house with his stick, muttering, "*Seka* dog, *seka* dog."

Just after midnight, the village was quiet and we were sleeping soundly. We awakened to, w*hine, whine, whine,* followed by *thump, thump. Whine, whine, thump, thump, thump.*

"That Snoopy," mumbled Cork. "Martinus must've tied her up." Snoopy was Martinus' and Lucia's dog.

I listened. "No, it's coming from the direction of our latrine. Maybe it's Toetie."

"That dumb dog." Cork was unpleasantly awake now. "I took the board away. The dumb dog probably wedged herself in and can't get out."

"Hope this doesn't go on all night."

A few moments of silence, then *whine, whine, thump, thump, thump.*

"Goddammit." Cork slapped his pillow in annoyance.

175

I reminded him that afternoon Martinus had tried unsuccessfully with the casaba stick to drive her out from under our latrine, and frightened, she had disappeared.

Cork swore again. He'd had a "bath" with hot water heated on the table top gas stove, was comfortable, and didn't want to get up to "mess with some stupid dog that can't find her way out the way she got in."

A half hour of quiet passed, just enough time to begin drifting back to sleep. Then, *thump, thump, whine, whine, whine.*

Mumbling and swearing, Cork crawled out from under the mosquito net, put on his socks and shoes and new bathrobe with the red, turquoise, blue, white and purple cow pattern. He lit the kerosene lantern, left the house and trudged across the white, moonlit sand.

Dressed for battle in cow bathrobe, shoes and socks, Cork said later, "I felt like Diogenes searching for the truth."

I laid in bed and listened to distant sounds of whining and thumping, combined now with grumbling and more swearing, while Cork tore off the front panel of the toilet seat bench.

After several minutes he returned with the story.

The latrine, "built to specs" that had been made up as they went along, was not the sealed model it should have been. There was an eight-inch gap between the top of the old diesel oil barrel that formed the hole and the toilet seat bench. When Martinus poked under the walls with his stick, he only succeeded in frightening the dog, who took what looked to her like an alternative escape route—over the edge of the barrel. She had landed in the hole and been trapped all those hours, wallowing in old excreta, unable to jump out of the shitter.

Cork's idea had been to get a rope and make a noose, with which he had tried several times to lasso the little dog. This combination of lasso and lantern light only served to further frighten the already traumatized Toetie. In exasperation, Cork had gotten down on his knees, reached his arm as far he could into the dark depths of the hole and felt around until he managed to catch the dog by the scruff of her neck. More swearing through clenched teeth.

As soon as he caught her, hauled her out and released her, she scampered off toward the river. Cork washed his hands, came back inside and dropped the cow bathrobe to the floor, to be washed the next day.

He crawled back under the mosquito net into the comfort of our bed, and I asked the stupidest question in the universe.

"Was she a mess?"

My dear husband snapped, "Whadda *you* think?!"

Zwartenhovenbrugstraat

By February 2000 the yellow government bus was no longer crossing the Carolina Bridge. The government had decided the old wooden bridge was too dangerous for the weight of cars and trucks and busses.

Vehicles now had to park alongside the road, and people had to walk across the bridge and get to the farther villages of Redidoti and Cassipoura as best they could. On our side of the bridge a small taxi business of private cars and trucks sprouted.

Because the bus had been running irregularly for several weeks, Cork and I decided it would be more cost-effective for us to find a little apartment to rent in *foto*. We realized we had been spending a couple of hundred dollars a month on overnights at Stadszending. With our own little apartment, we could save restaurant money by cooking and not have to carry clothes and toiletries with us each time we went to town.

As we walked the streets with our errands, Cork began to ask our favorite shopkeepers and friends if they knew of anything we could rent. This was how we found a furnished multi-level apartment we adored, better than our wildest expectations.

Ronald, manager of duPoort, a Dutch restaurant we frequented on Zwartenhovenbrugstraat, told us his family owned the entire building, and the apartment was, of all convenient places, next door above Guido's Galaxy men's store. It was clean, the kitchen was modern, and it included a new color television. Each floor had its own bathroom. From the window in the expansive third-floor walk-in shower we could enjoy a full view of the mosque and synagogue. The second-floor balcony overlooking the street ran the width of the building.

Ronald told us the narrow, steep, winding stairs to the second and third floors of the apartment were 150 years old.

We made the deal for $250 a month beginning March 1st.

The first night we slept in our new apartment, in the king-size bed and with air con, we slept really well.

The Devolution of Coffee

After drinking tea every morning for weeks, the idea of coffee became tantalizing, nostalgic and a symbol of everything we left behind when we came to this equatorial South American country.

On our next trip to *foto* we were on a quest: coffee, a coffee maker, and coffee filters. Coffee was easy to find, filters much more difficult, and no coffee maker could be found which wasn't electric. I got the idea of boiling the coffee in a pan on our two-burner tabletop gas stove, putting a filter in a metal strainer and straining the coffee into two cups.

While the idea was sound, not so the reality. The grounds backed up in the filter, creating a sludge no liquid could reasonably penetrate. The drink went into the cup droplet by droplet—way too slow for spoiled Americans. And, the droplets subsided before the cup was half-full. Using the strainer by itself, sans filter, didn't work, as the holes were too big to filter the grounds.

In the end I boiled the coffee in a pan, let it sit for a minute to allow the grounds to settle, then poured the liquid directly into the cups, where any remaining grounds again settled to the bottom.

Acceptable-tasting coffee, made just the way you see the Cowboys make it in old western movies.

To their delight, I showed the village children how to fold and cut snowflakes out of the filters.

Projects

We found Peace Corps procedures to be confusing at best. The preservice training manual stated, "You do not work for Peace Corps. You work for your host agency." Yet everything we did had to be approved by the country director. And though each month we received a "stipend", not a "salary", that money was considered taxable by the IRS.

In order to go forward with any project not related to the Blakawatra *stichting* or the Jodensavanne *stichting*, we needed special PC programming approval.

I discovered, over a hamburger lunch with the three medical volunteers who were lecturing in various interior villages, that they had asked the office for visual aides to help in their presentations. Of course, none existed, and over the Parbos with our hamburger lunch, the girls and I designed on napkins what they would like to have—three wide canvas banners with grommets so the banners could be strung between trees.

Approval for me to create these banners required a meeting with Eddie and Judith, during which we would also discuss my possible illustration work for a bird guide to be produced by another *stichting*, Stinasu (Foundation for Nature Conservation in Suriname). The Sur 4 volunteer who worked there had told them she knew an artist (me), and they could probably get the illustrations done for free.

Cork opened the meeting with, "Are we going to need guns or knives?"

The bird guide discussion went nowhere, but I did receive permission to create the three visual aid health banners, plus a small budget to buy a roll of canvas, brushes, acrylic paints, and hemming and grommeting.

One afternoon I was so engrossed in painting the canvas spread out in the living room of the Zwartenhovenbrugstraat apartment, I didn't even notice when a monkey came in the open window, pooped on the carpet below the window, and scooted out.

* * *

Cork discovered a myriad of new, little, fix-it projects for the apartment. We rearranged the furniture so the dining table was now on the third-floor with the kitchen and also the bed, which made an usual arrangement in a small area, but it was only floor of the apartment that was air-conditioned.

In our Peace-Corps-standard-issue cabin, Cork turned the second entrance into a Dutch door, and with wood from the outhouse added two handy shelves to the cooking corner.

For two afternoons in a row I worked on my photo journal pages. The Dutch doors were a godsend. Now children could look in, but they couldn't come in. They were consumed with curiosity when they saw the pictures laid out on the table but I was firm. I would not let them see until I had finished with the pages. I hadn't minded them in the house but sometimes it had become so crowded—and they wanted to *touch* everything. I didn't even want my darling husband touching my stuff.

The Green Chair

After bringing home more provisions for our little jungle home and storing them on shelves and in hanging bags, with nothing left to do, we hit the rum and pineapple juice. Before we knew it dusk had come, and we were shitfaced.

Cork rose from his chair to go outside to pee, lost his balance and fell against one of our two plastic chairs. It snapped in two places like it had been made of plastic matchsticks. "Your penance now ith to live w'out a chair," I slurred. "If you wanna sit, use the wooden shtool you built."

In a store in *foto* selling household things, we purchased a sturdy dark green plastic chair to replace the one Cork fell on. We carried the chair with our grocery purchases to the bus stop at Saramaccastraat to wait for the bus to our village. There we met several neighbors also waiting. Many commented on our shiny new plastic chair. The story of how Cork had been drunk and broken the previous chair had already circulated the village, and waiting for the bus with our new chair provided an opportunity for our neighbors to share the story again and have a good laugh.

When we arrived at our house and had put away the groceries, we put on hold the celebratory we're-back-in-Pierrekondre ceremonial drinking.

One Room Marriage, Continued

One morning while Cork was playing with the cassette recorder, the batteries died. I made a stupid remark about how things are never the same after he fucks with them, and he was understandably pissed off the rest of the day.

Outside, he raked leaves and hauled the broken canoe, which I thought made a rather rustic outdoor still life, into a pile and set it all on fire.

Days like that made us crazy, trying our patience.

* * *

The fight was on before I even knew what happened. We had just finished a great dinner of the succulent Suriname river whitefish, *anumara*, and squash. The sun was setting. We were sitting at the table watching dusk settle in.

These things are truly unpredictable. I don't remember what I said, but what Cork heard was, "You are boring to talk to." He exploded into an angry, defensive stream of verbal abuse. For the rest of the evening he sulked. His last words of the day before retiring at 7:30 p.m. were, "I'm going to town tomorrow on the bus. We need some days apart, and I need to think about this marriage."

These outbursts always left me numb and emotionally exhausted. I had little energy for anything. At the moment, I didn't care one way or the other what he did.

The following morning represented a new day. All was certainly not forgotten but much more rational in the light of the new morning. We were able to talk about what happened between us the previous evening.

Cork admitted to being afraid he was losing it, feeling useless, unproductive and wasted out here. This didn't surprise me, given his type-A personality. He said he's feeling his age all of a sudden with pressure to act in case he didn't have a lot of years left.

He said, "I don't want to die out here." He looked forward to the vacation in French Guiana we had in mind, around his birthday in July.

Wisdom, as often it does, prevailed, and he did not take the bus to town. In the midst of these discussions over morning coffee, Cork suddenly jumped from his chair, grabbed the flyswatter and yelled, "Stay over there!"

"What?!" I envisioned a snake in the house–my worst nightmare.

"Tarantula!"

The large, furry, black visitor with pink toes had emerged from under the plastic covering on the table. It scurried off while Cork swore and beat the table with the killer flyswatter. He didn't crush the spider, and now we couldn't figure out where it had gone. I got a flashlight. Cork began to move, with care, a few things around the table.

The great tarantula hunt was in full swing.

I spotted a furry leg partially hidden behind the vertical wall beam. I nudged it with a pencil, sending the tarantula in Cork's direction. It alluded us for a few more minutes until it met its final moment behind the peanut butter jar. On the flat of the flyswatter Cork carried the body outside and placed it in the sand. I scooped it with a spoon and threw it to the nearest chicken. The chicken grabbed it and ran, chased by a second jealous chicken. When the first one dropped it, the second one picked it up, then changed her mind and dropped it, too. They clucked off in search of tastier treats.

Who would think chickens would eat lizards, giant grasshoppers, cockroaches and their own skin, but not a fat little tarantula?

The Money Argument

My old fear of what-if-I-loose-everything rose its ugly head the day we got down to 80,000 guilders, and a wire transfer we had initiated from Nevada State Bank had not yet arrived.

I've always joked that I'm the daughter of parents married during the great depression. The truth of that is that I grew up listening to my laundry-truck-driver father and housewife mother worrying about everything, especially finances. Their greatest fear was that someone would come and take everything they'd worked so hard for away from them.

And one day, someone did.

On a Sunday afternoon while we were dining at my aunt's house, thieves broke in and stole everything loose: the family silver, linens, picture frames, candlesticks, dishes, my mother's tiny jewelry box, my father's guitar and all the food in the refrigerator. The police recovered nothing.

I think I carried this fear of losing everything in my genes.

Nancy at NSB had said the wire transfer would take seven to ten days. I suspected she knew nothing about wire transfers and had probably never done one before.

Claudette at Hakrinbank said the money could arrive on Monday, but it would be two more days before Hakrinbank would release the cash to us. At this point, I didn't trust anything anyone said anymore, either in America or in Suriname. The last wire transfer had gotten screwed up, so I had little faith for a simple transaction this time.

Meanwhile, Cork was cavalier, saying I could go back to Pierrekondre, and he'd sit in the apartment and wait for the money. With some business calls yet to make locally and the phone card down to $10, he called a friend in Vegas and chatted away. A few minutes later I entered the room to find him now talking to daughter Kathy in California.

When he said, "Oh here, I'm sure Carolyn wants to say hello," I lost it.

I screamed, "NO! I don't want to talk to anybody! We're running out of money, and you're talking on the telephone!"

He said goodbye to Kathy and began his regular argument: "These are my daughters, and I'll talk to them anytime I want."

Livid, I screamed more until I went downstairs to cry. I felt embarrassed as well as angry. I could've kept my mouth shut—the calls were only .44 cents and the money would probably come.

All of a sudden, I was tired of being culturally sensitive, tired of being maritally sensitive, tired of being told how to cross the street. Like the reasons for cancer, it wasn't any one thing—it was everything.

Indeed, the wire transfer had gotten screwed up, but the money came and was available to us at Hakrinbank on Wednesday.

After more arguing Cork and I agreed to live on 75,000 guilders a week and split it down the middle. I agreed to buy all the food with my half, and we would split mutual expenses like cabs, busses and dinners out. He contradicted each point I made in favor of this arrangement, trying to convince me "It will never work."

"This argument is ludicrous," I said. "Teachers here make $100 a month, other Peace Corps volunteers are living on $260, and we can't live here on $760 dollars a month?"

In the end, he was right. Our agreement on how to spend the money didn't work. He would not be "told how to spend his" money, and I continued to worry that we'd run out of money.

Hello Outside World

We agreed to purchase a cell phone.

With one of the good long poles from a nearby abandoned, decaying *kampu*, Cork erected the biggest telephone antenna he was able to buy at Teltronics, topped with a square solar panel. Now our village neighbors would certainly think we were CIA spies, in spite of our protestations that we were way too old for our own government to hire us for such things.

Discovering our new cell phone worked, we woke up daughter Kathy in California to share the news. Cork repeated several times how thrilled he was to be able to talk with his daughters, and the rest of his day was upbeat and enthusiastic.

When Woni wanted to call her sister in Paranam, we had to establish rules. We told our neighbors the phone was for emergency only, and they could only come to us to use it if blood was involved.

Rainy Season

By summer the rainy season was well upon us. For four days, we had awakened to gray skies and overcast days marked with sudden downpours. After ten to thirty minutes of torrential rain, it would stop as if someone turned off a faucet. Nights were cold, and I slept in sweats and socks. Durotanks and buckets were overflowing, creating in me a surreal feeling of comfort and abundance. We heated lots of pans of water and enjoyed warm bucket baths.

Passing through the Peace Corps office one day, one of the volunteers said to me with envy in her voice, "Wow! At your site you have hot baths!"

I had no clue what she was talking about. Then I realized she had been talking to Cork. No wonder she was confused. He had given her the impression that we had built some trick bath. She envisioned *spa*.

For Cork, the real downside to the rain was that it appeared to affect the telephone transmission. The clouds made conversations break up and even disconnect. And there was not much sun to power the solar panel.

The Urine Cure

When one of the dogs went into heat a new dog showed up in our village. Woni said he was from a village across the river.

For several days we watched him cry and rub his right ear in the sand, as if something in there hurt him.

Remembering the PC health presentation, Cork and I looked at each other and said at the same time "urine."

Two times a day Cork lured the dog close with a tidbit, poured warm urine into his ear and rubbed it with the palm of his hand.

We felt amazed that the dog let us, and even more amazed when it worked. The dog began to spend nights sleeping under our cabin.

Cork mumbled, "Now the damn thing thinks it's found a new home."

The Secret is Out

By July our apartment above Galaxy was no longer a secret. We had not admitted to anyone that we had rented an apartment. Our answer to questions about it had been that "we made an arrangement with a guy."

Naturally one of our fellow volunteers had reported this to the office. I'm sure PC staff saw Cork and I as troublemakers, as they had just had to deal with the rumor that we had a cell phone. In the resulting office meeting to confirm this, it had been made clear that while they weren't happy about it, there was no written Peace Corps rule that said we couldn't have a cell phone.

The Peace Corps' idea of a volunteer's living situation was that we should "live at the level of our counterpart," which in this case was probably Martinus.

Cork had said to Eddie, "So yeah, we have a cell phone. But Martinus has a truck. We aren't buying ourselves a *truck*."

In the meeting about the apartment rumor, Eddie said, "Where you live has to be vetted by the Peace Corps medical officer, to be sure it meets our health and safety standards."

There were standards for health and safety? I remembered Sylvia's house in Powaka, but for once, I said nothing.

Cork asked, "So what constitutes safety standards?"

"Well, for instance," Judith said, "if the place had a swimming pool, that could be considered unsafe."

"A swimming pool?" This time I couldn't keep my mouth shut. "The *ambassador* has a swimming pool."

Eddie said, "Let's schedule a time for Dr. Legiman to come and see your apartment."

The date was set, Dr. Legiman and Judith arrived, and Cork offered them each a glass of wine. They declined, as they were "working," looked around the apartment, and a friendly conversation ensued around our favorite Javanese restaurants.

After they left no more was said about our apartment.

New Country Director

Eddie had developed a serious case of leishmaniasis and had to go for an extended period of time to Walter Reed hospital in Washington DC. We would have a new country director.

Enter Shelby Matthew Givens, to whom Cork took an immediate dislike.

A 62-year-old African American, Shelby Givens had done a PhD dissertation in the eighties at the University of California Berkeley entitled "An Ethnographic Study of Social Control and Dispute Settlement among the Aluku Maroons of French Guiana and Suriname South America." He also spoke Sranan Tongo, which I'm sure endeared him to the DC office.

* * *

A barge coming down the Suriname river recently had hit a piling and the ancient wooden Carolina Bridge had collapsed.

Two versions of how this happened emerged. The newspaper reported that the barge captain had tied up to the piling for the night and the weight of the barge in the current had pulled it down. The locals reported that the barge captain had been drunk and in the middle of the night accidentally steered the barge into the piling. The only facts both reports shared were that this involved a barge and had happened in the middle of the night.

Because of the new lack-of-transportation situation with the now-defunct Carolina Bridge, Shelby Givens and Judith wanted to move Cork and I from Pierrekondre to a small Amerindian village on the Afobaka highway, just before the turnoff to Powaka. They also felt there we would have a better opportunity to get some projects going.

Cork and I were not thrilled with this idea. We knew that no matter what explanation the Peace Corps would give to Martinus and the three villages, our neighbors would say we had moved because we didn't like them. And because the families of all these Amerindian villages in this area of the Suriname river were interrelated, this idea would spread, fast.

In our first meeting with Shelby Givens to discuss this potential village move, he told us we must stop handing out our business cards.

"They are too self-aggrandizing," he said.

I was proud of Cork because unlike me, he had been able to keep his mouth shut in this meeting. Later he told me, "What a pompous ass. It was all I could do to keep from dragging him across his desk and punching him out."

Vacation to French Guiana

Like everything Peace Corps, this village move would not happen in the next ten minutes. Privately Cork and I were already discussing the possibility of leaving the Peace Corps. In order to have some time to think about this, and not wanting to lose our vacation time, we suggested we take our entitled vacation and discuss the move after our return.

This was approved, and off we went for eighteen days to French Guiana, the country east of Suriname.

* * *

While we waited at the border town of Albina to cross the Marowijne river into French Guiana, Cork exclaimed, "Wow—look at *that*!"

Official transportation back and forth across the river consisted of motorized dugout canoes, each manned by two men. At the river's edge we watched a group of men preparing to move a red Toyota truck across the river. To accomplish this, they had spread two wide planks across two canoes. The truck had somehow been placed with two wheels on each plank. As we watched in awe, they revved up their motors and headed out into the river.

"Where there's a will, there's a creative way," Cork said.

We showed our passports and yellow fever certificates at a raggedy wooden security shed, secured our dugout transportation, and crossed to Saint-Laurent-du-Maroni in French Guiana. There we visited the Camp du Transportation where we saw the cell, with its wall scratchings, where Henri

"Papillon" Charrière had been imprisoned when he had first arrived in French Guiana.

We visited the largest Island of the Îles du Salut, Île Royale, where Papillon was actually imprisoned. From there we had a view of Devil's Island, one of the three that comprise the Îles du Salut. Trivia: Papillon never set foot on Devil's Island itself.

At Kourou we toured the European Space Station, where about fourteen Ariane rockets were launched annually.

In the capital, Cayenne, we indulged in French food, French wine, Vietnamese food, and I bought real lacy French lingerie, made in Paris.

We perused a French bookstore where a man behind me pinched me on the ass before he hastened to leave the store. I found Cork in another aisle and said, "You're not gonna believe what just happened to me."

Cork smiled when I told him. "You're hot in any country."

* * *

While in Cayenne, we received news from Kathy that Louise, their mother, had died unexpectedly. This news devastated Cork, who had reverence and only good things to say about Louise, and who accepted a hundred percent responsibility for the end of their marriage. I had always felt had she and I met under different circumstances we could have been best friends.

"Do you want to go home and be with the girls?" I asked.

He shook his head. "There's nothing I can do."

Cork's Solution

Back in Paramaribo, another meeting with Shelby and Judith, and a trip to see the house where we would live and to meet the captain of the Amerindian village where they now wanted to place us.

A few weeks earlier, Sur 4 had left the country, and a post in the public relations office at Stinasu had become available. My participation in the production of the bird guide as an illustrator had been nixed by the Dutch project adviser in

Holland, a picky bird scientist who felt they should pay a professional bird illustrator. Meanwhile the entire project had stalled.

I wanted that public relations position, and we had discussed it with Judith and Eddie before he left. They had responded that they could not move me into the city because they did not have a position there for Cork.

This had added to Cork's anger and frustration. "All they have to do is pick up the phone and call somebody, and they could find me a post in the city." This led to more grumbling about lazy government officials.

Now that our vacation was over and we were close to being moved, we had decided it was time to leave the Peace Corps. We had always had the agreement that if one of us woke up one morning in hysterics and said, "Jesus, who do I have to fuck to get out of here?" we would go together.

That time had come.

One afternoon, on the bus bumping down the Afobaka highway with my boobs tightly bound, I watched jungle greenery pass and thought, *I don't want to leave. I want to stay and work at Stinasu. I want Cork and his kvetching to leave.*

As if he had read my mind, Cork touched my arm and said, "I have an idea. You don't have to give me an answer right now. Let me tell you what I have in mind and you take a day or two to think about it."

I turned my attention away from the jungle and looked at him.

"Why don't I leave and go home and you stay here?" he said. "If you're here alone they'll give you that Stinasu job. Now don't tell me right now what you think. Just think about it."

Yes! Yes!

I smiled. "Well, that is an interesting idea. Let me think about it. We won't see Shelby again for a couple of days so there's time."

* * *

By now, type A personality and obsessive-compulsive that he is, Cork had become disillusioned with the entire Peace Corps experience. He had developed a hate-on for Suriname, our "lazy" Amerindian villagers, the "arrogant prick" new country director, the "deer-in-the-headlights" office staff and most of our fellow volunteers.

I accepted his idea to leave the country while I remained.

Together we decided the best first step to accomplish this would be to have a conversation with Dr. Legiman about how it would work and to ask for his support for our request. We knew anything we told Dr. Legiman would be under medical confidence, whereas if we went directly to Shelby Givens, he could decide on the spot to put us both on the next flight out of the country.

We arranged a meeting with Dr. Legiman and explained that a year of living in different locations would not adversely affect our marriage because we were already accustomed to spending periods of time apart because of Cork's career. This would be no different from Cork working a year on the road while I remained at home.

"I understand," he said. "You can tell Shelby you have spoken to me and I approve of your request."

In our meeting with Shelby Givens, we outlined how this would work. I would go home to Las Vegas to visit Cork during the two-weeks-vacation I would have coming in January, he would come to visit me in Suriname around April, and I would be home again at the end of my service in August, 2001.

When a Peace Corps volunteer decides to quit earlier then his or her two-year commitment, the status of this is called "early termination" or ET. Some volunteers see ET-ing as "quitting" in the negative sense, while others could care less.

While Cork didn't care, I felt he deserved better than that. Unlike Cork, I had read every single missive sent from DC. I knew there was a "higher" category called "interrupted service" (IS).

"You really have no job for Cork," I said to Shelby. "Therefore we are asking that he leave as IS rather than ET."

Shelby expressed reluctance and I pressed. Maybe blackmail could work?

I laughed and said, "Really, Shelby, you know he is a standup comedian. I don't think Washington wants him going out on stage making negative jokes about the Peace Corps."

Shelby did not laugh. But he did grant Cork Interrupted Service and granted me the post in the publicity department at Stinasu. I would be moved into the capital where I would be housed in an apartment of Peace Corps' choosing. When Sur 6 arrived and completed their training in October, I would receive a roommate from that group.

Cork and I returned to our apartment on Zwartenhovenbrugestraat, opened a bottle of French wine to celebrate and began to plan what he would pack to take home and how we would close out this city apartment.

He had already repainted the steps of the stairwell and now he borrowed an industrial vacuum cleaner from our friend who managed the Dutch hotel around the corner, Krasnapolsky. Cork was obsessed with leaving the apartment spotless. When we went to duPoort to return the keys to Ronald, Cork looked forward to showing him how well we had left the apartment.

"Oh, that's okay," Ronald said, "You've been great tenants. I don't need to see it."

When we were alone Cork continued to rant against the Peace Corps and Shelby Givens. Cork couldn't wait to get out of the country and I couldn't wait to see him go.

* * *

I will always be so grateful to Cork for suggesting I stay in Suriname to work for Stinasu and finish my PC commitment after he went home with Interrupted Service.

I felt profoundly changed by my two years in Suriname, though I couldn't begin to say how.

Here are just a few of the adventures I wouldn't otherwise have experienced: Ate monkey, met Miss Suriname, peed in a bucket in an open dugout on a river in the middle of the night in pouring rain, read *Newsweek* faithfully cover to cover, squeezed *seka* eggs out of my husband's feet, ate margarine that came in a can, heard howler monkeys at dawn, slept in a hammock, learned to make Bailey's Irish Cream from rum, swam in rivers where piranha live, learned to make *cassaba* bread, gave information to Dutch tourists in English at a historic Jewish site, lost twenty pounds, learned an Amerindian dance, battled a six-inch wolf spider, screamed in Sranan Tongo at a speeding bus driver, ate Chinese chicken feet, produced a bird guide, saw the rare orange cock-of-the-rock, created banners as visual aids for rural health education, drank native bush medicine for diarrhea, learned to weave a hammock, painted 400-year-old brick synagogue ruins that are on the list of "100 Most Endangered Sites in the World", kicked a dog, flew in an Australian Nomad over an endless green carpet of Amazon jungle, picnicked at the Ambassador's home, watched a tarantula crawl up my friend's leg, sharpened a machete, drank *cassiri*, watched a squatting man wash his genitals in the gutter after a rain, observed an Amerindian healing ceremony, learned how to make jello shooters, saw a Harpy eagle catch a lizard, taught a textile design class, killed a six-inch centipede with a machete, planted a disastrous garden in the sand, lived with an Amerindian family, inscribed and painted a cement gravestone, wrote an "Amazon eco-romance" novel and got pooped on by a baby capuchin monkey.

I also received the kindest and most insightful thing Cork ever said to me. "I now see in you a strength of character I didn't know you had."

QUE HUEVOS. Literal Spanish for, *what eggs*. In the Mexican street slang he'd picked up as a child in East Los Angeles it meant, *what balls.*

The graphic designer in me couldn't help herself. I made
Cork a number of "personalized" greeting cards.

In the freezer, I found an exploded beer bottle and the missing lid to his blender.

"So, what's the craziest, oddest experience you've ever had as a cruise ship captain?" I asked.

"You want me to go where and do what?"

A ladder in the warehouse led to my sleeping loft, which also stored some of Cork's old publicity posters.

Cork does his income taxes in my office.

At the Gold Coast Hotel Casino in Las Vegas, "Comedy Under the Balls" with Kelly McDonald

A rare Cork moment in a bathtub, at Garza Blanca in Puerto Vallarta

Our engagement photo.

No wedding would be complete without a bachelor roast.

The weeping groom

Best party I've ever been to. I came home with a husband.

Christmas card photo with Puck, during our *ranchita* remodel.

"Will work for laffs" – marching on the Strip when the
Bally's marquee had burned.

Formal portrait on the Crowne Dynasty

Cork works with the audience during his performance on
the Crowne Dynasty

As we released it Cork said, "Godspeed and swim as fast as you can."

Fun with Phyllis Diller and a bottle of Chivas.

Michael Gaughan opened his new hotel/casino, The Orleans, on December 13th, 1996. Since Cork was Entertainment Director, this was our 1996 Christmas card.

Al Rapone,, leader of Zydeco Express, and his wife, Alice,
cook Cajun in our kitchen.

Swimming at Wangi Falls, in Kakadu, Northern Territory, Australia, where "Crocodile Dundee" was filled.

A sixteen-year-old boy showed us how to throw a spear at the Tjapukai Cultural Center. Under his guidance, I felt quite proud that my spear went further than Cork's.

Our seventh wedding anniversary in 1998 at Dunn's River
Falls, Jamaica.

"A girl made it for me, and then she died."

With British eco-activist, Captain Clive Kelly, on the
Suriname River.

Aboard *Survival*, Captain Clive Kelly's trimaran moored in the Suriname river, Cork signs his guest book.

Carolyn V. Hamilton

From my Suriname art journal, a watercolor painting of a Maroon woman paddling her dugout canoe on the Afobaka lake.

It's official. We swear in as Peace Corps volunteers.

Carolyn V. Hamilton

Daf trucks take us and all our new household goods to our site in the village of Pierrekondre, Suriname.

With a lot of time on our hands, Cork rebuilds our latrine.

Cork enjoys lunch with a Parbo beer outside our jungle
cabin in Pierrekondre

At our cabin in Pierrekondre, Cork takes a gutter shower.

Dressed to the nines, from, the ankles up, for Thanksgiving dinner at the ambassador's residence.

My first Peace Corps project, painting a cement headstone,
while our Amerindian neighbors look on.

With a lot of time on his hands, Cork repainted the 100-year-old stairs in our apartment on Zwartenhovenbrugestraat.

I landed at McCarran airport to be greeted by Cork carrying
a big sign that read, "WELCOME JUNGLE SLUT!"

In Paris near the Hotel du Paris, Cork found a neighborhood
do-it-yourself laundromat where he could wash his 100
percent wool sweater in hot water.

Cork washes his hands in Manzanilla, Mexico.

When I won a cruise for two with Carnival down the
Mexican Riviera, I bought a third ticket and invited Kathy
and Luann to go with me as a Christmas present.

Jazz singer Joe Williams in concert, raising funds to provide music scholarships for CSN, the Community College of Southern Nevada.

Cork's 80th birthday comedy roast and memoir debut at Las Vegas' Southpoint Hotel Casino, raising funds for Opportunity Village.

Cork "relaxes" in the big, red velvet chair during his 80th birthday comedy roast.

Showgirls escort Cork to the podium during his 80ᵗʰ birthday
comedy roast.

Cork and Carolyn at his 80th birthday
comedy roast at Las Vegas' Southpoint Hotel and Casino.

Comedian Bob Zany, roastmaster at Cork's
80th birthday comedy roast.

Long-time friend and singer/comedian Carme Pitrello takes
the podium to roast Cork on his 80th birthday.

Showgirls and friends gather to roast Cork on his 80th birthday
and memoir debut, in a benefit for Las Vegas' favorite charity, Opportunity Village.

Backstage with award-winning, international Elvis tribute artist, Pete Storm, and Cork Proctor as "the ghost of Elvis" in "Rendezvous With the King," at Harrah's in Reno, Nevada.

It's wonderful
having you in my life

From a collection of greeting cards Cork has sent me over
the years.

PART FOUR - AND THEN...

Back in the US of A

Because of my work with Stinasu and WWF, I knew there were laws about transporting animals and animal parts from one country to another. Souvenirs I had collected to bring home included Maroon wood carvings, Amerindian beading and basketry, and the skull from the capuchin monkey Woni had stewed.

To get a legal document to take the skull out of Suriname I made four visits to the appropriate wildlife office. Each time I had been thwarted with an unannounced office closure or told the right person wasn't there. "He's not here right now, I don't know when he'll be back," or "He left early today," or "He's on vacation."

I never got the document and worried that when I listed "monkey skull" with the craft items on my US customs declaration form, customs would take it away from me. In the end, no one asked any questions about anything, leading me to wonder if they ever read those forms.

* * *

The Peace Corps office decided that they wanted to bring new volunteers in in the third fiscal quarter rather than the fourth fiscal quarter of the year. In order to make that budget work, they had to get rid of Sur 5 early.

Of the original twenty-six volunteers in our group, only twelve of us remained. We were offered the option to "early out," meaning we could leave in July with the PC version of "honorable discharge," the official completion certificate (on which they misspelled my name) and entitlement to the government benefits available to volunteers who completed their service.

Eight of us took it.

* * *

At the end of July I landed at McCarran airport to be greeted by Cork carrying a big sign that read, "WELCOME JUNGLE SLUT!"

When Cork had come home from Suriname, he had moved into the free-standing apartment he had built in the back yard.

"Everything is over code," he announced. He had done all the plumbing himself and prided himself that it "never leaked a drop."

The Huffers had moved out of our house, and Cork had rented the apartment to Cheryl, a pretty young lawyer.

My first full day at home, Cork took me to lunch and to see an exhibit of comedian Steve Martin's paintings at the newly-opened Guggenheim Hermitage Museum in The Venetian Hotel Casino.

When we arrived home a little after four p.m, I noticed a lot of cars parked on the road in front of the house and in our driveway. Cork explained Cheryl had just graduated from law school and was having a little celebration party in the garage which, in the nine months I had been gone, he had painted yellow.

"Why don't we pop in?" he suggested, "You can meet her, and we can say hello."

When we walked in, about seventy of our closest friends screamed, *"SURPRISE!"*

Tears flooded my eyes. When the laughter and clapping abated, I turned to Cork and in a loud voice asked, "Who *are* all these white people?"

* * *

At home in Las Vegas I found many surprises. After a year of inhabitance by—surely there must have been more than one—bachelor pigs, my house was almost indescribable.

I found drawers full of mouse poop and pistachio shells. I found balls of clean sheets in the hall cupboard out of which fell jockey shorts, several clothespins and one sock. I found not a matching lid and pot in the same cupboard.

There were plastic grocery sacks full of little pieces of paper Cork informed me were "our taxes for 1999, 2000, and 2001." Strange kitsch had been gifted to him by well-meaning friends because the house looked "empty" to them—because he had yet to unpack any of the boxes in the big yellow garage.

I had assumed a return to hot showers, but no, Cork had the water heater turned off for the summer on the theory that the water comes out of those artesian wells at eighty-eight degrees, which it does at *noon*, not at eight a.m. or eight p.m., other times one might want to shower.

The best surprise had been the garage party. It had been a terrific homecoming, mouse poop notwithstanding.

My days now were spent sorting and cleaning and throwing away. It's amazing what people will take when you leave it out on the edge of the road. I became the housefrau Nazi.

Thank goodness I didn't have to go job-hunting. I committed to being the kept woman I knew I was always meant to be.

One night we were watching television when a mouse ran across the floor and disappeared behind a bookcase. Cork grabbled a BB gun and pointed it into the space between the bookcase and the wall and fired. There had been no time to think about this, and he didn't hit the mouse.

It took six months to get rid of all the mice.

Puck's Fate

During the year that Cork and I had been gone from the ranch, JD and Karen had to make a tough decision. They had brought with them two dogs of their own, one of which was also a border collie.

It had never occurred to any of us the four dogs might not get along. There had ensued confusion among the four, accompanied by much barking and growling and fighting, as to who would be the alpha dog. Puck bit their border collie.

JD and Karen's older son Jason, in his early twenties, lived in a rented house with a big yard, and he liked Puck. They all agreed Puck would go to live with him until we came home from the Peace Corps.

When Cork came home early he couldn't bring Puck back to the ranch as long as the other dogs were there, and didn't have the heart to separate Jason and Puck. Jason loved that dog and had even taken him up to Mount Charleston with his buddies and taught him how to snowboard.

We never saw Puck again.

Christmas With Trombones

We celebrated Christmas the Sunday before with a few close friends, a honey-glazed ham, goat-cheese scalloped potatoes, green beans, candied yams and hot eggnog.

Cork was surprised when his friend Ralph Pressler dropped by with three other trombonists and did an on-the-spot Christmas trombone concert in our living room. Each year at UNLV's Judy Bailey Theater Cork had emceed their fund-raising concert, "76 Trombones", and the guys wanted to do something special for him. It couldn't have been a nicer Christmas present.

Christmas Eve we attended two parties, didn't drink and were home fairly early. The following morning, Cork announced he had to go to Home Depot for something. He was shocked to learn they closed for Christmas Day!

Special Collections

My long-time friend, Joyce Moore, who had graduated from UNLV with a history degree, got hired by the university to work in their Special Collections and Archives department. By collecting maps and menus and books and manuscripts and photographs and contracts and oral histories, they documented the history of gaming, entertainment, Las Vegas, Southern Nevada and the University.

I could not wait to share this good news with Cork. I announced it in our kitchen. "Isn't that great? We can get rid of all those boxes of stuff and all your career memorabilia that's in the garage! We can donate it all to the university!"

Cork looked at me in shock. "Don't you think you could wait till I *die*?"

"No," I said with a smile. "When you die, I have other plans..."

The Saga of the Cell Phones

Life was back to normal—pretty much— with Bingo and Cork at *La Villita de Sapo Volado*.

Cork planned to realize his life dream of driving the length of route 66. He invited Mack to join him, and with Cork's agreement, Mack invited two of his Marine Corps buddies. I envisioned a combination of Harry and Tonto and Thelma and Louise go on the road.

A few days before their scheduled departure in February 2002, Mack came up from San Diego.

Cork had a question about a 1099 and decided we should all go to the Social Security office on West Sahara, get the question answered, and then go to lunch at a favorite nearby restaurant.

In our Taurus wagon, we had just exited the freeway onto West Sahara when we heard Cork's cell phone ring.

Since Cork was driving, Mack searched the console and the front seat. Not there. He turned to me in the back seat and said, "Check his jacket."

We could still hear it ringing. I turned the jacket inside out. "It's not here."

"Where is it?" Cork snapped. "I just had it."

"Well, I don't know what you did with it," I snapped back.

The ringing stopped, and all the rest of the way down Sahara we could hear the periodic beep that says you have a call.

In the parking lot of the Social Security office, we got out of our respective sides of the wagon.

"You go on ahead," Cork said, "I'm going to look for my phone."

We looked at each other across the top of the wagon. At the same time, we saw his little black cell phone, sitting on the roof. The metal luggage carrier strips on the top of the Taurus wagon had kept it from rolling off during the drive.

* * *

We had another cell phone incident at home. I had just prepared dinner and set the table. Earlier I had placed my cell phone on one end of the long table.

When we sat to eat, I noticed it was no longer there.

"Did you see my cell phone?" I asked. "I set it right there at the end of the table."

"I haven't seen it," Cork said. "I don't know what you did with it."

"I didn't do *anything* with it. I left it right there."

"Let's eat. You don't need it right now." We had an agreement neither of us would talk on the phone while we were eating.

"That is so weird," I insisted. "I know I set it right there."

Cork picked up his fork and dug into the mashed potatoes. "Eat while it's hot. You can look for it later."

"I've got an idea. Why don't you call my number, and I'll be able to locate it with the ring."

Through a mouthful of mashed potatoes, he said, "That won't work."

"Why not?"

"Because I turned it off so it wouldn't bother us if it rang while we were eating."

"So—you *touched* it," I exclaimed. "What did you *do* with it?"

"Well *of course* I had to touch it to turn it off."

"So, then what did you do with it?" I persisted.

Cork wanted to eat, not deal with my "misplaced" cell phone. He became angry, indicating this conversation was over.

Later I made a complete search of the house and couldn't find that cell phone. I had to buy a new one, and this time I bought a cover for it in the form of a little black and white dog. I figured it was so cute no man would ever touch it.

I also figured if we ever moved that phone Cork had "touched" would make an appearance. It never did.

Craig

In March Cheryl moved out of our backyard apartment. We didn't need to advertise it for rent because after mentioning it to a few friends, right away we had a new tenant.

Ann Geno recommended a young man, Craig Tomlinson, a former soccer star who free-lanced as a construction manager and was engaged to a Thai woman.

Craig's outgoing, comedy-loving personality—and love of a good glass of wine—endeared him immediately to Cork, and Craig would become a longtime dear friend, especially after we attended his wedding in Bangkok the morning of the 2004 tsunami.

The Fifteen-Year Tune-up

Cork decided we would do marital therapy for what he called "a fifteen-year tune-up" (even though we had been married for just eleven years). Because it was his idea it impressed the hell out of my girlfriends. He said he didn't want us "to be the couple that sits around waiting for the old guy to die so the wife can get on with her life."

I told the therapist, Nona, that I didn't have any issues—I'd read all the books and done all the seminars and was not interested anymore in "fixing" anything or anybody. I would welcome some new coping skills because I was just tired.

"I hear that a lot from women in their sixties," she said.

So, Cork talked, Nona laughed, and for this audience he paid $125 an hour. I'm now convinced a comic will do ANYTHING for an audience!

I told her, "We count ourselves fortunate to have a paid-for house, excellent health, nice cars, no demanding jobs, two border collies," —we'd bought a second one, Annie, from a cowboy— "four parakeets, and two dollars and forty cents in the bank."

When I came home from a private session with her, Cork asked, "What did you talk about? What did she say?"

"We agreed on one thing," I said. He gave me a quizzical look. "You really, really love me—"

"Well, of course I do!"

"And I have never asked you to do anything that wasn't in your best interest."

Nona told me that new studies had come out indicating men revert to childlike behavior as they age. It seems only men do this. It manifests itself in less care with personal habits and dress, loss of table manners, more swearing, and obsessive talk about sex.

This is what I have to look forward to?

Auctioneering School

Cork, disillusioned with the idea of going back on the road and trying to get back on the cruise ships, decided he wanted to become an auctioneer.

Our friend Jim marsh, who owned a Chrysler Jeep dealership, also had a business on the Strip two blocks from our house, Jim Marsh's Las Vegas Auto Auction. Through the guys there, Cork discovered Paul Behr's World Wide College of Auctioneering in Mason City, Iowa.

Cork knew a lot about cars and had professional theatrical and vocal training. Over afternoon wine Craig encouraged him.

"I gotta go get a degree in this shit," Cork said, "and come back and do this."

Off he went to spend two weeks and two grand at auctioneering school. Afterwards he told me, "The best part of the trip was seeing the Surf Ballroom, the last place the Big Bopper, Buddy Hollie & Richie Valens performed before they died."

There was never any doubt on the part of Cork or the instructors at World Wide Auctioneering that he could be successful as an auctioneer. While he came home enthusiastic about the act of auctioneering, he began to have doubts about the practicality of pursuing an entirely new career. He realized it would be just like starting all over again in comedy, getting the gigs, building up the connections and references, and as salesmen say, "pounding the pavement."

He could have gone to work immediately for Jim at the Las Vegas auto action, but now he had second thoughts about the place.

"Too much noise, too much bullshit, yelling and screaming, standing in a tower while a hundred cars go by, all spewing gas fumes you breathe." He decided he was too old and had no incentive for that style of auctioneering.

Together we began to envision a little weekend auctioneering business where we would rent a little warehouse like the one I had lived in, take in all kinds of estate odds and ends. We would have Saturday and Sunday afternoon auctions where we would also serve complementary wine and cheese.

Auctioneers need state licenses to work, so we looked into what it would take for Cork to get an auctioneering license in Nevada.

It turned out to be just like getting a gaming license—you had to be able to list every single (exact) address where you had ever lived in your entire life. I thought of my former advertising client, John Fulton, manager of the Colorado Belle Casino in Laughlin, who told me how he and his wife had driven around neighborhoods in Los Angeles to find the house where they'd lived twenty years earlier because they couldn't remember the house number.

For an auctioneering license in the state of Nevada, you had to sign a waiver for the state to be able to drill your safety deposit box on a whim if they ever thought you were hiding undeclared cash. Plus, the form gave the state freedom from any liability if in the course of said drilling of your safety deposit box any cash and/or your grandmother's antique diamond brooch went missing.

I had a theory about how that law came about. Cork said there had been issues a few decades earlier with some Armenian rug dealers, and the state had decided they needed laws for auctions. My theory was that they went to the most established and famous-at-the-time auctioneer in Nevada (whom I won't name here), and this man had helped them set up laws that effectively would eliminate any competition for him.

Who would sign something like that? Not us. So much for work as an auctioneer in Nevada.

Never Drink and Dress

The occasion was the Star Chefs of Las Vegas Cirque de Cuisine benefiting the March of Dimes at the Rio Hotel Casino. We had been invited to sit at a table with our friends Rod & Kristine Maly, who owned the gallery, Art Encounter.

The dress was black tie and Cork, whose favored attire since the fifties had been Hawaiian shirts and shorts or white Levis, decided it was time to buy a new tuxedo. He made his purchase at the last minute and blew off the free tailoring, saying, "My wife will hem the pants."

We planned to be ready by five for cocktails at home and leave for the Rio at six. Confident in our scheduling, we invited my friend Linda to come by at five for a cocktail.

But we ran late.

At five I was still hemming the tuxedo pants, and Cork was wearing only his tux shirt.

"You can't be half-naked when Linda gets here," I said.

Because we expected her at any minute, he put on his yard shorts while he waited for me to finish.

Linda arrived, we had martinis, I threw the finished pants at Cork and hurried to dress myself. We arrived at the Rio on time.

All evening Cork kept wiggling in an attempt to adjust his clothing, thinking, he told me later, *boy that addition I had to my shirt sure is a lot of fabric.*

When we got home, he discovered he had worn his yard shorts all evening under his tux pants!

Middle of the Night

At a certain age, you begin waking up in the middle of the night for various reasons which would be TMI—too much information—here.

"Let's go get strawberry shortcake," Cork said one morning at three a.m.

The nearby Silverton Hotel Casino had a special offer for strawberry shortcake for $1.50 from midnight to six a.m. No need to dress fancy or put on makeup. Who would we meet that we knew at Silverton in the middle of the night? This became a favorite thing to do when we had both awakened and couldn't go back to sleep.

Except one night, Cork turned on the television. We watched three hours of "Animal Planet" and ordered $200 worth of mail order vitamins.

Ultimately Cork made an astute deduction. "We're better off eating strawberry shortcake than watching television."

The Art Studio

Before we had gone into the Peace Corps, my office for Graphic Communications had been set up in the sunroom we had built adjacent to the kitchen side of the house. Since I no longer had Graphic Communications, the sunroom was now our bedroom. One day in June Cork announced he needed to keep his clothes "closer to the bed" rather than in their current closet close to the bathroom.

He eyed my two gigantic craft cupboards next to the bed and said, "Why don't you clean out that shit so I can put my clothes in there?" When I made a negative response, I was "unreasonable and stubborn."

He suggested the craft cupboards be moved to the big yellow garage, to which I made another negative response citing the presence in the garage of dust and bugs.

Now I was "unreasonable, stubborn, and selfish." After a few days of stilted communication, the husband announced, "I'm building you an art studio in the back yard so we can get all that shit out of the house."

Who was I to argue?

"So we won't be falling over it," he added.

I felt intrigued and excited to have a special creative space like that. A real art studio!

Tuff Shed had already built the little shed out by the well, so we visited their show yard to look at different Tuff Shed models. This seemed like an easy way to build.

I could visualize this. Ten-by-twenty feet, with no telephone, water or bathroom, just electricity and a swamp cooler. It could have a real French door. And it would have a wooden floor just like our little cabin in the jungle...

Cork rationalized he would be "saving our marriage" by building me this separate art/writing studio in the backyard under the trees.

One day I went inside the Tuff Shed to look at the progress. Our electrical engineer friend was finishing up the installation of the electrical sockets. I noticed there were only two.

"I thought we outlined six outlets, two each on three of the walls," I said.

"We did," he said, without looking up from his work. "But Cork said you don't need that many."

I felt torn between being given the gift of a custom-designed art studio, and not having final say in that custom design itself. In any case, the construction was too far along, and it was too late to add four other electrical outlets, so I decided it wasn't worth mentioning.

The end result was my 200-square-foot Goddess House— the exterior painted purple, with two skylights, a French door and a little porch in front. My two large craft cupboards fit perfectly side-by-side against the back wall.

It was fun to finish the inside of my new art studio. I hung silk plants from the skylights and wallpapered the walls with brown grocery bag paper, a process I'd seen on a home decorating TV show. It became a place where I could do beading, paint with watercolors, listen to new age music, write, do scrapbooking, and just be quiet when I needed to.

The childhood playhouse of my dreams… oh, and Cork's clothes?

On a recent trip to Snohomish, Washington he had bought a gigantic antique armoire and had it shipped down to Vegas where, with its full-length, oval, beveled mirror, it now housed his clothes where he wanted them, right next to the bed.

Las Vegas First Topless Wedding

Greg Thompson had decided to renew his marriage vows with entertainer Sunny, a blond, vivacious impersonator of Mae West, Marilyn Monroe, Madonna, Britney Spears, and Joan Rivers. One of the reasons for this renewal was that when they got married the previous year, Sunny had had laryngitis and could not sing to Greg the special song she had written for the nuptials.

Not a couple to miss out on a promotional opportunity, this 2002 wedding was billed as the "First Topless Wedding" in Las Vegas, and the press was dutifully called in.

This vow-renewal would take place at Special Memory Wedding Chapel—Sunny wearing a white skirt big enough that it could have been in *Gone With the Wind*, a white bra-like top so her midriff was tastefully exposed and a poufy hat as big as an umbrella.

She descended a staircase with microphone in her bosom and powerpack strapped to her ankle, singing her special song while gracefully balancing that hat as only a seasoned performer can.

Sunny's maid of honor was best friend Frank Marino, star of the Riviera drag show *La Cage* and impersonator of Joan Rivers. Frank wore a cobalt blue dress almost as spectacular as Sunny's.

A dozen bridesmaids wore only heels, mesh hose, spangled g-strings, and beaded headdresses. They hid their bare breasts behind big, cobalt blue, ostrich feather fans.

Shannon, lead dancer in *Skintight*, Greg's show at Harrah's, wore a flesh-colored, gauzy, form-fitting gown with just a few spangles here and there. The back was cut way down to there, but was decorous enough to stop just before we saw butt cleavage. She carried her pet Pomeranian, which miraculously did not throw up after being fed many tidbits of wedding cake.

The Tina Turner impersonator from *La Cage* was six feet tall and wore the shortest miniskirt possible. The special "star" of *Skintight* was Miss Nude America. Petite, blond and buxom, she wore pink bell bottom hip huggers and a matching crop top, midriff and pierced navel flagrantly exposed. We had not seen the show so we had no idea what she did in it.

A wasn't-quite-a-rock star from the sixties who shall remain unnamed wore a white suit, white fedora and, not to be outdone by Shannon's Pomeranian, carried a white, floppy, stuffed bunny.

Naturally your standard Elvis impersonator was in attendance, breaking out with "Viva Las Vegas" after the bride and groom said, "I do."

Sitting in the third pew during the ceremony, Cork turned to me, smiled and whispered, "I'd forgotten how many freaks there are in show business."

At the last minute, as guests outside the chapel blew bubbles at the departing wedding party, ABC television balked at the "Topless Wedding" bit, and insisted the bridesmaids properly bra themselves in order to be filmed.

The Garden Nazi

It was the third week in October—our short fall in the high desert. The week before had been summer, and the following week would be winter. We had lit our first fire, changed to flannel sheets and made our winter selections from the *Lands' End* catalog.

Southern Nevada has two growing seasons, so now it was time to plant the winter garden. Our raised beds had been totally neglected since we left for the Peace Corps in 1999. We had cleaned out one of the back corrals and rebuilt raised beds inside so they would be fenced off from the border collies. What could we plant in the winter in Vegas? Carrots, radishes, broccoli, cauliflower, Brussel sprouts, and lettuce.

A few months later we'd had a bountiful harvest, and some of the plants had died off. Only the Brussel sprouts had yet to be picked—they had a week or two to go to full maturity.

Cork had been eyeing the dead plants and had asked me several times when I planned to "get out there and clean out the garden."

No rush, I thought.

Midday on a Saturday I came home from shopping and, as I drove into the driveway, I saw Cork, shirtless, pushing a wheelbarrow heaped with what looked like yard clippings.

"Look," he announced. "I cleaned out the garden for you."

There was not a plant left. He'd cleared everything to the ground, including the Brussel sprouts. Furious, I said, "You didn't need to do that. I would have done it. You tore out all the Brussel sprouts that were just getting ripe to pick!"

"Brussel sprouts?" he asked in an innocent tone. "What do they look like?"

"They look like *Brussel sprouts*," I shouted. "Growing on a stalk!"

"I was just helping," he shouted back.

"Get *permission* to help!" I stalked into the house.

Gene Paulson came by a couple of days later. Amused by the Brussel sprouts story, he brought yellow police crime scene tape and wrapped it around the raised flower beds.

In jest, he dubbed me, "The garden Nazi."

From Paris to Amsterdam

For six weeks in August and September of 2003 we traveled throughout France and Holland.

We had no hotel previously booked in Paris. When we arrived at Charles de Gaulle Airport, I wanted to find a hotel booking window and Cork said, "Come on, we'll just ask a taxi driver." I loved that "we" part since I was the only one of us who spoke French.

Reluctantly I followed him outside where we found a taxi. I didn't trust the driver to take us to a safe place, but Cork was insistent.

The driver took us to the charming small hotel, Hotel du Paris, near the Bois de Boulogna, which I knew was a good neighborhood. Once again, I took a deep breath and thanked God Cork's winging-it-through-life approach hadn't gotten us into trouble.

We love museums and music and soon found the Musée de la Musique, filled with historical instruments like Chopin's piano and a collection of Stradivari violins.

That day we were the only people in the 19th-Century Room. A museum employee appeared and seemed to note our interest in the exhibit of the evolution of stringed instruments.

In English he asked, "Would you like to see Django Reinhardt's guitar?"

This caught Cork's interest since he has always been a huge fan of the Belgian gypsy jazz guitarist. The museum attendant explained that they had just received this guitar from Django Reinhardt's family. While we waited, he left the room and returned a few minutes later, holding an old battered Selmer guitar.

How curious to think that we touched the same guitar strings that Django Reinhardt played with only two good fingers on his left hand.

* * *

Back at the Hotel du Paris, Cork wanted to do laundry. I didn't pay much attention until he showed me his blue sweater that he had washed himself. He held it up and it was about the size of a sweater for a three-year-old.

"What happened?" I asked.

While I had relaxed and read a book, he had found in the neighborhood a French do-it-yourself laundromat.

"Maybe I shouldn't have washed it in the hot water."

This blue sweater was 100% wool. He gifted it to the lady who owned the hotel.

* * *

The day Cork wanted to go to the airplane museum, I rebelled, so we decided to spend the day apart. With a limited amount of time in Paris it seemed sensible that he should be able to go to the airplane museum, and I could choose to go to an art museum. We both got to do what we wanted. After all, where does it say, just because you're married you have to do every single thing together?

I enjoyed a special exhibit of the clothes and jewelry and luggage of Marlene Dietrich.

When Cork found a tour of the sewers of Paris, I said, "Yes, I'm in."

One of the most impressive city sewer systems of the world, the underground network that mirrors the city streets stretches 2,100 kilometers beneath Paris. Though they began building an underground system in the 14th century, it was Napoleon Bonaparte who commissioned engineers to design a formal, expanded sewer system for the city.

I wanted to go to Père Lachaise Cemetery to see the elaborate and famous graves—including the grave of Jim Morrison.

I could tell this did not excite Cork when he said, "I'm not interested in some stupid cemetery."

* * *

I had some magazine assignments, and in Paris we stayed our last two nights, compliments of the magazine, in the stately Hotel Ampère in the 17th Arrondisement, a historically prestigious district. From there we would depart on a Sunday afternoon for a luxury European Waterways barge cruise of the Nivernais Canal and the beautiful Yonne Valley of Burgundy (also compliments of the magazine).

Nick, our European Waterways guide, picked us up in a minivan for the two-hour journey through post-card-pretty

French countryside to the medieval town of Auxerre, where the barge, *La Belle Époque,* and her crew waited.

Once a working canal barge, *La Belle Époque* had been elegantly redesigned for canal cruising. Because the tourist season wound down in September, this barge that normally carried twelve passengers and six crew carried six passengers and five crew. This turned out to be one of our all-cruise favorites.

After a week of eating and drinking fine French food and wine, we gave new meaning to the old cruise ship joke, "The passengers came on as guests and came off as cargo."

* * *

In Amsterdam we discovered a comedy club that did improv shows, Boom Chicago, situated among the bars and restaurants of Leidseplein Square.

It amazed me to see how much the Leidseplein had changed since I had visited it in the seventies. Then, it had been a dirty, trash-ridden square full of drugged-out hippies and other suspicious people. Now there were upscale bars and restaurants and street performers and mimes and no trash.

At the Boom Chicago box office, we purchased the best seats we could get and found ourselves sitting in a little raised box with a great view of the stage.

In an opening bit, the players showed a silent video they had taken earlier of people in the audience waiting for the show. As the video played, they improvised comments and dialogue.

Imagine our shocked surprise when Cork and I saw ourselves on that big screen talking to each other, but with hilarious voice-over dialogue. This delighted Cork because years earlier in Vegas, opening for the Unknown Comic at the Landmark, he had done a similar bit. He took still photos of people as they entered the showroom, then projected them on the screen. With each headshot he ad-libbed a criminal description. He had called it, "The Ten Most Wanted."

The two American comics who had founded Boom Chicago in Amsterdam riffed equally on both American and

Dutch culture. One of my favorite lines was, "Only the Dutch would name a banking chain, Rabobank."

* * *

Being in Holland and able to visit friends from Suriname made our visit there special. It made me feel so international, so worldly, so sophisticated. Why, I could now country-name-drop in the most-educated of company.

We had dinner in Den Haag with Judith Voigt (my Paramaribo landlady) and her three children. She was getting them established at University. In Amsterdam we met the father of our photographer and graphic artist friend, Plu. Plu's wife, Evy, was visiting him and we all enjoyed high tea at Blake's Hotel. In Wageningen we had lunch with Harrold Sijlbing, the director of Stinasu, on a sabbatical to attend a ten-month course on tourism and the environment.

These Sranan friends made me feel at home in Holland.

* * *

When I saw all those people riding around on bicycles in the cold wind and rain, I decided you have to be tough to be Dutch!

For our last nine days in Holland, Cork rented a car. I would read the map to help him navigate. I found myself totally confused by long Dutch street names that are oddly abbreviated because they don't fit on the map. I discovered that some streets changed names five times within a kilometer—maddening. *Whose idea was this car rental, anyway?* Definitely a guy thing. Pass me a joint.

While France had the best bread and cheese, Amsterdam had great dope. A few doors from the Boatel where we stayed, we found a head shop selling various strains of marijuana with names like "White Widow" and "Devil's Blush." I invested twelve dollars and bought some loose weed and a packet of papers.

We left Amsterdam and drove to Scheveningen in the Hague district. Cork wanted to show me Madurodam, a place he remembered fondly from his visit to Europe fifty years earlier.

Madurodam was a park with little model replicas of Dutch landmarks and historical cities. As a crafter who had dabbled in miniatures for a short time, I appreciated the work that had gone into constructing Madurodam.

In our Scheveningen hotel room I rolled a nice joint and lit up. Cork did not smoke weed, but he didn't mind if I did. I took my first inhale and fire alarms blared, quickly followed by loud knocks on the door. Cork shooed me and my joint out onto the balcony.

A young man and young woman in neat, hotel front-desk uniforms entered the room and began to look around in an attempt to figure out what had set off the fire alarm.

Cork shrugged and gave them his most boyish innocent look. "I have no idea."

A bit more conversation ensued and the two hotel employees seemed completely confused. Surely, they could smell the pot in the room? I leaned in from the balcony and said, "It happened right after I lit up this cigarette."

"Oh, of course," the woman said. "Next time, smoke on that side of the room." She pointed at the ceiling smoke detector. "Away from *that*."

And they left.

Cork sighed with relief. "I was sure you were going to get us arrested!"

"For what? We're in Holland, for God's sake."

* * *

I have to say it was easier to ride in the car with my husband when I had a buzz.

We had heard there was a wonderful hostel in the woods outside of Amsterdam. With Cork at the wheel and I at the map, we set off in our rental car to find it. At a division in a major road, Cork insisted we take the road to the left. I insisted the map showed the hostel was down the road to the right.

He turned to enter the road on the left, and we drove through miles of forest with no hostel. The only building we saw was a restaurant, the Kust House. We parked and went inside to check it out. A century before, the structure had been the coach house for some fabulous estate. Now it featured fine dining in the middle of nowhere.

We retraced our drive back to the road division, and found the hostel on the other road. We made a reservation for that evening and drove back to dine at the Kust House.

Here is a good example of how in a marriage there can be a his-version and a her-version. While I will insist I said, "The *hostel* is not down this road," Cork will insist he heard, "There is *nothing* down this road."

The PT Cruiser

At the end of December, 2003, Cork's long-time friend, Blackie Hunt, died. He had met Blackie in the sixties when Blackie was one of four funny guys in the group, The Characters, popular in all the Vegas lounges. They did musical comedy and Blackie played accordion. Cork and Blackie had worked together on the road. Years later when Blackie married singer Lorraine Hunt, they opened a popular Las Vegas Italian restaurant, the Bootlegger. We loved the Bootlegger, which featured lots of Italian recipes from Lori's grandmother.

"God, life is short," Cork announced. "I'm going to buy that PT Cruiser I want."

Within a few months of Cork's return from the Peace Corps he had sold the big Ford truck, *Que Huevos.* He loved old Chevy El Caminos, and at one time had four of them parked around the property, prompting his friend Kenny Harkins to say, "Why don't you sell this shit and get a life?"

The PT Cruiser after which he now lusted had been sitting on Jim Marsh's lot for almost a year. Dark blue, it sported all the snappy additions: moon roof, cruise control, CD *and* cassette player, leather seats, shiny hubcaps.

I thought the PT Cruiser was a stupid-looking car, but I had to admit it was easy to find in parking lots, and later I would come to love it, kind of like the ugliest puppy in the litter.

264

Even though it was what car guys call "loaded," it did not have a turbocharger, or "turbo" induction device for the engine. Cork took it to his favorite pin-striping guy, and on the back, Wink hand-lettered, "Turbo? We don't got no freakin' turbo!"

The Turkey in the Driveway

Craig had been raving about how great a turkey tastes when it's been deep-fried. Thanksgiving 2003 approached, and Craig volunteered to cook the turkey this way. He actually owned an electric deep fryer specifically for turkeys. I was skeptical, but he insisted and volunteered to buy the bird, so I agreed.

Craig set up the big deep fryer in the driveway because he said it would be safer, since it involves so much hot oil, than cooking it in the house. This was a good idea because I think Craig misjudged the amount of oil needed for the size of the turkey and hot oil overflowed onto the chat that composed our driveway.

I prepared all the usual sides, and the turkey meat tasted savory, with just the right moistness. Making gravy was the challenge, with no gravy drippings from an oven-roasted bird. In retrospect I would not cook a turkey that way again, because part of the Thanksgiving experience is that mouth-watering, roasting smell that fills the house all day. Plus, the drippings necessary for a great gravy.

Bingo and Annie, also attracted by that tantalizing turkey meat smell, ate the cooking oil-soaked chat. For the next two days, their doggy-do was full of tiny little rocks. Never underestimate the resilience of a dog's digestive system.

The Atrial Fibrillation

On a Saturday afternoon in March, 2004, I was preparing spaghetti while Cork puttered in his big yellow garage.

He entered the kitchen with blood on his arm, and told me he had fallen in the garage.

265

"What happened?" I exclaimed.

"I don't know—I tripped over something."

When he mentioned this to a couple of buddies, they said, "Hey man, at your age, you might have had a heart attack and don't even know it. You should go see a doctor *right away*."

For Cork, "right away"—if the blood has dried and there's no immediate, excruciating pain—means any time in the next few days or weeks when he gets around to it.

Given the state of that garage, anything was possible.

On Monday Cork visited his cardiologist, who said, "Your heartbeat is dancing all over the place." He immediately checked Cork into St. Rose de Lima for tests.

My friend Maggie and I had obtained visas to travel to India. Cork's phone call a few hours later from the hospital interrupted and destroyed my India plans.

"Guess where you're not going?" he said.

"I'm not going to India?"

He told me the doctors had him on oxygen and some kind of drip. It took three hours to stabilize his heartrate.

I drove to the hospital, where I could sit next to his bed and keep him company. The first thing Cork complained about was that when he left home with his pajamas and reading glasses, he had forgotten to pack his favorite hot sauce.

I sat for hours, and minute by minute the chair seemed to harden under my butt. In his cozy jammies, my husband fell asleep in his warm, horizontal bed. At midnight I went home for my own good night's sleep.

He had lots of tests, including a cat scan, was diagnosed with an atrial fibrillation and, thirty-six hours and fourteen thousand dollars later, they sent him home. A home health care nurse came daily to draw blood while the doctor tried to balance his dosage of his new medication, Coumadin.

"It's rat poison," Cork told me. "It's in the stuff they put out to kill rats. It thins their blood, and they bleed out to death."

The conclusion was that he had not, in fact, collapsed in the garage from a heart ailment. He had, in fact, tripped over some box or tool on the floor of the garage. What did he learn from this experience?

"I can confirm the rumor that hospital food sucks."

Maggie and I never went to India, and neither of us was that disappointed.

The Bionic Book

In the summer of 2004, my first book was published by a small Chicago publisher.

Elisabeth Sampson Forbidden Bride is a novel based on the true story of the first black woman in Suriname in the 18th century to get legal permission from the Dutch to marry white. Elisabeth Sampson is an iconic figure from Suriname's turbulent past. During my two years in Suriname, I had become intrigued by her story and the plantation and slave history of the country itself. I had even visited the building that had been her five-story Dutch colonial home in Paramaribo.

In October, carrying gift copies of my book, I returned to Suriname to visit friends. One of the gifts was for my friend Donna at Vaco Press. Unknown to me at the time, after my vacation the company ordered forty copies from the publisher and made it their book-of-the-month with a full display in their front window.

A week later I received a demanding email from a friend of Cynthia McLeod. Cynthia had published (in Dutch) a reference book of historic documents and papers pertaining to Elisabeth Sampson, which I had paid to have translated so I could access the information. I am convinced the Dutch originated the paper trail, and I had found her book most useful in my historical research. It is listed at the end of my book in the bibliography of my research.

In the email, this man demanded $100,000 and my books "to be removed from all of the bookstores in America." He claimed I had "plagiarized" Cynthia McLeod.

When I did not respond within twenty-four hours he emailed again, this time threatening me with a six-million-dollar lawsuit for "stealing Suriname's black culture."

He also contacted my publisher in Chicago who freaked. I tried to reassure him I had done nothing wrong, but I began to wonder myself. What did I really know about plagiarism and copyright infringement?

I found an intellectual properties attorney, but could not get an appointment until the following week.

While I waited, I received two media phone calls, the first from the Paramaribo newspaper *de Ware Tijd* and the second from a literary journal in Amsterdam. They wanted me to comment on the lawsuit. It seemed Cynthia McLeod and her supporters had held a press conference at Torarica Hotel, announcing her lawsuit against the rich American author who had stolen their black culture. I told them I could not comment until I had spoken to my lawyer and asked them to call me back in a week. I did not hear from them again.

Cork began to call *Elizabeth Sampson Forbidden Bride* "the bionic book."

I hustled to the library to check out books and learn as much as I could about plagiarism and copyrights before I met with the lawyer.

The intellectual properties attorney advised me I'd done nothing legally wrong.

"Don't overreact," he said. "They're fishing for money and publicity. Go home, get a good night's sleep, get on with your life, write another book."

Imagine the loss to the world if only one writer were allowed to write about a historical person such as Mahatma Gandhi, Queen Elisabeth I, Thomas Jefferson, or Marie Curie. I felt grateful that in America we are don't have such educational limitations. Unfortunately, it's this kind of limited thinking that in many ways holds Suriname back.

I began to notice new reviews at Amazon accusing me of plagiarism and written in bad English, rather like those Nigerian email investment offers. I called Amazon to file a formal complaint. Amazon has strict rules about attacking an author personally, and they removed each one of those reviews.

Having my novel attacked in such a way by Surinamers left me with feelings I wished I didn't have. Along with being saddened by such a hateful attack on my character, integrity, and creativity, I felt a new disillusionment towards Suriname. I had to remind myself I still have many supportive friends there, though I felt like a wonderful love affair had just diminished because I discovered my lover picks his nose. Granted, I had probably been viewing Suriname through rose-colored-romance glasses, choosing not to see realities, willing to "forgive his faults in the name of love."

A Wedding & a Tsunami in Thailand

Craig and Pukie planned to marry in December 2004 in Bangkok so her family could attend. In October, over martinis in our kitchen, Craig invited us to the wedding, and Cork, without hesitation, responded, "Sure! We'll be there!"

That was the beginning of our plan to visit Thailand for six weeks. The wedding was scheduled for Sunday, December 26, 2004.

Craig and Pukie had arranged for us to be greeted with flowers and dancing girls when we arrived at the airport in Bangkok. But as happens with international travel, times and flight numbers can get confused, and they waited in a different reception hall.

Craig's brother, Paul, and sister-in-law, Rachel, and their thirteen-year old daughter, Brittany, had flown in from Detroit.

The days before the wedding, Rachel, Brittany, Pukie and I spent shopping in the narrow, alley-like *suks*. Individual, tiny stalls displayed silk dresses, silk skirts, silk jackets, silk blouses, silk slippers and silk slacks at amazing low prices. While we shopped, Paul and Craig and Cork hung out at an open beer plaza, with pretty, young, Thai beer maids. There I saw my first beer tower. Only a guy could design such a thing.

Craig insisted we visit one of the nightclubs in Patpong, a world-famous district home to Thailand's infamous "go-go" culture. He described bar girl entertainers who could perform amazing tricks with their vaginas. Because Brittany was thirteen, she couldn't go, so Rachel—I imagine not that enamored anyway with the idea of bar girls doing vagina tricks—agreeably stayed in the hotel with Brittany.

269

In the bar we visited, beautiful hostesses wandered around to sit on a guy's lap for tips and let him buy them drinks. Paul and Cork and Craig found all this fascinating.

"Some of these bar girls aren't really women," Craig explained, "They're called, 'lady boys.' Men in drag."

These smart bar girls could see Craig and Cork were with women, so they swarmed over Paul, the "available" man in our group.

The show commenced, and we watched in fascination as one girl pulled needles on a string from her vagina, another placed a cigarette in her vagina and blew smoke rings from it, and from her vagina another popped ping-pong balls across the room. The latter was so clever that in her dance you didn't see her insert the ping-pong balls. On the other hand, she may have inserted them before she came on stage.

This was just one of the many speculative conversations between Cork, Craig and Paul. The needles particularly amazed them. I figured she tied them to the thread and inserted them, eye-side out, in a round Tampax container. As for the ping pong balls—for any woman who's reclined in a warm bath and with her muscles blew water in and out of her vagina—how she expelled the ping-pong balls seemed easily explained. But the guys couldn't figure it out, and I wasn't about to tell them.

* * *

On Sunday morning a van took us from the Pinnacle Hotel to the Monks Hospital where Craig and Pukie's wedding would take place.

The "hospital" was actually a home where monks lived. Monks can only eat at seven a.m. and eleven p.m. so festivities began at seven a.m. when five wedding couples served the monks their breakfast bowls. On the main marble-tiled floor, family and friends sat at long tables with pomegranate-colored tablecloths, while the wedding couples went upstairs to serve breakfast to bedridden monks. This is considered good luck, as the monks will pray for you.

At one end of this reception hall, nine monks sat on cushions on a cement bench along the wall. Each couple approached an altar where they received a long candle with which to light a bundle of incense, after which they kneeled to pray.

A moderator with a microphone spoke of this homage to Buddha, and then moved one couple's bundle of sticks back on the altar to make room for the next couple's bundle.

One by one, each wedding couple approached each of the nine monks for a blessing. They presented each with flowers along with their breakfast bowl. Each monk splashed water from a little pot onto their heads while he chanted a special prayer.

"I love the color orange, but I don't think I could be a monk," Cork whispered. "I don't care for the haircut."

The monks spoke with their hands in the prayer position, and the room hummed with a monotone rhythm.

Afterwards the wedding couples went outside to pour water from a silver cup onto the ground at the foot of two trees to honor the departed. These dead people in their family would pass on some of the good prayer, plus giving water to something living and keeping it alive was more good luck.

The whole thing lasted two, un-air-conditioned hours.

* * *

When we returned mid-morning to the Pinnacle Hotel, we passed a lobby television. We stopped to listen to a special broadcast about a tsunami that had hit Thailand's eastern coast at 8:30 a.m. It was reported a few people had actually been killed.

"Oh boy," Cork said. "People in the U.S. are going to see this and think we're all dead." He turned to me. "Why don't you get on the internet and email everybody we're okay. You know how Americans overreact."

At the computers in the lobby, I crafted a quick note. "By now you may have heard a tsunami hit Thailand. Not to worry. We are all fine." I dashed it off to about fifteen of our friends.

After lunch Pukie and Craig, in their Thai wedding costumes, sat at a table in one of the hotel's meeting rooms, where they officially greeted family and friends. Lots of photos were taken and blessings shared.

Afterward Cork took a nap, Craig and Paul went off to share a beer tower, and us girls sat in Pukie's room and watched a lady boy redo her hair and makeup for their wedding reception that evening.

Pukie explained it is not good luck to wear the same dress you wear to the wedding for other wedding-related events. Pukie had *three* white wedding dresses. The first for the formal wedding portraits, taken a week before the wedding. The second, for the actual ceremony, had been designed after traditional Thai dress. The third was for her western-style reception at the Ramada Tawana in Surawongse, Bangkok's Chinatown district.

As we departed for the reception, we noted the TV news in the lobby now reported as many as one hundred people may have been killed in that morning's tsunami.

* * *

The news the following morning was more devastating. Thousands has been killed and thousands were missing—a major disaster.

But we were celebrating a wedding, and we were off to the island of Koh Samed to celebrate New Year's with rose petals on our beds, huge paper lanterns launched from our dinner on the beach, and morning outdoor massages.

"*Sawadabimai!*" Happy new year!

* * *

Other tourists told us, "You should call your embassy and give them your names so people calling from your country will know you're okay."

I called the American Embassy and volunteered our names. "There are five Americans in our group," I said.

A bored young man said, "Oh, we're not doing that."

* * *

We returned to Bangkok where Craig and Pukie and Paul's family caught flights to return to the US. Cork and I traveled north to spend a few days in Chang Mai, where I took a Thai cooking class at the Sompet Thai cooking school on the banks of the Porn Ping River.

The last two weeks in Bangkok we had nothing planned. We decided we should spend the time volunteering to help tsunami victims.

Again, I called the American Embassy to ask where we could go to volunteer, naïvely thinking our U.S. people in Thailand would be involved in helping the Thai people.

The same bored young man said, "We are not involved with that."

So, could he point me in the direction of a local organization that might be helping?

No. As an afterthought he said, "I suppose you could call the Red Cross."

"Okay. Do you have a number for them?"

"No."

That was the end of my conversation with the not-so-helpful American Embassy.

Through the Pinnacle Hotel I learned there is a Thai Red Cross, and I was given their number. For the following ten days Cork and I worked with the Thai Red Cross sorting donated clothes, and I answered the phone when English-speaking people called with questions. There were no concrete answers for many of their questions, so mostly I listened and offered comforting words.

One day while we worked at the Thai Red Cross there was a special visit by one of the Thai princesses. Just like in the U.S., journalists and cameras accompanied her. Cork and I, though we hailed from jaded Las Vegas, felt honored to meet her.

Of all the countries affected by the tsunami, Thailand was in the best position to recover—they had money and good infrastructure.

The Sally Rand Model

After Cork sold our Ford Taurus wagon to Kelly McDonald, he decided to buy another PT Cruiser.

"It would be fun to have two of them," he said.

At Jim Marsh's dealership, where he had purchased the first PT cruiser, he discovered Jim only had black and red and he didn't want those colors. On impulse he stopped at Las Vegas Dodge on West Sahara, where he was approached by a handsome, mid-twenties Hispanic car salesman.

This time Cork wanted a "basic, no frills" car. When he explained this to the young salesman, he said, "Just give me the Sally Rand model."

The salesman frowned. "We don't have a model by that name. What is Sally Grand?"

With about a three-generation gap here, I'm sure the young salesman had never heard of the famous stripper, Sally Rand.

"You know, basic, nothing extra."

The young salesman took Cork out on the lawn and showed him a 2003, pale blue PT Cruiser. Since it was the end of the year, the car had not sold—probably because it had no extras—and Cork was able to bargain for a good price.

Later Cork began to periodically mutter, "There are no automatic windows," and "There's no cruise control," and "There's no CD player."

When he complained about all this on the phone with daughter Kathy, she said, "Oh Dad, you don't need all that stuff. It's just more things to break." Smart daughter.

Because PT Cruisers were being assembled in Mexico, Cork had Wink hand-letter on the back, "*Hecho* in Mexico."

Naming My Novel

After years of listening to show business stories involving magicians, I was now writing a new novel about the world's most famous—and hated—magician who dies in a roller coaster escape stunt on national television, and all the murder suspects are magicians. The book later became, *Magicide*.

But in the beginning, I had the working title, *Murder by Magic.* At Amazon I discovered another book already published by that name. Not a good marketing position, to have another book out there with your book's title.

One afternoon at our dining room table with Cork and Jac Hayden, I broached the subject of the title of my book. We began to brainstorm.

Jac and I were throwing out title ideas and Jac suggested, *"AbracaDeadly."*

From the end of the table, Cork said, "How about, *POOF! You're Fucked?"*

The Citizen's Police Academy

I thought if I were going to have an ex-showgirl-now-police-detective heroine for *Magicide,* I needed to learn more about how Metro operated. I needed to get first-hand information.

I discovered the Las Vegas Metropolitan Police Department's Citizens' Police Academy, a twelve-week program that involved both classroom and interactive instruction on the role of police officers. I also discovered there was a two-year waiting list to get in.

"Tell them you're a writer," our detective friend, Randy, advised. "You'll get right in."

When I went to the office to apply, I took autographed copies of *Elisabeth Samson, Forbidden Bride* and gifted the two girls at the desk.

"We have a class beginning next Wednesday night for twelve weeks, okay?"

Yes, of course, thank you very much.

One week we met at the gun range, where I hadn't been in thirty years, and with a Smith and Wesson I shot nine out of ten rounds within the ten-inch circle in the middle of the man-form. I thought the sergeant was impressed. Then the swat guys arrived, did equipment show-and-tell, and gave a demonstration. I was amazed to see they were all under my height. They were not amused when I asked why they were all under five-foot-ten. Honestly, I thought maybe there was a height policy for the job.

The night they did drug education I stumped the drug expert, who had never heard of Amyl Nitrite, a popular drug in the seventies. As he shook his head, an old guy on the other side of the room yelled, "poppers." I learned later from another source that it's still out there, only with another name—Locker Room. Aren't those drug guys creative?

I arranged for Cork to be the guest speaker at the official graduation of Las Vegas Citizen's Police Academy on November 6. He planned to talk about how his life of crime began and ended when he stole a car at fourteen and went to jail, and how over the decades he has survived five sheriffs.

At the graduation, when Sheriff Bill Young handed me my certificate of completion and shook my hand, he whispered, "Any time you want me to lock him up, you just call."

Why Not Move to Thailand?

From Yuma, Arizona to Hollywood, Florida, Cork viewed each place we visited as a great place to live.

"Hey, we could move here…"

No. We. Couldn't.

Cork and I had been considering a move to Florida, or southern California. Kathy and Luann lived in the valley north of Los Angeles, and would have liked to have us closer.

The fast-paced growth of Las Vegas saddened us. By 2005 it was a far different town from the one we had come to and enjoyed in the seventies. Along with the growth, the cost of living had risen and the traffic and smog had become more like L.A.

We had fallen in love with Thailand, and now entertained fantasies of living in Bangkok. We rosily ignored the smog and crazed, three-wheeled, tuk tuk drivers.

While it had been six months since I had been threatened with the lawsuit over my "bionic book," and I had heard nothing more, I still felt disturbed and could not erase it completely from my mind.

Cork had worried through this with me, and now he said, "Never mind, we'll run away to Thailand. They'll never find you."

We considered storage for our stuff or selling the ranch and getting a condo where we could lock the door and go rent a high-rise in Bangkok for a year to see how we liked it.

As had happened with joining the Peace Corps, Cork began to tell our friends we were moving to Thailand. Meanwhile I researched visas and budgets and the kind of paint to use to paint designs on silk clothing.

One day Cork complained, for the umpteenth time, that he was not getting "his beach" because I wouldn't move to the west coast of Florida (though I had been willing to move to the east coast).

I'd had enough of this complaint. "Guess what?" I said. "Not only am I not moving to Florida, I'm not moving to Thailand. How 'bout that?"

After a moment of silence, he said, "Where are we going?"

"Into a condo down the street."

Sedonas on the Boulevard

Eight years earlier we had watched a five-hundred-unit apartment complex rise from the desert at the end of our street. Called Sedonas on the Boulevard, the buildings are all eight-plexes among grounds of mature trees and shrubs and grass. It was the only complex on the Strip in a park-like setting.

The complex had recently been converted to condominiums, and we bought a three-bedroom upstairs unit. Cork did not want to live with people over his head. One of our friends said, "You bought a condo *upstairs* at *your* age?"

We paid $272,000, closed in August and began to move. The homeowners fee alone was less than Cork spent monthly on Mexican gardeners and trips to Home Depot.

Thus began the sorting and packing. This reminded me of packing everything up for storage when we left for the Peace Corps.

I got the Starving Students, a moving business of strapping young college guys, to move our household on three separate days. When I called to make the appointments, they said, "You're going *how far*?"

Only in Vegas can you move from a ranch to a condo on the Strip and only go two blocks!

Cork's contribution to the moves was staying out of the way. It was so refreshing when I made a request to hear the boys say, "Yes ma'am," instead of things like, "Why do you want it *there?*" and "Why didn't you think about this earlier?" and "You're moving *that*?"

* * *

Because during the construction of the big yellow garage, the rental house, and the art studio none of the plans had been registered with the county—"the less they know the better," Cork had said—these structures and square footage could not be included in the appraisal of the property.

"Screwed again," Cork grumbled.

Tommy Bast, who had been renting our front arena for his horse-boarding business, decided to get a lawyer to file an injunction against the sale so he could complete the three-year lease he'd broken in the summer of 2004. He refused to believe that even though he'd been notified in writing, he was on a month-to-month lease.

We got a bigger and badder lawyer. In the end we bought him off for $1,000 so he would take his fencing and go away. This bit of high drama delayed the closing by two weeks and turned Cork into a white-haired madman. Both Cork and Tommy were so angry, I had to negotiate the final deal with Tommy's father.

I was thrilled to be in the new condo with cushy carpeting, soft water, a Roman bathtub, a dishwasher, indoor washer and dryer, and all without dust and flies and cowboy neighbors.

Lunch in Barstow

During the move to the condo Cork wanted to give the Wernicke bookcase that had belonged to his grandparents to daughter Luann. It was arranged that we would drive it to Barstow—a good halfway point between LA and Vegas—and

Luann and Kathy and Luann's new boyfriend, Sean, would meet us there to pick it up.

Over lunch in Barstow Cork began a long, detailed story about Fats Johnson.

Fats had lost money on the Funny Farm in Temecula, divorced Beverly and moved back to Las Vegas. For years he suffered from diabetes, and now one leg had been amputated at the knee. Cork had been driving him from his assisted living apartment to the Veterans Hospital for various appointments.

Though Fats was not doing well, he had not lost his sense of humor. He would answer the phone with, "One-legged Johnson here."

Cork knew I wasn't a big Fats fan. Perhaps that was why when I tried to interject to share the positive way Fats answered the phone, he exploded.

"Go ahead." He snarled. "*You* tell the story. You know everything. I'm done."

"Dad—" Luann began.

"No, I'm done. You guys talk about whatever you want to talk about. Anything I have to say obviously isn't important."

I don't think I would have felt quite so embarrassed and humiliated if Sean hadn't been present. New to "the family," he wasn't yet accustomed to Cork's personality.

Stifling the urge to cry, I rose from the table, purse under my arm, and headed for the ladies' room. When I returned fifteen minutes later, the four of them were conversing about something else. No one said anything to me, and I was able to silently recite the serenity prayer for the remainder of this happy visit.

For some reason I have never been able to completely understand, the communication dynamics when Cork and I and both daughters are together has always been different from when it's just Cork and I and one daughter. I vowed to myself after that Barstow lunch I would be careful to never again enter into any activities that involved all four of us.

From Istanbul to Ankara

My ex-ad agency partner Rich and his wife Peggy had planned an amazing tour of Turkey, and they invited us to go along. We couldn't say yes fast enough.

That is how in October 2006, we found ourselves touring Istanbul, Ephesus, Troy, Cappadocia, and Ankara.

Cork was most impressed by the cistern under Istanbul and the whirling dervishes, which he said "look like dreidels on acid."

In Cappadocia we had an option to purchase a dawn balloon ride over the fairy-chimney rock formations of Göreme. This historical region of turkey covers a rugged plateau of volcanic rock north of the Taurus mountains. It's a world-famous, hot air ballooning destination, and I was eager to experience it.

Cork, not so much. I couldn't get him to actually say the word, yes. He seemed to have reservations he could not explain to me and I could not understand. At the same time, he wouldn't say, no. I cajoled and coaxed, and still he would not commit. Peggy and Rich and several others in our group had already signed up. I could not imagine why Cork would not be up for this exciting adventure and, because he had not said no, at the last minute I slapped down the credit card and signed us both up.

When I told Cork, he said, "Well, I'm still thinking about it."

When we got our wake-up call the morning of the balloon ride, he announced, "I'm not going. See if you can get the money back."

I told everyone Cork was sick, and I was assured by the balloon company I could get the money back. I would have to apply online in writing. I wasn't able to do this before we returned home, and my subsequent emails to the company were never answered.

In the breath-taking moments of dawn over Göreme, with rock formations accentuated by stark shadows, I thought, *Cork would have loved this*. Or maybe not. Maybe I suffered from fairy-chimney rock enchantment.

That morning I took one of my best all-time photos, a sky full of puffy clouds and hot air balloons punctuated by a burst of light that was the sun. It later would win first-place in an Expedia photo contest.

* * *

Always witty and gregarious with service people, Cork went to the bank in Istanbul and became enamored with the teller.

That afternoon our group visited the haram, one for men, one for women. Everyone except Cork. He's never been the sauna and hot tub and massage type. Once, when we had stayed in a suite at Catalina Island's Inn at Mount Ada, I had tried to lure him into an over-sized bathtub of bubbles, but he'd been more interested in watching television. Oh well.

At dinner that night plenty of "haram" jokes were shared. I stood and said to Cork, "You can have the bank teller, and I'll take that young man from the haram." Mostly, the women laughed.

On the bus when Cork did *shtick*, some people laughed, others stared.

"If you were a household name like Robin Williams," I told him, "you could get away with that, but these people not only don't know you as a professional comedian, but they're on a tour bus, not in a showroom prepared to laugh."

For a man obsessed with the timing of a joke, I could never understand how he could be oblivious to the timing of the *presentation* of a joke.

Washing Hands in Manzanilla

On December seventh of 2006 we arrived in Manzanilla, Mexico on Carnival's cruise ship, *Pride*. Cork was appearing as the featured comic that week, thanks to his ventriloquist buddy, Kyle Wayne, who had referred him for the job.

We loved exploring Manzanilla. After lunching in one restaurant we used the available bathrooms and afterwards asked the proprietor where we could wash our hands. In the bathrooms we had seen only toilets.

281

Though he spoke no English and our Spanish was limited to *"una cerveza mas por favor"* and *"donde esta el bano?"* he understood what we wanted. He led us to a wall outside the restaurant and opened a side door. He showed us a narrow room which contained the toilet tanks along one wall. The porcelain toilets themselves had been installed in the bathrooms right up against the wall, with their tanks on the other side.

The proprietor lifted the lid from one of the tanks and gestured that we could wash our hands in the water in the tank. Of course, there was no soap and no towels.

Cork shook his head and said, "Necessity may be the mother of invention, but God says, seek and ye shall find."

The Women's Cruise

At a holiday fund-raising event for Las Vegas Women in Communication, I won two cruises to Mexico on Carnival. Both the first and second names drawn were mine! The second one I donated back into the drawing.

When Cork came home from another road gig, I told him, "Good news and bad news!" I described winning the two cruises. "The good news is I won, the bad news is I'm not taking you."

After working for nine years for RCCL and watching the quality of dining and service deteriorate, Cork had developed a cynical view of cruising. I could see his point of view. On my first cruise on the *Song of America*, we were treated like royalty, getting on and off the ship with the passengers. On a later cruise, they separated us; I could go with the passengers, but Cork had to go with the crew on the crew gangway. And still later, we both had to embark and disembark on the crew gangway. The company explanation was that technically Cork was "crew."

"So's the Captain," Cork had declared. "So, shouldn't he be using the crew gangway as well?"

"Oh no," the Cruise Director said. "He's the *captain*! What would the passengers think?"

I bought a third ticket on the Carnival cruise down the Mexican Riviera and invited Kathy and Luann to go with me as a Christmas present. We had a great time laughing at and dissing men.

From Madeira to Madrid

That Grand Circle Travel company really has their marketing act together. Those brochures are so bright and colorful they make you want to start a file and keep every one of them for "someday." Though as Cork often says, "Someday is not a day of the week."

GCT not only puts together a comprehensive affordable tour—our favorite part is the home-hosted lunch arranged with local families— but they always offer a four- or five-day extension on the front end and the backend. Our latest brochure, "Portugal and Spain", offered a pre-trip extension to the island of Madeira. We like wine and a whole island named for one had great appeal. Again, slap down that credit card. We are in.

We landed at Cristiano Ronaldo Madeira International Airport, commonly known in Portuguese as Aeroporto da Madeira, just outside the capital of Funchal.

"That's the most exciting airport I ever flew into," Cork said. In the airport gift shop, he bought a refrigerator magnet with an aerial view of the landing strip showing how it simply ends at one edge of the island.

We wandered and dined through Funchal, already in love with their tomato and onion soup, Black Scabbard fish fillet with bananas, wine and garlic pork and fried sardines.

Wonderful restaurants line the Funchal waterfront. Waiters in black pants, white shirts and wrapped white aprons, holding menus, stood in front of several eateries to entice the tourists inside. One day after lunch as we passed other restaurants, a waiter hailed us.

"Eat here, eat here," he called in English.

We smiled and told him we had already eaten.

He smiled back and said, "Eat again."

* * *

Funchal was hilly. One of Cork's favorite exploratory methods is to get on a city bus and see where it goes. Ride it all the way to the end, pay again, ride it back.

It was mid-afternoon when we boarded the bus that meandered through the streets along the waterfront. Eventually it turned away from the waterfront and began an uphill climb. I glanced across the aisle and noticed a little aged Portuguese woman in a coat and a babushka. She had had her hands crossed in her lap, and she began to mumble and make the sign of the cross in front of her face.

"She must know something we don't," Cork whispered.

As the bus climbed further into the Madeiran hills, the sun rolled lower in the west. From our bus we enjoyed a sunset splashed in multi shades of orange and purple.

We reached the end of the line and told the driver we wanted to pay for the return. The driver did not speak English, but made it clear this was the end of the line, and he was going home for dinner. We looked around a simple crossroads that did not look like the center of anything and spotted three or four restaurants, all closed.

"I have to pee," Cork announced.

If the driver was annoyed by having his dinner delayed, he made no sign to us. He knocked on the door of one of the restaurants, spoke to the owner, and we were invited inside to use the bathroom. He also called a taxi to come and take us down to the center of Funchal, which as I recall was far more expensive than any of our dinners, including glasses of Madeira wine.

* * *

Our Portugal and Spain tour was filled with ups and downs.

In Malaga, one of our tour members died suddenly. It was quite impressive to see how our guide, Filipa, and GCT handled this. The couple had trip insurance, but his wife could not continue with the tour, because she had to stay in

Malaga and wait for company and international death certificate paperwork.

GCT paid for their daughter and son-in-law to fly in immediately from the United States and stay with her until everything was finalized. They even arranged for special short tours so the three of them did not have to spend days sitting in their hotel room waiting for the Spanish embassy and the US embassy—not known to be hasty and I imagine even slower with a dead body involved—to make the required arrangements.

* * *

By the time we reached Madrid, Cork and I were both sniffling and coughing from some Spanish flu bug. We went to a *farmacia* and armed ourselves with pills and syrups.

The last day of our tour we were really too sick to go out that night, but we agreed we could "rest when we get home" because "after all, we aren't coming back here tomorrow."

We had tickets for a flamenco music and dance show. I loved the dancing and the costumes but decided a little strident and shouting flamenco goes a long way. By the end of the performance I had an overpowering headache that prevented me from focusing on anything. I couldn't wait to get to my bed in the hotel.

In the lobby we passed the musicians selling their CDs at special tables.

"Just a minute," Cork said, and headed for the nearest table. While I stood by, he began a long monologue to one of the guys explaining that years ago he had been a drummer in Las Vegas, etc, etc. The Spanish musician nodded and smiled, and it was evident he did not speak or understand English.

After a few minutes I touched Cork's arm and said, "Please, my head is splitting, can we go back to the hotel now?"

He made it clear he did not appreciate being interrupted. "You got some place to be?" he barked. "Wha' do I look like, I got a clock in my ass?" I was already so sick I didn't have the energy to snap back.

In retrospect, we should have extended a few days in Madrid to recover and not taken the flight home the next day. Stuffed up heads and high-altitude pressure kept us miserable for the entire flight. In LA we went immediately to an emergency clinic near the airport where we were both diagnosed with borderline pneumonia.

The Girl From the Union Plaza

Jazz singer Joe Williams, famous for performing with big bands like the Count Basie Orchestra and the Lionel Hampton Orchestra, and his English wife, Jillean, had made Las Vegas their home until his death at eighty-one in 1999.

Cork had met Joe in the sixties at Reno's Harold's Club. I always thought Cork identified on a subconscious level with Joe's hit, "Every Day I Have the Blues."

At the end Joe had been in Sunrise Hospital. One afternoon he got dressed, walked out, and collapsed dead on the sidewalk walking back to his house. Cork said he could appreciate that "he didn't want to die in the hospital."

Cork had gone to his funeral at the Church of Religious Science. "Goddam, he was a good singer," Cork said, "and not a bad bone in his body. He was a sweet human being."

For years Joe had done an annual benefit concert to provide music scholarships for CSN, the Community College of Southern Nevada. After his death the college continued the concerts in his name. They now became "Joe Williams Memorial Concerts."

The last one Cork emceed was a memorable afternoon.

Unlike some entertainer wives, I never tired of watching Cork work. Because he had no act and worked off the top of his head with the audience, each performance had unexpected highlights. As a joke I once said to him, "I never met anybody who built a career and made so much money just running his mouth off." He didn't think it was funny and scowled when I said, "Hey, you're a comedian. Where's your sense of humor?"

In the lobby after the concert, we mingled with friends and had casual pictures taken. An attractive woman approached me and asked, "Are you Cork's wife?"

"You're not going to hold that against me, are you?" This was a standard line I had developed over the years for this question.

She laughed. "Oh no, I just wanted to tell you how much I enjoyed the show. My name is Nancy and I was a cocktail waitress in the lounge at the Union Plaza when Cork first worked there in the seventies. We all thought he was so cute and so funny. It was really fun to see him today and to see he is still just as cute and funny as ever!"

"Do you have two dollars and fifty cents?" I asked.

She looked startled. "What?"

"If you have two dollars and fifty cents and you think he's so cute and so funny, I'll sell him to you."

Without missing a breath, she responded, "Oh no, honey. I've been watching him for years and I can tell—he's high maintenance."

From Beijing to Hong Kong

I have never felt so alone as I have when I was married. In 2008 I again visited the therapist, Nona. I described my jumble of feelings for Cork and my marriage, how confused I felt by the way he treated me, how sometimes I felt like I overreacted, and how other times I felt like I just didn't give a shit.

"You're suffering from mild depression," she said. "There are drugs for that, but I'm not licensed to prescribe them."

"That's okay. I don't want to take drugs, anyway."

My biggest fear was that I would meet an attractive man who would speak kindly to me, and I would fall into an affair and ruin the marriage. Or what was left of our marriage. I tried to focus on the positive in my life: I lived in a beautiful ranch, I didn't have to work, I was married to a man admired in the community, we had talented, entertaining friends, I had no financial pressures, and I enjoyed good health. I was free to devote my time to artistic and creative things. Yet I wasn't doing that. I had no interest, and often asked myself, *what's the point?*

I didn't want a divorce. I didn't want to feel like a failure for the third time. There must be something I missed in all those self-help books I'd read, like *Women Who Love Too Much, Codependent No More, I'm Okay, You're Okay, Adult Children of Alcoholics, My Mother Myself, Bradshaw on the Family* and a bundle by Wayne Dyer.

I felt there was something wrong with me that I couldn't fix this marriage, couldn't seem to make my husband happy, couldn't make this marriage work.

* * *

By May 2008 I had sworn to myself I would never travel with Cork again. The experiences had become too unpredictable and personally stressful. But those color brochures from Grand Circle advertising a tour in China were too enticing.

I agreed to go with him to China.

A girlfriend, to whom I'd shared my vow, called me on my words. "So?" I said, "I'm a travel whore."

Again, we slapped down the credit card, booked the tour to China and flew from Los Angeles to Beijing.

The first day of the tour, we befriended seventeen-year-old Evan, whose grandmother had brought him on the tour as a present for graduating from high school. At first, I felt sympathy for Evan, traveling with this group of old people, but he was a curious young man, and he and Cork took an instant liking to each other.

In Beijing we visited the Great Wall of China, which I had no idea was near the city. Being the usual geographically-challenged product of the American school system, I envisioned it being somewhere out in the Chinese boonies.

Both Evan and his grandmother laughed at Cork's observations at the Great Wall. "When they built this wall, why didn't they build in a bathroom every couple hundred feet?" That was definitely Cork, the practical construction guy. "'Great Wall' means nowhere to pee," he said.

"So, where do you think they peed?" Evan asked.

"Off the top of the wall to scare off the Manchurian barbarians. It wasn't the wall that scared off the Manchurians—it was the sight of all those Chinese guys peeing off the top."

Listening to this, I didn't even want to think about what they did with number two.

In Shanghai, Evan found an Internet café and befriended some young Chinese students who he told us spoke excellent English. He had been delighted to discover they played the same computer game. He explained that people from all over the world, and even in different age groups, played it. This gave me the idea that in a hundred years there will be world peace, and the history books will credit the internet, because young people will say, "I can't go to war against that country. I have friends there I play 'Age of Hyborian Adventures' with."

On the five-day Yangtze River Cruise, Evan met a young Israeli brother and sister, and the three of them spent a raucous night below decks with the crew drinking snake wine.

Cork and I had tasted it, and Cork concluded, "You have to be young and stupid to drink that stuff."

It was true that the snake coiled in the bottom of the bottle made the worm in a tequila bottle look like amateur time.

* * *

As can happen with a group of older folks, the subject one evening at dinner around the Chinese lazy susan was dysfunctional children. With no children of my own, I had nothing to contribute, and besides, I came from a family that avowed, "If you can't say something nice about somebody, don't say anything at all."

After hearing a particular dysfunctional story, Cork said, "Oh yeah, I have two daughters like that—One's a drug addict and the other one hasn't been laid in twenty years."

The other parents laughed, and the conversation continued, but I felt horrified, embarrassed for the daughters who weren't present to defend themselves, and angry on their behalf. Their father's comment seemed so harsh and judgmental, beyond rude.

Later, when we were alone, I told Cork how I felt, and how inappropriate I thought his public comment about his daughters had been.

He tried to defend himself with his usual argument that "Hey, those are the facts," I had no cause to have an opinion since I didn't have children, and I was over-reacting. I objected, and another argument no one could win ensued.

* * *

Three days before our flight from Hong Kong to Los Angeles, our tour guide, Nan made regular announcements regarding our passports:

"Be sure you have your passport handy."

"Be sure you know where your passport is."

"Now be sure your passport is in your carry-on luggage."

In the Hong Kong International Airport the morning of our departure, in line to check-in, eight people in front of us, I discovered Cork could not find his passport.

"Where did you have it last?" I asked.

"Right here... I think ... in this sleeve... no... maybe in here..."

He bent to his unzipped carry-on bag and began to remove items and spread them around on the floor. Our fellow tour members watched in amazement. A few looked at me, as if, as the wife, it was my duty to know at all times the location of my husband's passport.

The line moved. Seven people in front of us. I stepped in the space in front of Cork.

More stuff on the floor. Hotel stationary. His shaving kit. A stuffed and embroidered Chinese hanging, refrigerator magnets. Two ceramic figurines of a couple in a humorous sexual position. I had no idea he could pack all that stuff in his carry-on.

The line moved. Five people in front of us. Cork stood, and with his foot scooted his stuff forward on the floor.

I couldn't believe that after all of Nan's announcements, he couldn't find his passport. What if we got to the counter and he still hadn't found it? What if they wouldn't let him board the flight? What if I had to decide whether or not to stay behind with him? Watching him fumble-fuck through his carry-on, jacket and pockets, I began to feel more amazed than worried.

Well... what if?

Thoughts of the nature of personal responsibility filled my mind. How much responsibility for this situation was really mine? As wives, are we really our husband's keeper? I asked myself, *what is the worst that can happen here?* The worst was that he would not able to board the plane.

At that moment, I made a conscious decision that I would go to Los Angeles on the flight without him. I was not a baby-sitter, a secretary, a mom, or my husband's keeper. Nan, representing Grand Circle Tours, would take care of it. Part of her job was to manage customer emergencies like this. Cork would be in capable hands, and I had nothing to worry about.

As miracles are wont to happen, at the last minute, with one person in front of him in the line, Cork found his passport. He kicked his carry-on and all the loose items to one side so he could repack after he checked in.

Trouble in Comedy Paradise

In late summer I did a road trip to Seattle in the PT cruiser with the "no turbo" pinstriping and bullet hole decals Cork had placed on the fenders. This was now my car since he had sold the PT cruiser, "*Hecho* in Mexico", and bought a Dodge Magnum wagon.

The first full day I was back home in Las Vegas, Cork wanted to take my road-dust-covered car to the car wash. I had not yet unpacked one thing and said, "No. Please wait. Let me unpack first."

I don't remember if he actually said okay, nothing, or if he didn't hear me. I brought a few things up from the car and puttered around the condo while he went out for a few hours. When he returned, he said, "I got your car washed for you."

In Seattle I had found a perfect fifteen-inch long blue heron feather. I'm not normally a feather collector, but this

291

one was so striking, in such perfect condition, it seemed almost magical. It made me think of a place called Blue Heron Beach where my parents had taken me as a child for my first picnic.

When I went down to the car to bring up more stuff, I saw the feather, which I had laid across the dashboard cover, was gone. I looked around the seats and the freshly cleaned and vacuumed floor of the car.

Back upstairs I said to Cork, "Where's my blue heron feather?"

Even at seventy-six, he could still summon boyish innocence to his face. "What feather?"

"The big, long, blue feather that was on the dashboard cover in the car."

"I didn't see any feather."

I realized it had been extremely windy that afternoon. "When you took the car to the car wash, did you have all the doors open at the same time?"

"Well of course," he said. "How do you think I cleaned out the inside?"

"Ah. I think I know what happened. The wind blew the feather out of the car."

"So, what's the big deal?"

I couldn't find the words that would explain to him how attached I had become to that special feather. I sputtered and mumbled and tears came to my eyes.

"It's just a feather," he said. "And I never saw it."

"It was so pretty…and so big. I can't believe you didn't see it."

I could tell he was getting annoyed with my questions. He waved a hand. "I'll get you another one."

That's when I lost it.

"Like you're going to, *what*? Go buy one at *Kmart*? I can't believe you took the car and got it washed when I *specifically asked you* to wait until I unpacked."

"It was dirty."

In frustration my voice rose. "So what? I *asked you* to wait, and you couldn't wait just one day or two!"

"So, you like driving a dirty car?"

"Not the *point!* I asked you to *wait,* and it's like you didn't pay any attention to what I said, what I asked you to do didn't mean anything!"

"You're overreacting." He glared at me. "I did you a favor by washing your car for you, and this is what I get. It was just a feather, for godsake. You're starting to piss me off."

We didn't speak for the rest of the day. In a numb daze I finished unpacking my car and putting things away. I wandered from room to room in the condo, unable to find any spot where I could sit or lie down and not feel frustrated and powerless and lonely and helpless.

* * *

In my head I ran what felt like a million change scenarios, none of which I had the energy to initiate. The idea of a third divorce made me feel like a complete failure as a woman. I thought about how my high school health education teacher had said, "Making a marriage work is eighty percent the woman's responsibility." Logically I knew this was dated thinking, but the fact that I remembered it now made me realize how those things stick in your mind and can affect your thinking decades later.

One change scenario seemed workable. I dressed up so I would feel good about myself and took Cork to lunch and presented it like this:

"I know things have been tense between us lately, and I sense you are just as uncomfortable as I am, so I have an idea that might be really great for both of us. I don't want a divorce, but we could live apart for a while and see how that works. We have enough income from the investments from the sale of the ranch to support two separate households. I'm thinking this could be the perfect time for you to go to LA, get a little apartment, and pursue the dream you've always talked about of getting a part in the sitcom. You could devote your days to the go-sees and networking and maybe even get yourself a manager."

Cork had never had a manager—he didn't trust them and didn't want to give them money. Even though his favorite story was how B.B. King said he never made any money until he got a manager and even though the manager took fifty percent, "Fifty percent of a couple hundred thousand dollars is better than a hundred percent of nuthin.'" I don't know why I thought perhaps this time around Cork might really do it.

He thought it was a great idea, and we began to make plans for his move. Luann had moved in with Sean, and arrangements were made for Cork to rent her furnished condo. The daughters were thrilled that he would be living close to them, he looked forward to living near his comedy buddies, and I anticipated living in the condo in peace and daily predictability.

* * *

The summer passed. From what the daughters and my girlfriends in LA told me, Cork mostly invited them to lunch and to museums. This was frustrating for him because they were busy working, so he had a hard time making "dates." I suspect he was simply comfortable and not up to experiencing the rejection that is ninety percent show business. As Fran O'Bryan, a modeling agency owner had told me in the sixties, "The most successful model is the hungry model," and Cork simply wasn't "hungry."

I didn't press because I too was comfortable, he seemed happy, and it wasn't my place to try to make him a star.

Then the unthinkable happened.

The Disappearing Investments

Neither Cork nor I were particularly savvy financially. We had both bought and sold a lot of houses, and while he profited a little on his, my m.o. seemed to have been "buy high sell low." I think I was too emotional and frightened of losing money to ever be successful in the real estate market.

When we came into the hunk of money from the sale of the *ranchita*, we consulted several friends on the best way to invest it: a self-made millionaire, a bank president, a lawyer, two financial planners, two accountants, and a former bellman who had prospered in real estate.

Neither of us wanted to be landlords, and Cork didn't want to hire a property management company, so besides buying the condo, we invested in two annuities, and with three different investment groups that loaned development money on unimproved land. We were averaging twelve to fourteen percent return in the form of monthly interest checks.

Then one day we weren't.

Two interest checks stopped coming. The investment company explained the borrowers had defaulted on their loans.

Then the third stopped coming. Same story.

It was September 2008 and within a couple of months we no longer had enough income to support two households with two people without jobs.

Cork had to come home.

Cork's First Accident

In the basin country of northwestern Montana lies Flathead Lake, and the home of Cork's cousin Syd. They weren't particularly close, and I had never met him. In September Cork decided since they were both old guys now, they should connect.

Syd and his wife, Lynette were thrilled to hear from him and a visit was arranged.

We flew from Las Vegas to Kalispell, Montana. At the Kalispell City airport, we rented a car to drive the seven miles to Big Arm and their home on the lake.

We were hungry—the food on Allegiant Air had been paltry—and wanted to grab a quick bite before we hit the road. We drove into a parking lot, checked out the coffee-shop style restaurant and decided we didn't care for their fare and would find something else.

At the exit driveway from the parking lot to the street, we waited in our rental car to enter the traffic. In his side mirror, Cork saw a parked Kalispell police car begin to back up towards the driver's side of our rental car. We couldn't go forward into the traffic, and with a car behind us we couldn't back up. Cork laid on the horn and we watched in horror as the police car backed right into our rental car, smashing the door on the drivers' side.

Unable to open his door, Cork had to crawl over the console to get out on the passenger side.

The Kalispell cop was young and embarrassed and repeatedly apologetic. We had to wait while he called the Montana Highway Patrol, which had jurisdiction over the Kalispell police department. Questions were asked, statements were given, Cork made jokes, and we were "released."

He crawled back across the console and into the driver's seat, and we drove back to the airport to return the damaged car to the rental agency.

Back on the road in a new vehicle, I was so stressed I looked at the map and vectored us off course. We drove eighty miles in the wrong direction, which we discovered when we saw a sign for Boise, Idaho.

Cousin Syd, concerned because we hadn't shown up on time, called and directed us to his house via a "shortcut" through a beautiful valley we would not have seen otherwise.

Afterwards, Cork wrote the Montana Highway Patrol a nice thank-you note, they had been so polite.

Gas Money

By November the distance between Cork and I in our marriage had become apparent to both of us. We hardly spoke, and when we did, we argued. Over. Every. Little. Thing.

At one point he said to me, "If you think you're going to find another guy who *lets you do* all the things I *let* you do…"

Let's me do? As in, I'm not allowed to do anything without his permission?

I had no energy and no interest in anything. I felt old, my emotions detached, my body lethargic, my mind indifferent. Sex had been off the table, or perhaps I should say out of the bed, for a long time. I had no interest, no desire. I felt like I was floating through life on a sea of indifference.

In an effort to understand, to cope with my frustrations, I'd devoured two new books, *The Verbally Abusive Relationship: How to Recognize It and How to Respond* and *Why Does He Do That?: Inside the Minds of Angry and Controlling Men*. Both gave me profound insights. But I compared myself to women with small children who were trapped in abusive marriages, and told myself I really didn't have it all that bad. I minimalized my situation, and felt guilty because it still felt so painful, and I still felt so sad.

* * *

A few days before our November 3rd anniversary, in a moment of emotional rebellion, I decided to take off my wedding ring and see if Cork would notice. He didn't.

On the day of our anniversary I blurted, "You didn't even notice I'm not wearing my wedding ring!"

He shrugged. "That's okay," he said. "I sold mine."

WHAT?

Stunned, I couldn't speak. Emotions I thought were dead exploded. A spinning sensation rocked my head, my eyes blurred, and for a moment it seemed like I couldn't see.

He continued in a casual tone. "When I was in L.A. I sold it for fifty dollars. I figured I could use the money for gas."

And *I* hadn't noticed. What a sham we were playing. I couldn't believe how calm I sounded when I announced, "I want a divorce."

He shrugged again. "I'm not surprised."

I walked into our bedroom, found my purse and car keys, and left. I did the one thing a person should never do in a hysterical state—I got in my car and drove. And screamed. And cried. And pounded the palm of my hand on the steering wheel. Five blocks later I parked in front of the neighborhood coffee shop. Inside, I ordered a cappuccino and phoned four girlfriends.

"How could he *do* this to me?" I wailed. "What was he *thinking*?"

"He wasn't thinking," one of them said.

We had a long conversation about emotional and verbal abuse and the cruel things people say to each other. She said her ex- husband used to "call me a stupid cunt and then buy me a mink coat."

"I told him I want a divorce."

"I'm surprised you lasted this long," she said. "You're a better woman than I."

* * *

Over the next three days I decided to move to Seattle, as if fleeing back to my home town would magically revive me. With the PT Cruiser packed so that only a little tunnel allowed me to see through the rear-view mirror, I left.

I had a lot of time on the drive to think. It occurred to me that when we mourn at the end of a relationship, we don't mourn for the relationship itself, but for how it *could have been, if only…* If only he/she had been…would have done…had treated me…. hadn't said…

My choreographer friend, Mistinguett, who lived in a gorgeous condo above the Pike Place Market, offered a stay until I could find a permanent living arrangement. Then it happened that she needed to move temporarily to Las Vegas to help her aging mother, and my temporary stay turned into a five-month sublet housesit.

Later when I thought about it, I realized that when Cork sold his wedding ring, it was not about *me*. As a person, I didn't exist in the equation. I realized he had decided *his* (not *our*) marriage was over. His life had always been about *him*: his daughters, his career, his cars, his wife, his dogs, his house, his dick. Even in conversations about Louise, he had never referred to Kathy and Luann as *our* daughters. And nowhere we had lived had ever been *our* home.

As a man for whom stuff has never had a lot of sentimental value, I suppose it made sense to him to sell the ring. It was not an act of anger or revenge towards me. I could see how he probably did look at it and, in that moment, see it not as a representation of a marital relationship, but as gas money.

I also felt guilty that in my indifferent poor-me state, I had not noticed that since he'd returned from LA, his wedding ring had been absent from his finger.

PART FIVE - LIFE AFTER DIVORCE

Money, Mortgages and Sneaky Moves

During my three years in Seattle I fell into an encore career as a grant writer and lived in a vintage sixties apartment in Lake Forest Park with a deck and expansive view of Lake Washington and the Cascade mountain range.

Those eastern sunrises over the Cascades were so magnificent that I told myself, *This is God's gift to me for making me get up at the crack of dawn at my age to go to a job.*

On Lake City Way, behind my building, was a barbecue rib restaurant, Casper's. On Friday and Saturday nights the owner, a Cajun from New Orleans, hosted a Dixieland jazz band, and I enjoyed hanging out there.

With the divorce final, I began to date and found a new boyfriend.

In Las Vegas, Cork took in a roommate to help make the condo payment. In our phone conversations about paperwork involved to divide the finances and investments, Cork told me how messy, inconsiderate and slovenly the roommate was, and I was not surprised when he soon moved out.

Our mortgage had been with Countrywide, through the Bank of America. Cork applied for a new restructuring loan at a lower monthly payment and stopped making the mortgage payments.

Even though I had signed over the condo in the divorce agreement, I worried about any financial responsibility I might have since my name had been on the original mortgage. When he told me he'd stopped making payments, I was so frightened I screamed into the phone, "If you ruin my credit, you cocksucker, I'll hunt you down and make your life a living hell *forever!"*

Because in all our years together we had never called each other bad names, to this day he remembers not the subject of the telephone conversation, but that I called him a "cocksucker."

It took the Bank of America eighteen months—during which they lost the paperwork three times—to decide that Cork's monthly income—which had not changed during that time—was not high enough to qualify for a restructuring loan at a lower monthly payment. He called our realtor Mary, they put the condo on the market for a short-sale, and he began to look for a place to rent.

Our beautiful $240,000 condo sold fast for $75,000, and escrow was opened.

One morning a few weeks later Mary got a call informing her the condo was no longer for sale—the Bank of America had sold it at auction for $60,000. She was shocked and the young couple who had made the escrow deposit were devastated, even though they were given back their escrow deposit.

I thought the right hand of the Bank of America had no idea what the left hand was doing, because none of it made sense. I fantasized about getting on *60 Minutes* where we could tell this outrageous story of how the Bank of America had screwed this poor seventy-eight-year-old senior. I'm confident that with all our media connections we could have done it. But I felt that I was creating a new life for myself, and I didn't want that negativity to be part of it.

Cork moved with a public relations friend of ours into an apartment in a senior complex Cork dubbed, "Wrinkle City."

* * *

Years later Cork told me that through a friend at Metro (I never asked who because if it was our detective friend Randy, I didn't want to know) he'd been introduced to a cop in Seattle whom he'd hired off-duty to follow me and take pictures.

"Really?" I shook my head in disbelief. "Where are the pictures?"

"I threw them away."

I wouldn't have believed him but for the facts that he knew the name of the BBQ joint and he knew the name of the new boyfriend, which I had never mentioned. How creepy to think a strange man had been sneaking around stealing pictures of me.

"That's stalking," I declared.

Not in Cork's view. "I wanted to be sure you were okay."

* * *

Cork has always prided himself on the fact that he has never hit a woman. I suspect one reason is that he's smart enough to know that behavior could get you arrested, and after his teen-age jail experience, he's clear that he never wants to go there again.

And why would you need to hit a woman when you can cut her off at the knees in ten words or less? With kidding on the square? With phrases presented as jokes? With behaviors that confuse and demoralize? With cruel words disguised as comedy?

I have never been physically abused. The only incident in my family was when an older cousin's husband gave her a black eye. My parents said, "She fell in the shower." I don't know how we kids knew that wasn't true, that he had actually hit her. It wasn't something you talked about. If you didn't talk about it, it wasn't real.

Only later in life did I learn that there are other kinds of abuse. I've always wondered, *does it hurt more to be slapped or punched? Is the pain we feel from sarcastic, unkind words any less real?*

Author and Unitarian Universalist minister Robert Fulghum has written: "Sticks and stones may break our bones, but words will break our hearts."

I don't think most people realize that words can also kill love and sexual desire.

Why Not Move Abroad?

In September 2011, I was unceremoniously fired from my fun grant-writing job in Seattle. Escorted out of the building with my box of personal things, just like you've seen in the movies! I was emotionally mortified. Later I suspected my fund-raising success had been tainted by discoveries of what I prefer to call "slopping bookkeeping."

Job-hunting at sixty-eight revealed that age discrimination is alive and well. I was excited about my strong recommendation for a position as Communications Director at United Way. In the subsequent interview with five thirty-somethings, I was told, "We want to establish up front that there won't be a lot of eye contact in this interview because we will all be taking notes." So why did I dress up when we could have done a phone conference? From there the interview went nowhere.

I can't do this, I thought. *I'm exhausted and over-qualified and have no heart for this.*

Ever since the Peace Corps I had fantasized about living abroad again. I began to think about moving to Puerto Vallarta, where I have friends. But my monthly social security and tiny annuity income was twenty dollars short of the Mexican income requirement for retirees.

"Oh, come on anyway," my friends said. "They don't really care."

But I would be nervous every day worrying about being in the country illegally.

I'd been subscribing to *International Living* magazine, and Ecuador came onto my radar. Requirement within my means, 110 voltage, and American currency. How bad could it be? You need a round-trip ticket into the country, so I figured if I didn't like it, I could always come back.

For the next six months, with both Social Security and unemployment income, I was able to take my time sorting, selling and packaging for storage in anticipation of a February move to Cuenca, Ecuador.

The Roast

My longtime friend Gertie had come with me to Cuenca. Today we joke about how we each came with four suitcases, and now we each have a three-bedroom home full of *stuff*. We arrived in Ecuador in February, 2012.

That same month I woke up in the middle of the night with an idea that changed my future.

Five years previously I had received a grant from UNLV to edit Cork's autobiography for publication. Joyce had been assigned by Special Collections to do audio interviews with him and the resulting transcript had been 130,000 words. During the divorce I had stopped working on it. The University had never pressed me to finish, but I had felt guilty. During my last six months in Seattle, I had finished the work and given it to Stephen's Press.

Cork would be turning eighty on July 22, 2012, and lying awake in the middle of the night I fantasized and formulated a spectacular Las Vegas birthday event.

The next day I called him—after the divorce we had amicably kept in touch—described my idea and asked if he would be interested. No use going to all that work if he wasn't onboard.

He loved it. We kicked around some scenarios, and I assured him he wouldn't have to do anything except show up. I would be responsible for all the logistics and the details.

Afterwards I made three phone calls and things went into motion.

My idea was that on Sunday afternoon, July 22, 2012 we would throw a comedy roast for Cork's eightieth birthday at a major hotel, donate the proceeds to Opportunity Village, and debut his book the same day. Opportunity Village would handle the marketing, Stephens Press assured me the book could be printed by then, and Mistinguett would handle the stage production.

Cork went to Michael Gaughan to ask for the showroom at the Southpoint. Michael was happy to donate the room for the fundraiser but told Cork, "I don't think you'll draw anybody."

* * *

After our fund-raising wedding, Cork's 80th Birthday Comedy Roast at the Southpoint Hotel Casino in Las Vegas was the most fun party I've ever been to. Cork and I felt like a team once more, and I began to envision a possible life with him in Ecuador. I knew he'd love the country. When I suggested he might come visit and check it out, he got so enthusiastic he told everybody.

* * *

Mistinguett created a fabulous poster, Opportunity Village sent out news releases and emailed their extensive list, and Carolyn Hayes Uber, president of Stephens Media, manned a book sales booth. Mistinguett had found an enormous, oversized, red velvet chair and supplied two showgirls to escort Cork on and off stage and book-end the chair.

The bar opened and the showroom filled.

Comedian Bob Zany was the perfect Roastmaster. Roasters included comedians Peter Anthony, Gerry Bednob, Carme, Sammy Shore, Kenny Davis, Kelly McDonald and Jeff Wayne, comedy magicians Fielding West and Jac Hayden, corporate satirist Bob Ross, comediennes Kathleen Dunbar and Kim Richards, award-winning journalist and author John L. Smith, and me. Carrot Top made a surprise guest appearance.

Carme's words:

"How can you roast a guy that's been your best friend since 1973? A man who will give you the shirt off his back and never let you forget it the rest of your life?

Cork Proctor is actually a left-handed, dyslexic, anal-retentive person. Now for those of you who don't know what anal-retentive is, I shall enlighten.

It means exhibiting a tendency towards excessive neatness and obstinacy. This results in attitudes, associated with an infantile pleasure in the retention of feces. Dr. Spock attributes this condition to traumatic

305

experiences during early toilet training. That could explain why Cork went through life never giving a shit about anything.

I do believe when Cork was born, he came with a built-in wordometer. He figures if he doesn't use enough words in a day, he'll either implode or his dick will fall off.

Cork once spent ten days with me in Florida. My girlfriend asked, 'What do you talk about all day?'

'He talks, I listen,' I said.

She said, 'But what does he talk about?'

I said, 'Everything from Einstein's theory of relativity to how to make gasoline out of horseshit.'

I have been at most of Cork's firings. The best one was when he opened for Johnny Harra, a big fat Elvis impersonator at the Silverbird. He walked out on stage and said, 'I've always wanted to work with Porky Pig in a Dracula cape.' They fired him, and I got the job.

So Cork, this is for you:

All the years I have known you.
The laughs and tears we shared was an experience
With somebody who's mentally impaired.
But one thing I can say about you, Cork
You never try to make amends
When I asked you how you want to be remembered you said,
'Hey, I was good to my friends.' "

* * *

I talked about how Cork and I met and got laughs with, "He's the only man I've ever met who can change subjects mid-sentence," and "He was the only man I've ever met who could talk and give head at the same time."

But the most memorable line from the roast came from Fielding West: "People wonder why Cork is following Carolyn to South America—he just can't stay away from that seventy-year-old pussy."

* * *

Mistinguett and I had arranged with the hotel to have the show taped so we could sell CDs to raise more money for Opportunity Village. But after the show she came to me, tears in her eyes, with dreadful news.

The guy in charge of the showroom, with whom all the production arrangements had been made, had taken off for the weekend, delegated the management of the show to some kid, and either neglected to tell him about the video recording, or the kid just forgot to push a "start" button.

When Mistinguett had gone to ask when we could see the video the kid had shrugged and told her he had no idea what she was talking about.

Because we had advertised that there would be a CD for sale, only a few people took video on their smart phones. Mistinguett and I were devastated and angry beyond words, especially by the cavalier attitude of the head of the showroom production staff.

You can see snippets on YouTube. Just google "Cork Proctor Comedy Roast."

Cork Comes to Ecuador

In the months before the roast, Cork and I had talked about what it was like to live in Ecuador. When I had arrived in Las Vegas three weeks before the event, I had been appalled to see how he was living. The apartment he shared with a public relations friend made me think of two Oscars from *The Odd Couple*.

I began to think perhaps we could live together in Ecuador under better circumstances. Combining our social security incomes we could live quite well, in fact.

Cork had always wanted to see Vilcabamba, since 1976 when he had read Grace Halsell's book, *Los Viejos: Secrets of Long Life from the Sacred Valley*, about her experience living in Vilcabamba for a year. So, when I had suggested he come down for a few weeks to visit, I had said I would take him to see Vilcabamba, and if he liked what he saw we could talk about living together in Ecuador. Naturally, he had told his friends he was going to Ecuador with me, hence Fielding's infamous line.

During the weeks he visited, we explored Vilcabamba, Guayaquil, the coast from Salinas up the Ruta Spondylus to Mantanita, as well as Cuenca.

As I knew he would, Cork loved Ecuador. A date was set for him to leave Vegas, make the permanent move at the end of December, and join me in this new adventure.

Modern Living in the Andes

Cork and I found a modern, unfurnished, three-bedroom apartment up in the Andes in Cuenca, a UNESCO World Heritage site. We enjoyed shopping to furnish it and finding craftspeople to build custom furniture to our design.

"Just so you understand," I told him when we began to shop, "My home decor taste has changed. I'm not into Mexican Country anymore. I'm into Asian Deco. So, no bright colors and woven orange llamas hanging on the walls."

He laughed and agreed. "But you know orange is my favorite color," he said. "It signifies love of change."

After a few months it became apparent that it didn't work for us to sleep together in the same bed even if it was queen-sized. Old people get up in the middle of the night, sometimes more than once, and not always at the same time. Since one person bouncing on the mattress to move out of bed wakes the other person, it meant we were both being awakened at least twice in the middle of the night.

I also had to arrange myself to avoid the air that blew from his sleep apnea machine.

"I thought you liked *Star Trek*," Cork said with a smile. "Surely you've always fantasized about sleeping with an eighty-year-old Borg."

That sounded like a Fellini movie for sure.

We both agreed that the best solution was for me to move into the guest bedroom.

Though we had our usual moments of love and discord, we were managing well.

Last Drive

On a visit to Vegas to see our friends and brag about our cushy Ecuador lifestyle, we rented a white Chevy Malibu. Cork, who prided himself on having never caused the accident, drove and I had no reason to object.

When he drove into a mall parking space and did not stop the car until the wheel touched the cement barrier and the front of the Chevy bumped the car parked in the opposite space, I laughed.

Cork muttered, "My depth perception isn't that good."

When he made a U-turn on Rainbow Boulevard and bumped over the curving curb of the center strip, I said, "Jeese. Cork. Watch where you're going."

He laughed. "Welcome to Mr. Toad's Wild Vegas Ride."

We drove to LA to visit the daughters and stayed with Luann in her Valley condo. When he pulled into the parking space under the building, he sideswiped the wooden support post. Now there was a major Redwood-stain-colored slash on the right side of the white Chevy Malibu.

"No problem," Cork said. "I can rub that out." In an automotive store he bought some kind of rubbing compound which removed the redwood color, but left a large patch that was white matte instead of shiny white, like normal car paint.

Back in Las Vegas, I was horrified when he nearly sideswiped a police car on the freeway. Luckily the cops were focused on some important destination instead of an old guy attempting to change lanes.

Because the car had been rented in my name with my credit card—Cork had walked away from all his credit cards before he left the country—I worried that when we returned the car, there would be a big repair expense.

I held my breath while the young girl, carrying a clipboard, came from the Enterprise office to walk around the car for the customary damage inspection. Perhaps she had only been trained to look for dents, because she did not notice the matte area of the paint. Guess she had never been to Hot August Nights or had had a boyfriend to rave on to her about the fine details of a quality car paint job.

"Wet," Cork had always said. "It should look drippy wet."

I escaped with no extra charges and a silent conviction that that would be Cork's last drive.

The Prodigal Husband

Towards the end of 2015 little disagreements began to escalate. I sensed Cork wasn't happy. It occurred to me that, at eighty-three, there might be something mental going on, but with a man always given to squirrely behaviors, who could tell?

He dropped his bomb in January, 2016. He announced he had too many grievances against me and could no longer live with me. He announced that he planned to move back to Las Vegas.

His major grievances were:

1 - I always had my nose in the computer

2 - (Eleven years ago) I made him sell the *ranchita*, and

3 - I wouldn't let him have his music

(It was true that I've always objected to mariachi-like horns with no melody or rhythm, first thing in the morning.)

At first, I didn't believe him. I had a vacation in Panama with a Vegas girlfriend scheduled for mid-February, and I began to wonder if he would disappear while I was gone. Before I left, I pressed to learn more about his plans. He announced he would stay until I returned from Panama and leave on March 1. No talking him out of it. He was adamant.

In a daze, I helped him pack and on March 1 he flew to Las Vegas. He kissed me at the door and told me he was leaving because he knew he was getting older, and he didn't want me to be "a full-time caregiver." He wanted to save me "from that terrible fate."

When I closed the door, I believed I would never see or hear from him again.

* * *

For two days I wandered the apartment and cried. With perfect logic my head understood the situation. But my heart still asked, *what could I have done differently? What more could I have done to make him happy?*

On the third day I made arrangements to sell the queen-sized bed and repaint the entire apartment. I would turn his bedroom into a classroom where I could teach writing and watercolor painting classes to offset the loss of his half of the overhead. I moved each photo and object that reminded me of him into a dark cupboard. I bought three tables and six chairs and wrote outlines for class ideas.

Three productive weeks later, Cork called and said those words every woman wants to hear: "You were right."

He told me how surprised he had been to find Vegas so expensive. "Just a beater car would be three thousand dollars and a single apartment is twelve hundred. I can't *afford* to live here. I have to come back to Ecuador."

I was too dumbfounded to feel anything. "Well, I suppose you can come back..." I said, "but you can't come back *here,* because I've turned your bedroom into a classroom."

He said he understood. He would just "find a little place."

In the first year of his return, I helped him find new places and move three times. His first apartment, in a charming, vintage, former Ecuadorean country home, had too many smokers and a barking dog.

His second apartment, on the top floor of an office building, had a modern design and an amazing view. We spent a romantic and drunken New Year's Eve there. But the elevator went out a few times, and we realized it wasn't a practical apartment for an eighty-four-year-old single man. In typical Ecuadorian style, the elevator was so small that if there had been a serious emergency, he would have to be carried in a stretcher down nine flights of stairs. Assuming he would be conscious, that experience alone would give him a heart attack. Plus, the office building was locked at street level on evenings and weekends. How could the *bomberos* get in?

His next move was around the corner to a room at the vintage Hotel Orchidea. He didn't need a kitchen because he didn't cook, and now there would be someone nearby twenty-four hours a day if he needed help. While charming and a great location, the Hotel Orchidea proved too noisy. Late night slamming doors and sounds echoing off tiled floors made it impossible to get a full night's sleep.

Ladronas

After buying some large plastic storage containers for the business building high-rise apartment, Cork had been carrying them in two black plastic bags across Cuenca's outdoor market, San Francisco Plaza.

Two women approached him, smiling and speaking rapid Spanish. The older one grabbed his crotch while the younger one moved behind him to unzip his cloth backpack.

Cork dropped both shopping bags and yelled, "*LADRONAS!*" (Spanish for "thieves"). At the same time, he put both hands under the older woman's shoulders, lifted her to move with him, and twisted to the right. This sudden body twist foiled the younger woman's attempt to get into his backpack.

As soon as he set the first woman onto the pavement, still yelling "*ladronas*", the two women sprinted across the plaza.

"I had no idea drunk women could run so fast," Cork told me later. "They both smelled like a brewery."

From their store a couple ran to his aid, assuring him that those thieves were "not Ecuadoreans. They are Colombians." Cork said he felt so grateful, he went into their shop and bought twenty dollars-worth of stuff he didn't need.

He laughed and added, "I wonder how many guys in Cuenca can say they've been cock-jacked?"

The Ghost of Elvis

What could possibly be more fun than going on the road with the ghost of Elvis, plus the handsome *young* Elvis?

When Cork got the call to play the ghost of Elvis Presley, he invited me to go with him. A Greg Thompson Production, the show, *Rendezvous With the King*, would run for three special nights in Sammy's Showroom at Harrah's in Reno, Nevada.

For decades, Cork had been the comic relief in many stage shows designed and produced by Greg Thompson. In *Rendezvous With the King,* the ghost of Elvis comes back to advise the young Elvis tribute artist to "update your act, son. That's what I'd have done." It was a high concept story line created by Greg. This would be a kind of old-home-week for Cork, since he already knew the company manager, the back-up singers, Sammy's Showroom, some of the crew, and the producer.

In his high-rise apartment, we rehearsed the lines. We recorded him speaking them.

Before we left for Reno, I made Cork a business card he could pass out to advertise the show that read, "This is what Elvis would have looked like at eighty-four!"

Pick up at the Reno airport in a Harrah's limo made up for the bus tire explosion delay in the Andes crossing the mountains to get from Cuenca down to Guayaquil for the flight to the US.

Here's how our last week in show business went down:

Day one, Monday, 12:00 noon.
79.5 hours to *SHOWTIME!*
We meet Number One Worldwide Elvis Tribute Artist Pete Storm. Pete is from London, England, so it was bizarre to hear "Elvis" speak with an English accent! When I asked him how tall he is, he said, "Oh, six-three and a bit."

Pete Storm and Cork Proctor—the latter as the ghost of Elvis—read through the show dialogue for the first time together.

While Pete can patter between Elvis songs, he has no formal theatrical training and I hear that now, with story lines to memorize, he is terrified.

Cork, our old Elvis, hasn't performed in a play in twenty years, and at eighty-four is having trouble memorizing lines. He has major senior stage fright—he's also terrified.

Greg says: "Sheesh—I have *two* stars who don't know where they're going…"

That evening in our Harrah's hotel room, I sit nervous old Elvis in a chair, make him close his eyes, and do some hypnosis and repeat positive affirmations. I hold his hand and do my best to calm him.

Day two, Tuesday- 4:30 a.m.
63 hours to showtime

Yesterday's preliminary rehearsal for *Rendezvous With the King* went well, even though at five a.m. old Elvis woke up worrying that the costume pants are a little snug, there's no belt, how will he tuck in his shirt, maybe he can leave the coat open, and are they really going to spray his hair white?

2:00 p.m. – 53.5 hours to *SHOWTIME!*

Lead back-up singer and company manager Sheldon Craig drives Cork and me to Posh Salon, where stylist Jessie will make Cork's wild two-month growth of white hair into an Elvis-like updo. There will be fat sideburns, and I'm given a can of white hair powder to make them really stand out. Spraying triangular sideburns with a handmade template on Cork's face appeals to the artist in me.

Day three, Wednesday, 1 p.m.
30.5 hours to *SHOWTIME!*

Old El was awake again at the crack of dawn, worrying, worrying, worrying…

The rehearsals are going well. So fun to hear people banter back and forth with off-script quips.

Greg's script note to Old El: "Now you need to pause here because there will be applause—something you may not have been familiar with in your career—and then deliver that line."

Cue lines on white paper are placed along the stage side of the footlights so Cork can follow the story line. But Old El is still flustered and having trouble with the flow. He's so afraid of letting everyone down—especially Greg—that in the middle of the rehearsal, center stage, he has a meltdown.

Greg Thompson to the rescue. "We'll wire your ear and Carolyn can feed you the lines from backstage." Old El is visibly relieved. "And for about the fiftieth time," Greg adds, "She'll save your ass."

The backstage crew sets up a lighted music stand for the script with a microphone wired to the earpiece old El will wear. The music stand isn't too stable because the floor seems to slope. One of the stage crew guys explains, "That's because in the olden days this area used to be a parking garage, before they built Sammy's Showroom."

After the first rehearsal we enter the elevator to go to our sixteenth-floor room with a bellman carrying a gift basket. We chit-chat, make the usual "is that for me?" joke. He gets off on our floor and heads down the hall. We see him stop in front of our door!

It's an opening night congratulatory gift basket from our comedian friend, Jeff Wayne.

And it's all CHOCOLATE! Chocolate candies, chocolate bars, gourmet hot chocolate mixes, chocolate coffee—just the drugs I need. I had no idea there would be such major hand-holding involved to combat senior stage fright anxiety.

The accompanying card from Jeff reads, "Break both legs!" That's show-biz speak for "good luck." Another comedian friend e-mailed, "Break a hip."

6:30 P.M. – FULL DRESS REHEARSAL
As I'm feeding Old El his lines, I notice Pete periodically glances over my shoulder to read the script and review his entrance cues.

Day four, Thursday, 2 p.m.
5.5 hours to *SHOWTIME!*
Only in show business do people show up for work at two in the afternoon and say, "Good morning!"

Old El complains the white shoes—that came with the white suit, white shirt, white tie and white underwear—are "killing" him. While sizes were provided in advance, a mishap has occurred and the shoes are two sizes too small. Greg says, "Ah, forget the shoes, then…just come out in your white-stockinged feet."

OPENING NIGHT, *7:30 pm. It's SHOWTIME!*
In the opening night performance, "Now, where'd I leave my shoes?" becomes a running "old-Elvis" gag line.

Pete's and Cork's lines flow together and the show goes well and the audience loves it and everyone is happy.

Day five, Friday

Old El has slept a full eight hours last night. Now he's feeling back in the fling of things. The afternoon full dress rehearsal progresses with a minimum of stops for Greg to comment.

In the Friday night performance, the "Where'd I leave my shoes?" line—now a running gag—continues to get laughs.

Day six, Saturday

There's no rehearsal today. Pete goes with his girlfriend, Abby, to work out—he has Old El's fabulous old body—while Old El naps.

The 7:30 p.m. show is sold out, which makes crew and cast excited to perform. When the show ends, at the curtain bow, Old El carries out one white shoe, waves it in a broad gesture, and says, "Hey, I found one!"

So, what was the highlight of my week in show business? Seeing tall, handsome Pete Storm—did I mention he has Cork's old body?—backstage wearing nothing but the male equivalent of a g-string…

Cashew Nuts

The day before our flight back to Ecuador, we visited Postal, Etcetera for one last check for mail. Roxanne, the owner, said, "There are new packages for you." She lifted a large box onto the counter and handed us a small, padded envelope package.

Inside the package was a tiny black lace bra edged in pink. I held it up for display. "I don't know anyone with tits this small," I said with a laugh. I told Roxanne I hadn't ordered that, and she agreed to return it to the sender.

The big box contained twenty-five pounds of cashews in one giant silver foil packaging bag.

"Those are for Mex," Cork announced.

In Cuenca we frequented a Thai restaurant, The Thai Connection, owned by an Austrian ex-pat, Mex, and his Thai wife, Wan.

In a conversation about our forthcoming trip to Vegas, Mex had asked Cork if he would bring back some cashew nuts.

"Sure, no problem." Cork had given him the address of our post office box in Las Vegas.

"Twenty-five pounds?" I exclaimed.

"I didn't know he was going to order that much," Cork said.

"How much did you *think* he was going to order?"

"I dunno. We never discussed it."

Since we were flying first-class, we had a 75-pound limit for each suitcase, but all four were already packed. No room in any one of them for an additional 25 pounds.

"I've got some zip-lock bags," Roxanne said. "Maybe we could divide them up and put some in each of your suitcases."

She produced bags and scissors, opened the packing bag, and on the counter, we separated the cashews into a dozen zip-lock bags. We were able to stuff three in each bag. Problem solved.

At home in Cuenca, when we opened our suitcases, we got another surprise. The pressure in the baggage compartment of the planes had caused each bag to explode. Loose cashew nuts fell out of our clothes.

"At least they're raw cashews, not salted," I said with a sigh. I got spoons and new zip-lock bags from the kitchen, and we spent an entire evening carefully removing each item from each suitcase and bagging loose cashews.

We decided it was best not to tell Mex what had happened. "Maybe we should avoid ordering cashew chicken for a while," Cork added.

The little black and pink lace bra? Wan had ordered it online. Too bad nobody had told us. She did ultimately get it, but not for several months.

Mattress in the Shower

One morning Cork called and said, "I have an idea I'd like to run by you, so if I wanted to come by this afternoon with a bottle of wine, would you say you're too busy, or would you say to come on over?"

"I'd say both. I'm busy and yes, if you're bringing wine, come on over."

We sat in my kitchen, poured two glasses of a nice Chilean red, and he proposed: "I was thinking I could move back in, because I know you need the money, but I would never ask you to give up your classroom. I was thinking I would just get a single mattress, prop it up in the shower, and just take it out at night to sleep on."

Talk about MacGyver. Who would think to live like that? A clever man who had scraped and scrambled and struggled to support a young wife and two babies. Cork had always been a master at the unusual solution.

"No, we're not keeping a mattress in the shower," I said. I thought of two small pieces of furniture in what had originally been the master bedroom/art room that I could part with. "Let me see what I can do, and we'll get you a decent bed."

He nodded. We poured ourselves another glass of wine.

"But this time," I added, "there will be a penalty for time out for stupid behavior." He gave me a curious look. I felt bold with power. "This time you will pay for *all* the overhead, not just half."

He agreed. The deal was done. I sold the two pieces of furniture, and at the consignment store we found him a good deal on a double bed, mattress and side table.

The Surfboard

Cork loves Cuenca Consignments. Lorie and Suzanne and Brenda, the women who run it, give him coffee and the occasional sandwich and laugh at all his jokes and stories. He takes them the occasional bottle of wine. Cork loves nothing better than a good deal and often comes home thrilled to have found something we don't need, but at a good price.

When he brought home *The Soup Bible*, 100 recipes in an oversized hard-bound book, he declared, "Look what I found for five dollars!"

I would thumb through the book like a magician shuffling cards, he would tell me when to stop, and I would make that soup.

"I love soup!" he said. "I could *live* on soup."

"Now you tell me? All these years I've been making you gourmet dinners, and all I had to do was make *soup*?"

One day I ran into Suzanne on the street, we cheek-kissed and she said, "Oh, we were so thrilled that Cork bought the surfboard!"

Surfboard? "He bought a surfboard?"

"Lorell brought it in. We had it for a long time."

"When did he do this? What did he do with it? Does he plan to come back later and get it?"

"Last week," she said, "He took it with him in a taxi."

"A full-size surfboard?" She nodded. "I can't imagine what he did with it—our apartment isn't that big! Every cupboard and closet is full. I would *know* if he brought home a surfboard."

That evening at dinner—not soup—I told him I had run into Suzanne, and she had told me he bought a surfboard. Like a proud little boy, he nodded, smiled and said, "Yes. It was only twenty dollars."

"Well, where is it?"

"Under my bed."

After that he brought out the surfboard and propped it upright in the corner window of his room. Now the place looks like a *real* college boy dorm room.

The Girl From Las Vegas

Old car dude that he is and huge fan of the Buenavista Social Club, Cork had always wanted to visit Cuba. I was referred by a friend to a tour company in New Zealand that organized tours in Cuba. Locally Sourced Tours created a special "we are old people so no hikes to waterfalls" two-week program and even provided the tour guide my friend had recommended. I limited the tour to twelve people.

Eight friends came from Ecuador and two from Las Vegas.

We have a lot of friends in the US, but here are the questions they asked about travel to Cuba:

"What about Trump's travel ban?"

"What about flesh eating bacteria?"

"How close is it to Santo Domingo?"

Peggy Newman brought with her a friend named Janice, who had also lived for years in Las Vegas. She was the only person on the tour whom I had never met

On the third day of the tour, Peggy and Janice and Cork were reminiscing about early days in Las Vegas and playing the usual game of, who do you know?

A prominent casino owner was mentioned whose long-time mistress had been his casino manager.

"Oh yes," Cork said, "I dated her daughter."

"That was me," Janice said.

Cork was forgiven for not remembering this woman he had had a fling with forty-five years ago.

Later he told me he thought it was odd when she first arrived and said to him, "So can I have a hug?" She told me she figured he didn't want to say anything because of my presence.

For the rest of the tour, every time he grumbled and stumbled, I said to Janice, "See what you missed?"

And every time she went off to smoke a cigarette, I said to Cork, "See what you missed?"

Take Me Out

At eighty-six, in a moment of heavy reflection, Cork asked, "If I were *really* old…and I was suffering from something incurable…and in *really* bad pain, with no meds helping…and there was no cure…would you help me take myself out?"

I didn't hesitate. "No."

He looked astonished. *"NO!?* Really? If I was *suffering* in *excruciating* pain—after all these years and everything we've been to each other—you wouldn't help me take myself out?"

"No. Here's how that would go," I said. "You would die and go to warm, pastel-colored place—and I would go to a cold Ecuadorean prison with bad food."

THE END

Postscript:
As I said in Part One, "On more than one occasion I wanted to *kill* him, but I have never been bored." And, he can still make me laugh!

* * *

Thanks for reading *HELP! I Married ~~An Alien~~ A Comedian*

Reviews are everything!

If you enjoyed this book, I would really appreciate it if you would go to Amazon, rate the book and write one or two lines about what you liked about the story.

Carolyn

www.carolynvhamilton.com

This book is dedicated to the one and only Cork Proctor, without whom it would not have been possible, and in memory of comedian Carme Pitrello.

ACKNOWLEDGEMENTS

Thank you so much to my helpful beta readers, whose comments helped me step back and "see the forest for the trees:"

Sandy McLuckie, Ingrid Triki, Erika Horn, John Gee, Dean Keyes, and Colleen Morrison.

If I missed your name, it's because I inadvertently set up the google beta form without names, and you didn't respond to the email I sent asking to confirm. Just let me know, and I'll gladly update this list.

And to my editor, Kathryn M. McCullough, I can't thank you enough for your insights and advice.

Cover Illustration: Iben Affan
Cover Photo of Carolyn: Keith Paul
Cover Photo of Cork: Lee McDonald
Cover Design: Swift House Press

Carolyn V. Hamilton

TO LEARN EVEN MORE ABOUT CORK PROCTOR
you can read his autobiography:

MY MIND IS AN OPEN MOUTH

With his outlandish, machine-gun rapid-fire humor, comedian Cork Proctor has been knockin' 'em dead for sixty years ... literally. From his first attempt at stand-up comedy as a gravedigger entertaining his co-worker to lounges and showrooms around the world—on land and sea—this left-handed, dyslexic, two-time high school dropout has not only seen it all, he tells it all.

PRAISE FOR MY MIND IS AN OPEN MOUTH:

Sit up, take a deep breath, pat down your hair, and straighten your tie. Cork Proctor is known for playing with the audience.
—Dick Clark, Television Host

Roastmaster General of the United States.
—Tip O'Neill, former Speaker of the House

Cork Proctor has been one of the funniest men in Las Vegas for many glowing years. Read his book: Giggle and laugh!
—Phyllis Diller, Comedienne

The fastest, funniest comedic mind and mouth in town.
— Las Vegas Sun

His observations are intelligent, his delivery original. He is in command at all times, and like the drums he plays, his mind works in a double paradiddle beat. In other words, I like him: Brash, bright, and brilliant!
—Shecky Greene, Comedian

Also by Carolyn V. Hamilton:

FICTION

Elisabeth Samson, Forbidden Bride
Magicide
Hard Amazon Rain
Implosion
Dare to Survive

NON-FICTION

Coming to Las Vegas, A true tale of sex, drugs &
Sin City in the 70s
Power Editing For Fiction Writers
Power Editing For Memoir Writers
The Big Red Power Pen Editing System: Kill These
24 Words
Throw Up Your Emotions on Paper! A Workbook
Planner with 21 Challenges to help you learn to
write about emotions in your memoir in 21 days.

ADULT COLORING BOOKS

The Art of Caro
Color Caro's Mystic Mandalas
Color Caro's Orchids of Ecuador

Printed in Great Britain
by Amazon